SAT*

7TH EDITION
VERBAL WORKBOOK

ARCO
™
THOMSON LEARNING

Australia • Canada • Mexico • Singapore • Spain • United Kingdom • United States

An ARCO Book

ARCO is a registered trademark of Thomson Learning, Inc., and is used herein under license by Peterson's.

About Peterson's

Founded in 1966, Peterson's, a division of Thomson Learning, is the nation's largest and most respected provider of lifelong learning online resources, software, reference guides, and books. The Education Supersite℠ at petersons.com—the Web's most heavily traveled education resource—has searchable databases and interactive tools for contacting U.S.-accredited institutions and programs. CollegeQuest® (CollegeQuest.com) offers a complete solution for every step of the college decision-making process. GradAdvantage™ (GradAdvantage.org), developed with Educational Testing Service, is the only electronic admissions service capable of sending official graduate test score reports with a candidate's online application. Peterson's serves more than 55 million education consumers annually.

Thomson Learning is among the world's leading providers of lifelong learning, serving the needs of individuals, learning institutions, and corporations with products and services for both traditional classrooms and for online learning. For more information about the products and services offered by Thomson Learning, please visit www.thomsonlearning.com. Headquartered in Stamford, Connecticut, with offices worldwide, Thomson Learning is part of The Thomson Corporation (www.thomson.com), a leading e-information and solutions company in the business, professional, and education marketplaces. The Corporation's common shares are listed on the Toronto and London stock exchanges.

For more information, contact Peterson's, 2000 Lenox Drive, Lawrenceville, NJ 08648;
800-338-3282; or find us on the World Wide Web at: www.petersons.com/about

ISBN 0-7689-0616-4

Printed in the United States of America

10 9 8 7 6 5 4 3 2 1   03 02 01

Contents

About the Scholastic Assessment Test (SAT)

Purpose of the SAT   1

Diagnostic Verbal Reasoning Test   13

PART ONE: VERBAL REASONING PRACTICE

1   Analogies   25

2   Sentence Completions   79

3   Critical Reading   149

PART TWO: PRACTICE VERBAL REASONING TESTS

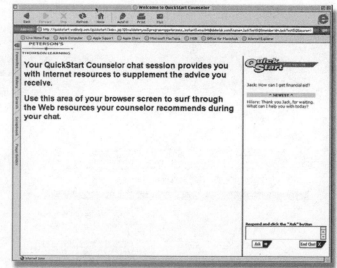

About The Scholastic Assessment Test (SAT)

Purpose of the SAT

The Scholastic Assessment Test (SAT) is offered by the Admissions Testing Program of the College Board to high school students. Well over 2,000 colleges and universities in the United States and Canada require their applicants to take the test. Since the SAT is a standardized examination that is consistent in difficulty and format, it allows colleges to compare the abilities of students from different high schools. According to the College Board, the SAT is designed to measure your aptitude for college work.

The SAT is now divided into two separate types of exams designated SAT I and SAT II. SAT I tests verbal and mathematical reasoning skills—your ability to understand what you read, use language effectively, reason clearly, and apply fundamental mathematical principles to unfamiliar problems. SAT II tests mastery of specific subjects essential to academic success in college.

Taking SAT I

SAT I is administered on several Saturday mornings throughout the year at established testing centers. When you apply to a college, find out whether it requires you to take SAT I and when. If you have not yet decided which schools you will apply to, take SAT I in the early winter of your senior year. You will then be sure of having your scores reported in time wherever you apply.

Registration forms for SAT I may be available from your high school guidance officer. You may also obtain the form by writing to:

College Board ATP	or	College Board ATP
CN 6200		Box 1025
Princeton, NJ 08541-6200		Berkeley, CA 94701

Along with the registration form you will receive a current Student Bulletin. It includes all necessary information on procedures, exceptions and special arrangements, times and places, and fees.

1

Format of SAT I

SAT I is a three-hour, mostly multiple-choice examination divided into sections as shown in the chart on the following page. One of the sections is experimental. The nonexperimental sections make up the scores that colleges use to evaluate your application.

The verbal sections test critical reading and vocabulary skills.

The mathematical sections cover arithmetic, algebra, and geometry. The formulas you need will be given in the test instructions; you are not required to memorize them. Although they can all be answered with basic math, the questions may, in some instances, seem unusual to you. They are designed to test your skill in applying what you know to unfamiliar situations.

The experimental section of SAT I may test verbal reasoning or mathematical reasoning. Your score in this section does not count; the results are used solely by the test-makers in devising future tests. The order of the sections of SAT I is not fixed. You will not be told which section is the experimental one, so it is important that you do your best on every section.

The following is a schematic representation of a typical SAT I. While the ordering of the sections—as well as the timing and number of questions within each section—may vary, the format will adhere to this basic scheme.

TYPICAL FORMAT OF SAT I

SECTION	NUMBER OF QUESTIONS	TIME ALLOWED
SECTION 1: VERBAL REASONING	30	30 min.
Sentence Completions	9	
Analogies	6	
Critical Reading	15	
SECTION 2: MATHEMATICAL REASONING	25	30 min.
Regular Mathematics		
SECTION 3: VERBAL REASONING	13	15 min.
Critical Reading		
SECTION 4: MATHEMATICAL REASONING	10	15 min.
Regular Mathematics		
SECTION 5: VERBAL REASONING	35	30 min.
Sentence Completions	10	
Analogies	13	
Critical Reading	12	
SECTION 6: MATHEMATICAL REASONING	25	30 min.
Quantitative Comparisons	15	
Student-Produced Responses	10	
EXPERIMENTAL SECTION	varies	30 min.
Verbal Reasoning or Mathematical Reasoning		

TYPES OF SAT VERBAL REASONING QUESTIONS

The verbal sections of the SAT test vocabulary, verbal reasoning, and the ability to understand reading passages. These skills are measured by means of three question types:

1. Analogies
2. Sentence Completions
3. Critical Reading

Analogies

This type of question tests your ability to see a relationship between a pair of words and to recognize a similar relationship between another pair of words.

Example:

> PAINTER : STUDIO ::
>
> (A) composer : piano
>
> (B) teacher : faculty
>
> (C) judge : courtroom
>
> (D) golfer : club
>
> (E) stage : theater

The correct answer is (C). A *painter* works in a *studio* as a *judge* works in a *courtroom*.

Sentence Completions

This type of question tests your ability to recognize relationships among the parts of a sentence so that you can choose the word or words that best complete each sentence.

Example:

> Conditions in the mine were ----, so the mine workers refused to return to their jobs until the dangers were ----.
>
> (A) filthy .. disbanded
>
> (B) hazardous .. eliminated
>
> (C) deplorable .. collated
>
> (D) conducive .. ameliorated
>
> (E) illegal .. enhanced

The correct answer is (B). The workers wanted the *hazardous* conditions *eliminated*.

Critical Reading

This type of question tests your ability to read and understand passages taken from any of the following categories: humanities, social sciences, natural sciences, and fiction or nonfiction narrative.

Based upon reading selections ranging from 400 to 850 words, critical reading questions may require you to

- recognize the meaning of a word as used in context
- interpret specific information presented in the passage
- analyze information in one part of the passage in terms of information presented in another part of the passage
- evaluate the author's assumptions or identify the logical structure of the passage

Some reading selections consist of a pair of passages that present different points of view on the same or related subjects. The passages may support each other, oppose each other, or in some way complement each other. Some questions relate to each passage separately and others ask you to compare, contrast, or evaluate the two passages.

Example:

SAMPLE PASSAGE

Private enterprise is no stranger to the American prison. When the United States replaced corporal punishment with confinement as the primary punishment for criminals in the early 19th century, the
(5) private sector was the most frequent employer of convict labor. Prisoners were typically either leased to private companies who set up shop in the prison or used by prison officials to produce finished goods for a manufacturer who supplied the raw materials
(10) to the prison. The former arrangement was called the contract system, while the latter came to be known as the piece-price system. In both instances, a private company paid the prison a fee for the use of prison labor, which was used to partially offset
(15) the expense of operating the prison. Blatant exploitation of inmates sometimes developed as a consequence of these systems.

Opposition to the use of prison labor from rival manufacturers and from the growing organized
(20) labor movement began to emerge in the latter part of the 19th century as more and more prisoners were put to work for the private sector. Opposition reached a peak during the Great Depression when Congress passed a series of laws designed to prohibit the
(25) movement of prison-made goods in interstate commerce, thus insuring that these products would not compete with those made by outside labor. Many state legislatures followed suit, forbidding the open market sale or importation of prison-made goods
(30) within their borders and effectively barring the private sector from the prison. As a consequence, prison-based manufacturing operations became state-owned and-operated businesses, selling goods in a highly restricted market.

QUESTIONS ON SAMPLE PASSAGE:

1. Prisons stopped producing readily available goods due to all of the following *except*

    (A) laws passed by state legislatures

    (B) laws passed by the Congress of the United States

    (C) opposition from organized labor

    (D) dissatisfaction of the prisoners

    (E) opposition from rival manufacturers

This question requires you to apply information given in the passage. The correct answer is (D), because there is no mention of prisoner dissatisfaction. Choice (A) is mentioned in lines 28–30, choice (B) is mentioned in lines 23–25, and choices (C) and (E) are mentioned in lines 18–20.

2. In the arrangement known as the "contract system",

    (A) companies set up shop inside a prison and used prisoners for labor

    (B) manufacturers supplied raw materials to the prison

    (C) all of the prisoners signed a contract to produce a certain amount of goods

    (D) prisoners with suitable skills would contact the companies

    (E) exploitation inevitably ensued.

This question requires you to interpret details. The correct answer is (A). In lines 6–7, the contract system is defined as a system in which prisoners were "leased to private companies who set up shop in the prison."

3. According to the passage, which of the following was instrumental in the development of the private sector in prison?

    (A) Seed money from the federal government

    (B) The replacement of corporal punishment with confinement

    (C) The crudeness of the original prison system

    (D) The constant exploitation of the prisoners by manufacturers

    (E) The piece-price and contract system

This question requires you to evaluate information. The correct answer is (B), as stated in the second sentence of the passage.

4. Which of the following statements can be inferred from the passage?

    (A) There is no longer any private sector work done in prisons.

    (B) Legislatures are ready to repeal the previously passed prison laws.

    (C) Prison systems were once fully supported by the fees paid by the private sector.

    (D) The Great Depression was caused by excessive prison labor.

    (E) Piece-price was more profitable than the contract system.

This question requires you to make an inference. The correct answer is (A), which follows from the last sentence of the passage.

General Test-Taking Tips

SAT I contains several verbal sections. On a typical test, the nonexperimental sections will contain 78 verbal questions. Of these, typically 19 will be sentence completions, 19 will be verbal analogies, and 40 will be critical reading questions.

THE SAT CONTAINS AN EXPERIMENTAL SECTION.

One of the sections of your SAT will be an experimental section. That is, the test-writers will be using it to try out new questions for future exams. The experimental section may contain either verbal or math questions. You won't be told which section is the experimental one, so you will need to do your best on every section.

EVERY SECTION OF THE SAT HAS A TIME LIMIT.

You are allowed to work on a section only during the time set aside for that section. You cannot go back to an earlier section and you cannot skip ahead to a later section. Since you only have one chance to answer the questions in a section, make sure you use your time wisely.

LEARN TO PACE YOURSELF TO GET YOUR HIGHEST SCORE.

Your verbal SAT score is based on a formula that takes into account the number of questions you answer correctly and the number of questions you answer incorrectly. The formula is:

Raw Score = Number Correct $- (\frac{1}{4} \times$ Number Incorrect)

Questions left blank do not affect your score. For example, a student who answers a total of 55 verbal questions correctly and 20 incorrectly (leaving 5 blank) would have the following raw score:

Correct $- (\frac{1}{4}$ Incorrect) = Raw Score

$55 - (\frac{1}{4}(20)) = 50$

The raw score is then converted to a scaled score (the 200 to 800 scale) using another formula. To give you some idea of how many answers you need for a certain score, here is a partial listing of raw score/scaled score conversions:

Verbal Raw Score	Verbal Scaled Score
(0 to 80)	(200 to 800)
80	800
75	750
60	610
50	540
30	470

PRACTICE UNDER TIMED CONDITIONS TO FIND THE BEST BALANCE BETWEEN SPEED AND ACCURACY.

Since your verbal score is based on the number of questions you answer correctly less an adjustment for questions you answer incorrectly, you can get your maximum score only if you learn to balance speed with accuracy. You can't afford to go so fast that you miss a lot of questions due to carelessness. On the other hand, you can't afford to be so careful that you just don't get to a lot of questions.

DON'T WASTE TIME READING THE DIRECTIONS.

By the time you take your SAT, you will have practiced on a lot of verbal questions. You will be able to recognize the three different types (analogies, sentence completions, and critical reading) and you will know how to attack them. Reading the directions for these questions on the SAT would be a waste of your time.

DON'T WASTE TIME ON SPECIFIC QUESTIONS.

Each verbal question counts exactly one point toward your raw score. The easiest question on the test counts one point, and the hardest question counts one point. So don't waste time working on a question that you can't seem to solve. When you reach the point at which you realize you're not making progress, leave that question. Come back to it later if you have time.

ANALOGIES AND SENTENCE COMPLETIONS ARE ARRANGED IN INCREASING ORDER OF DIFFICULTY.

Within both of these types of questions, the questions get harder as you go along. The first question will be one anyone can answer. By the middle of the section, you will find some questions that are difficult. By the end of the section, you will encounter some very difficult questions. Thus, work as quickly as you can through the earlier questions in a section; you can use the extra time to answer the difficult questions that come later.

YOU CAN VARY YOUR ORDER OF ATTACK WITHIN A SECTION.

Within the time limit, you can attack the questions in the section in any order you want to. You could do analogies first even though they are not presented first. Is there any advantage to doing the problems out of order? Maybe— critical reading questions are based on a selection that may be as long as 850 words. You can't answer the critical reading questions until you've done the reading. Wouldn't it be a shame to read a critical reading selection and run out of time before you have a chance to answer the questions? So, if you are having a problem with time, make sure that you answer all of the short questions (analogies and sentence completions) before you tackle the critical reading. But be careful that you mark your answer sheet correctly!

BRING A WATCH TO THE EXAM.

Your exam room may not have a clock. To keep track of the passing time, make sure that you bring your own timepiece. You don't have to have a fancy stop watch; a simple watch will do.

IF YOU ARE ABLE TO ELIMINATE ONE OR MORE ANSWERS TO A QUESTION, YOU SHOULD GUESS.

In the scoring system, the guessing penalty is calculated to eliminate the advantage of *random* guessing. It should not affect educated guessing. To prove this to yourself, ask what would happen if you guessed at random on 20 questions. Since there are five answer choices to each question, you would get one out of every five questions right and miss the rest. Since you would get four questions right and miss 16, your raw score would be:

Correct $-$ ($\frac{1}{4}$ Incorrect) = Raw Score

$4 - (\frac{1}{4}(16)) = 0$

A completely neutral result. But now think about what would happen if you make educated guesses. Assume that in each of the 20 questions you can eliminate even just one answer choice. That would leave four rather than five choices for each question, so you would expect to get one out of every four correct. Since you would get five questions right and miss only 15, your raw score would be:

Correct $-$ ($\frac{1}{4}$ Incorrect) = Raw Score

$5 - (\frac{1}{4}(15)) = 1-\frac{1}{4}$

That number will be rounded off to the nearest integer, so your net gain would be +1 on the raw score. And that could make you jump 10 points on the scaled score, e.g., from 510 to 520 or from 630 to 640!

MAKE SURE YOU MARK THE ANSWER SPACES COMPLETELY AND NEATLY.

The SAT is a machine-graded exam. You enter your responses on an answer sheet by darkening ovals. Be careful! The machine can only read what you've put down. If you make a mistake in marking your answer sheet, even though you know the right answer, the machine will read a wrong answer.

MARK YOUR ANSWERS IN GROUPS.

Instead of working a question and marking an answer and working a question and marking an answer and so on, work a group of problems in your test booklet, and then mark your answers. With this system, there is less chance that you will make a mistake as you enter your answers.

CREATE A RECORD-KEEPING SYSTEM FOR YOURSELF.

You'll find that there are some questions you can answer easily, others that you can't answer immediately but think you can if you come back later and do some more work, and still others that you can't answer at all. You'll probably be going back and forth a good deal. To help keep track of what you have done and what you haven't done, create for yourself a system of symbols. For example, circle the answer you think is correct. Or if you aren't able to answer a question definitely and intend to come back to it later, put a question mark by the number of that question and put an "x" over any choice you have already eliminated.

HOW TO USE THIS BOOK

This is not an ordinary SAT exercise book. Every test is graded for difficulty so that you can pace yourself according to your needs. Level A questions are slightly easier than actual SAT questions; level B questions are approximately equal in difficulty to real exam questions; level C questions are more difficult; and level D questions are of varying degrees of difficulty. Level D tests have a difficulty level approximately equal to that of a regular SAT.

The diagnostic verbal reasoning test on page 13 will serve as a reasonably accurate indicator of your SAT scores at this time. If the equivalent score on this test is below the level required by the college of your choice, you may need to improve your study skills or your understanding of the exam or both. The diagnostic test's explanatory answers will help you find out whether your vocabulary and critical reading skills are what they should be. In addition, by studying the test-taking hints preceding each section you will become more familiar with the actual exam format, which will in turn enable you to work on the questions in an efficient, orderly way. The guidelines below should be followed for maximum results:

1. Take and grade the diagnostic test.

2. Analyze your results to see how well you did in each question category.

3. Study the advice given as well as the pre-test and analysis in each category.

4. Apportion your time for the drill tests according to the amount of trouble you had in each category.

5. Retest yourself periodically between the time you take the diagnostic test and the time you plan to take your SAT. Use the three practice verbal reasoning tests. If, for example, there are nine weeks from the time you took your diagnostic test until your SAT, you should plan on taking the practice verbal reasoning tests in the third, sixth, and ninth weeks.

Your scores should keep climbing as continued practice gives you confidence and experience.

Diagnostic Verbal Reasoning Test

Answer Sheet

1. Ⓐ Ⓑ Ⓒ Ⓓ Ⓔ
2. Ⓐ Ⓑ Ⓒ Ⓓ Ⓔ
3. Ⓐ Ⓑ Ⓒ Ⓓ Ⓔ
4. Ⓐ Ⓑ Ⓒ Ⓓ Ⓔ
5. Ⓐ Ⓑ Ⓒ Ⓓ Ⓔ
6. Ⓐ Ⓑ Ⓒ Ⓓ Ⓔ
7. Ⓐ Ⓑ Ⓒ Ⓓ Ⓔ
8. Ⓐ Ⓑ Ⓒ Ⓓ Ⓔ
9. Ⓐ Ⓑ Ⓒ Ⓓ Ⓔ
10. Ⓐ Ⓑ Ⓒ Ⓓ Ⓔ
11. Ⓐ Ⓑ Ⓒ Ⓓ Ⓔ
12. Ⓐ Ⓑ Ⓒ Ⓓ Ⓔ
13. Ⓐ Ⓑ Ⓒ Ⓓ Ⓔ
14. Ⓐ Ⓑ Ⓒ Ⓓ Ⓔ
15. Ⓐ Ⓑ Ⓒ Ⓓ Ⓔ
16. Ⓐ Ⓑ Ⓒ Ⓓ Ⓔ
17. Ⓐ Ⓑ Ⓒ Ⓓ Ⓔ
18. Ⓐ Ⓑ Ⓒ Ⓓ Ⓔ
19. Ⓐ Ⓑ Ⓒ Ⓓ Ⓔ
20. Ⓐ Ⓑ Ⓒ Ⓓ Ⓔ
21. Ⓐ Ⓑ Ⓒ Ⓓ Ⓔ
22. Ⓐ Ⓑ Ⓒ Ⓓ Ⓔ
23. Ⓐ Ⓑ Ⓒ Ⓓ Ⓔ
24. Ⓐ Ⓑ Ⓒ Ⓓ Ⓔ
25. Ⓐ Ⓑ Ⓒ Ⓓ Ⓔ
26. Ⓐ Ⓑ Ⓒ Ⓓ Ⓔ
27. Ⓐ Ⓑ Ⓒ Ⓓ Ⓔ
28. Ⓐ Ⓑ Ⓒ Ⓓ Ⓔ
29. Ⓐ Ⓑ Ⓒ Ⓓ Ⓔ
30. Ⓐ Ⓑ Ⓒ Ⓓ Ⓔ

Diagnostic Verbal Reasoning Test

30 QUESTIONS · TIME—30 MINUTES
(Answers on page 19)

Directions: Each of the following questions consists of an incomplete sentence followed by five words or pairs of words. Choose that word or pair of words which, when substituted for the blank space or spaces, *best* completes the meaning of the sentence, and mark the letter of your choice on your answer sheet.

Example:

In view of the extenuating circumstances and the defendant's youth, the judge recommended ----.

(A) conviction

(B) a defense

(C) a mistrial

(D) leniency

(E) life imprisonment

Ⓐ Ⓑ Ⓒ ● Ⓔ

1. Gregory's face was ---- when he reported the loss of his ship.

(A) vivid

(B) somber

(C) animated

(D) pusillanimous

(E) antiquated

2. Since his clothes were soaked, his story of falling into the creek seemed ----.

(A) incredible

(B) absurd

(C) predictable

(D) plausible

(E) remarkable

3. You have a(n) ----; the test has been postponed for a week.

(A) absence

(B) holiday

(C) request

(D) assignment

(E) reprieve

4. The sheik's wealth was a matter of ----; nobody had the least idea of how much he possessed.

(A) conjecture

(B) conjunction

(C) divinity

(D) obloquy

(E) concern

5. During the 1923 German inflation, there was a ---- of paper currency; it took a wheelbarrow to transport enough marks to buy a suit.

(A) shortage

(B) supply

(C) dearth

(D) transfer

(E) plethora

6. Trespassing on private property is ---- by law.

(A) proscribed

(B) warranted

(C) prescribed

(D) eliminated

(E) forgiven

13

GO ON TO THE NEXT PAGE

7. Since you have just made a(n) ---- sale, this is a(n) ---- time to ask for a raise.

   (A) meager .. excellent

   (B) ostentatious .. precipitous

   (C) impressive .. opportune

   (D) plausible .. preposterous

   (E) pernicious .. reprehensible

8. People are ---- to confess such anxieties for fear of appearing ----.

   (A) reluctant .. virtuous

   (B) eager .. recondite

   (C) constrained .. derelict

   (D) reticent .. weak

   (E) hesitant .. prudent

9. They are a(n) ---- couple who cultivate many friendships among ---- people.

   (A) gratuitous .. frivolous

   (B) indolent .. impeccable

   (C) gregarious .. diverse

   (D) insidious .. intrepid

   (E) solicitous .. laconic

Directions: Each of the following questions consists of a capitalized pair of words followed by five pairs of words lettered A through E. The capitalized words bear some meaningful relationship to each other. Choose the lettered pair of words whose relationship is most similar to that expressed by the capitalized pair and mark its letter on your answer sheet.

Example:

DAY : SUN ::

   (A) sunlight : daylight

   (B) ray : sun

   (C) night : moon

   (D) heat : cold

   (E) moon : star

   Ⓐ Ⓑ ● Ⓓ Ⓔ

10. SANGUINE : PESSIMISM ::

    (A) absolute : relativity

    (B) unharried : optimism

    (C) frenetic : serenity

    (D) ardent : involvement

    (E) uncouth : rudeness

11. TACT : DIPLOMAT ::

    (A) courage : coward

    (B) widsom : investigator

    (C) cowardice : magnate

    (D) honesty : perjurer

    (E) prejudice : bigot

12. VEHICLE : CONVOY ::

    (A) ship : voyage

    (B) building : brick

    (C) train : tracks

    (D) fish : school

    (E) minnow : whale

13. TRITE: FRESHNESS ::

    (A) pedestrian : archetype

    (B) typical : laxness

    (C) banal ; boldness

    (D) prophetic : foresight

    (E) perfunctory : solicitude

14. DAMP : SATURATED ::

  (A) cold : gelid

  (B) calm : tranquil

  (C) dewy : moist

  (D) frigid : frozen

  (E) dank : satiated

15. PRODIGAL : PROFLIGATE ::

  (A) radical : temperate

  (B) invalid : protean

  (C) proponent : plaintive

  (D) scholar : exemplary

  (E) spendthrift : lavish

Directions: Each reading passage below is followed by a set of questions. Read the passage and answer the accompanying questions, basing your answers on what is stated or implied in the passage. Mark the letter of your choice on your answer sheet.

QUESTIONS 16–21 ARE BASED ON THE FOLLOWING PASSAGE.

Nancy Langhorne was born in the United States in 1879. She moved to England, married Viscount Astor, and became the first woman ever to sit in the House of Commons, a position she held from 1919 to 1945. As Lady Astor, her politics were often questionable—she was among those who sought to appease the Fascists in the 1930s—but her door-opening role for women in politics made her an important figure. The following comments are excerpted from a 1922 address at Town Hall in New York City.

My entrance into the House of Commons was not, as some thought, in the nature of a revolution. It was an evolution. My husband was the one who started me off on this downward path—from the fireside to
(5) public life. If I have helped the cause of women he is the one to thank, not me.

A woman in the House of Commons! It was almost enough to have broken up the House. I don't blame them—it was equally hard on the woman as
(10) it was on them. A pioneer may be a picturesque figure, but they are often rather lonely ones. I must say for the House of Commons, they bore their shock with dauntless decency. No body of men could have been kinder and fairer to a "pirate" than
(15) they were. When you hear people over here trying to run down England, please remember that England was the first large country to give the vote to women and that the men of England welcomed an American-born woman in the House with a fairness
(20) and a justice which, at least, this woman never will forget....

Now, why are we in politics? What is it all about? Something much bigger than ourselves. Schopenhauer was wrong in nearly everything he
(25) wrote about women—and he wrote a lot, but he was right in one thing. He said, in speaking of women, "the race is to her more than the individual," and I believe that it is true. I feel somehow we do care about the race as a whole, our very nature makes us
(30) take a forward vision; there is no reason why women should look back—mercifully we have no political past; we have all the mistakes of sex legislation with its appalling failures to guide us.

We should know what to avoid, it is no use
(35) blaming the men—we made them what they are— and now it is up to us to try and make ourselves—the makers of men—a little more responsible in the future. We realize that no one sex can govern alone. I believe that one of the reasons why civilization has
(40) failed so lamentably is that it has had a one-sided government. Don't let us make the mistake of ever allowing that to happen again.

I can conceive of nothing worse than a man-governed world except a woman-governed world—
(45) but I can see the combination of the two going forward and making civilization more worthy of the name of civilization based on Christianity, not force. A civilization based on justice and mercy. I feel men have a greater sense of justice and we of mercy.
(50) They must borrow our mercy and we must use their justice. We are new brooms; let us see that we sweep the right rooms.

GO ON TO THE NEXT PAGE

16. According to Lady Astor, the reaction of the men in the House of Commons to her being seated was one of

   (A) surprise and horror

   (B) polite consternation

   (C) resigned distaste

   (D) witticisms and good humor

   (E) amused acceptance

17. Lady Astor urges Americans to give England its due for

   (A) having a bicameral legislature

   (B) its tolerance toward women in politics

   (C) allowing an American into their Parliament

   (D) both A and B

   (E) both B and C

18. Women look forward, according to Lady Astor, because

   (A) the history of sexism makes their past insignificant

   (B) something may be gaining on them

   (C) they have made so many mistakes in the past

   (D) they have no real sense of history

   (E) men refuse to do so

19. Lady Astor sees the ideal government as a balance between

   (A) fairness and compassion

   (B) the past and the future

   (C) Christianity and force

   (D) honesty and courage

   (E) virtue and strength

20. When Lady Astor refers to "new brooms" (line 51), she means that

   (A) women belong in the home

   (B) there is now a fresh chance to clean up things

   (C) the tide of history has swept right by women

   (D) it is time to sweep men out of power

   (E) sweeping change is a thing of the past

21. Lady Astor's attitude toward men seems to be one of

   (A) chilly disapproval

   (B) lighthearted leniency

   (C) reverent deference

   (D) defiant contempt

   (E) weary indifference

QUESTIONS 22–30 ARE BASED ON THE FOLLOWING PASSAGE.

Sun Yat-sen (1866–1925) was a revolutionary who worked to overthrow the monarchy and install a republic in China. He served as president of the republic from 1923 until his death in 1925. This speech, which he gave in early 1924, shows his desire to bring China into the twentieth century and make it a world power.

Although we are behind the foreigners in scientific achievement, our native ability is adequate to the construction of a great material civilization, which is proved by the concrete evidence of past achieve-

(5)   ments. We invented the compass, printing, porcelain, gunpowder, and the curing of tea and weaving of silk. Foreigners have made good use of these inventions. For example, modern ocean travel would be impossible if there were no compass. The fast

(10)   printing machine, which turns out tens of thousands of copies per hour, had its origin in China. Foreign military greatness comes from gunpowder, which was first used by the Chinese. Furthermore, many of the latest inventions in architecture in the West have

(15)   been practiced in the East for thousands of years. This genius of our race for material inventions seems now to be lost; and so our greatness has become but the history of bygone glories.

I believe that we have many things to learn from
(20) the West, and that we can learn them. Many West-
erners maintain that the hardest thing to learn is
aerial science; already many Chinese have become
skillful aviators. If aeronautics can be learned, I
believe everything can be learned by our people.
(25) Science is only three hundred years old, and it was
not highly developed until 50 years ago. Formerly
coal was used as the source of energy; now the age
of coal has given place to the age of electricity.

Recently America had a plan for nationalizing
(30) the water-power of the country. America has hundreds of thousands of factories. Each big factory has
to have a powerhouse which consumes a tremen-
dous amount of coal. The railroads in the country are
busily engaged in transporting coal, and have little
(35) time for transporting agricultural products. As a
means of economizing coal and lessening transportation, a national central powerhouse is suggested.
When such a house is built, the entire nation will
receive energy from one central station. The result
(40) will be the elimination of enormous waste and the
increase of efficiency.

When we learn from the West, it is evident that
we should learn the latest inventions instead of
repeating the various steps of development. In the
(45) case of the powerhouse, we may well learn to adopt
the centralized plan of producing electricity, and
need not follow the old plan of using coal to produce
energy. In this way we can easily within ten years
catch up with the West in material achievement.
(50) The time is critical. We have no time to waste,
and we ought to take the latest and the best that the
West can offer. Our intelligence is by no means
inferior to that of the Japanese. With our historical
background and our natural and human resources, it
(55) should be easier for us than it was for Japan to rise
to the place of a first-class Power by a partial
adaptation of Western civilization. We ought to be
ten times stronger than Japan because our country is
more than ten times bigger and richer than Japan.
(60) China is potentially equal to ten Powers. At present
England, America, France, Italy, and Japan constitute the so-called Big Five. Even with the rise of
Germany and Soviet Russia, the world has only
seven Powers. When China becomes strong, she can
(65) easily win first place in the Council of Nations.

22. Sun Yat-sen lists past scientific contributions of
Chinese inventors (lines 5–6) to show that

(A) China deserves more credit for past
successes

(B) most important inventions are Chinese

(C) the Chinese have the ability to create and
achieve

(D) Chinese inventions have been stolen by
foreigners

(E) life would be difficult without scientific
exploration

23. Why has China lost greatness, according to Sun
Yat-sen?

(A) It has turned inward and lost its place in
the world.

(B) Its inventions are old and outdated.

(C) It cannot turn its inventiveness to
good use.

(D) The people are not interested in material
things.

(E) The people's genius for invention has
been lost.

24. Sun Yat-sen uses the example of aviation (line
22) to show that

(A) the Chinese have the skill to learn from
the West

(B) Western inventions are more complex
than Chinese inventions

(C) only aeronautics offers a challenge to the
Chinese

(D) science is not very old

(E) very few people can become inventors

25. A vital lesson the West can teach China is the
use of

(A) centralized electrical power

(B) coal to produce energy

(C) railroads to transport agricultural products

(D) both A and B

(E) both B and C

GO ON TO THE NEXT PAGE

26. It is important to Sun Yat-sen that the Chinese learn from the West without

    (A) repeating the West's mistakes

    (B) having to start from the beginning

    (C) acting aggressively

    (D) spending as much as the West has

    (E) becoming too Western in outlook

27. Sun Yat-sen compares the intelligence of the Chinese to that of the Japanese (line 52) to demonstrate that

    (A) Chinese spies are just as good as Japanese spies

    (B) China can become a Power as easily as Japan did

    (C) with a little education, the Chinese can surpass the Japanese

    (D) it was not easy for Japan to become a Power

    (E) it will not be easy for China to compete with Japan

28. By "critical" (line 50), Sun Yat-sen means

    (A) analytical

    (B) grievous

    (C) dangerous

    (D) picky

    (E) momentous

29. Would Sun Yat-sen approve of fast-food restaurants opening in China?

    (A) Probably, because he approves of Western inventions.

    (B) Probably, if they were run by the Chinese for Chinese profit.

    (C) No, because they are too Western in appearance.

    (D) No, because they have nothing to do with material achievement.

    (E) No, because he wants China to maintain its traditions.

30. A reasonable title for this speech might be

    (A) How China Lost Its Way

    (B) Military Strength

    (C) How the West Has Won

    (D) Learning from the West

    (E) Ten Times Stronger

STOP

IF YOU FINISH BEFORE THE TIME IS UP,
GO BACK AND CHECK YOUR WORK.

Diagnostic Verbal Reasoning Test

Answer Key

1. B	7. C	13. E	19. A	25. A
2. D	8. D	14. A	20. B	26. B
3. E	9. C	15. E	21. B	27. B
4. A	10. C	16. B	22. C	28. E
5. E	11. E	17. E	23. E	29. B
6. A	12. D	18. A	24. A	30. D

Explanatory Answers

1. **(B)** When a person loses anything as large and important as his ship, his face can be expected to look serious, "down," or depressed—not *vivid* (full of life), *animated* (lively), *pusillanimous* (cowardly), or *antiquated* (made to look old). *Somber* (dark and gloomy) is the ideal choice.

2. **(D)** The soaked clothes make the story believable, or *plausible*.

3. **(E)** Since the test has been postponed, the students have a *reprieve*—a temporary escape from taking it.

4. **(A)** Since "nobody had the least idea of how much he possessed," apparently one could only make a guess at the amount. *Conjecture* (theory, inference, or prediction based on guesswork) fits.

5. **(E)** If "it took a wheelbarrow to transport enough marks to buy a suit," there must have been a superabundance, or *plethora,* of paper currency.

6. **(A)** *Proscribed* means forbidden, outlawed. (B) means justified; (C), recommended. (D) and (E) are impossible.

7. **(C)** Both words in the answer choice must be either positive or negative, so (A) and (D) are eliminated. Neither (B) nor (E) makes any sense in the context of the sentence. The correct answer is (C): following an *impressive* sale would be an *opportune* (appropriate) time to ask for a raise.

8. **(D)** A sentence that includes *anxieties* and *fear* has a strong negative connotation, so two negative-sounding words are needed. Only (C) and (D) offer two negative-sounding choices. In (C), however, *constrained* (forced or compelled) and *derelict* (irresponsible) make no sense in the context. The correct answer is (D): people are *reticent* (hesitant) to confess anxieties for fear of appearing *weak*.

9. **(C)** People who have many friendships are *gregarious* (sociable) and are likely to have *diverse* (varied) friends. None of the other answer choices makes any sense.

10. **(C)** A defining quality of a *sanguine* (confident) person is a lack of *pessimism*. Similarly, a *frenetic* (frenzied) person lacks *serenity*.

11. **(E)** *Tact* is the defining quality of a *diplomat;* similarly, *prejudice* is the defining quality of a *bigot*. None of the other choices illustrates a similar relationship.

12. **(D)** A *vehicle* is one small part of a *convoy,* just as a *fish* can be one small part of a *school*.

13. **(E)** Something that is *trite* (stale) lacks *freshness*. Similarly, something that is *perfunctory* (careless) lacks *solicitude* (care).

14. **(A)** *Saturated* means "filled with water," a much greater degree of wetness than *damp*. Similarly, *gelid* (extremely cold or frozen) connotes a much greater degree of chilliness than *cold*. None of the other choices illustrates a comparable relationship.

15. **(E)** A *prodigal* is a person who is careless with money, or *profligate*. Similarly, a *spendthrift* is a person who is extravagant, or *lavish*.

16. **(B)** "… They bore their shock with dauntless decency" (line 12), says the speaker. They were shocked, but polite.

17. **(E)** In the end of paragraph 2, Lady Astor commends the English for these two things.

18. **(A)** She is unfailingly polite in her discussion of sexism, but lines 31–32 explain her position.

19. **(A)** This is an accurate translation of "justice and mercy" (line 48).

20. **(B)** The reference is to the adage "A new broom sweeps clean." Lady Astor implies that women, the "new brooms," have the power to change things for the better.

21. **(B)** She thanks her husband for getting her into politics (line 3), and she blames women for making men what they are (line 35). Despite the "appalling failures" of sex legislation, Lady Astor lets men off the hook.

22. **(C)** The point of the opening paragraph is to demonstrate that China once had the power to build and invent, and that it may regain this past power.

23. **(E)** This is implied by the correlation of clauses in lines 16–18; Sun Yat-sen says that "our greatness has become but the history of bygone glories" because the genius for invention is lost.

24. **(A)** Although aviation is hard to learn, many Chinese have mastered it; therefore, they are up to any task.

25. **(A)** Paragraph 3 is all about this centralization of power.

26. **(B)** Line 43 at the beginning of paragraph 4 states the speaker's desire to learn from the West without repeating all the stages of development.

27. **(B)** China's rivalry with Japan is used here to indicate that China can do anything Japan can do.

28. **(E)** Only *momentous* makes sense in context.

29. **(B)** Sun Yat-sen approves of Western inventions (A), but here he appears to approve only if they can be adapted and used by the Chinese for "material achievement."

30. **(D)** Most of the speech deals with the fact that China has much to learn from the West if it wants to become a Power.

PART

ONE

EVERYTHING YOU NEED!

Verbal Reasoning Practice

 PREVIEW

Chapter 1
ANALOGIES

Chapter 2
SENTENCE COMPLETIONS

Chapter 3
CRITICAL READING

Analogies

What Is an Analogy Question?

In each SAT Analogy question you are given a pair of capitalized words followed by five other word pairs as answer choices. You must select the answer-choice pair that best expresses a relationship similar to that expressed by the capitalized pair.

> SPARROW : BIRD ::
>
> (A) trout : fish
>
> (B) bear : fur
>
> (C) giraffe : neck
>
> (D) dog : pet
>
> (E) snail : aquarium

The correct answer is (A). All the answer choices are word pairs that have a logical relationship, but only (A) expresses a relationship similar to that expressed by the capitalized pair. A *sparrow* is a kind of *bird,* just as a *trout* is a kind of *fish.*

Analogy questions test your verbal reasoning ability—the ability to see relationships between words and to make comparisons. How well you answer analogy questions will depend on the size of your vocabulary, your knowledge of the different meanings and connotations of words, and your ability to express logical connections between them.

How to Answer Analogy Questions

Make up a sentence that states the relationship between the capitalized words. Use the capitalized words in a sentence that expresses the relationship between them. Then test the answer choices by substituting them for the capitalized words in your sentence. The choice that makes sense in your sentence will be the correct choice. Here are four examples of the kinds of sentences you might use.

DROP : WATER	A drop is a very small amount of water.
PEN : WRITER	A pen is a tool used by a writer.
JUDGE : COURTROOM	A judge is found in a courtroom.
PREFACE : BOOK	A preface is a part of a book.

Eliminate choices that do not fit in your sentence

DROP : WATER ::

(A) oil : engine

(B) mountain : snow

(C) milk : glass

(D) grain : sand

(E) lumber : tree

A *drop* is a very small amount of *water*.
(A) An *oil* is a very small amount of *engine*. (Wrong)
(B) A *mountain* is a very small amount of *snow*. (Wrong)
(C) A *milk* is a very small amount of *glass*. (Wrong)
(D) A *grain* is a very small amount of *sand*. (Correct)
(E) A *lumber* is a very small amount of *tree*. (Wrong)

PEN : WRITER ::

(A) tooth : dentist

(B) chain saw : mechanic

(C) antenna : actor

(D) cake : oven

(E) scalpel : surgeon

A *pen* is the tool used by a *writer*.
(A) A *tooth* is the tool used by a *dentist*. (Wrong)
(B) A *chain* saw is the tool used by a *mechanic*. (Wrong)
(C) An *antenna* is the tool used by an *actor*. (Wrong)
(D) A *cake* is the tool used by an *oven*. (Wrong)
(E) A *scalpel* is the tool used by a *surgeon*. (Correct)

If necessary, revise your sentence to make the relationship more specific. Your first statement of the relationship between the capitalized words may not eliminate all the wrong answers.

JUDGE : COURTROOM ::

(A) scientist : laboratory

(B) lawyer : client

(C) student : cafeteria

(D) patient : hospital

(E) plumber : sink

A *judge* is found in the *courtroom*.
(A) A *scientist* is found in the *laboratory*. (?)
(B) A *lawyer* is found in the *client*. (Wrong)
(C) A *student* is found in the *cafeteria*. (?)
(D) A *patient* is found in the *hospital*. (?)
(E) A *plumber* is found in the *sink*. (Wrong)

This successfully eliminates two choices, but there are still three left. So you must state the relationship more carefully: A judge is not just "found" in a courtroom; a judge works in a courtroom.

A judge works in a courtroom.
(A) A *scientist* works in a *laboratory.* (Correct)
(B) A *student* works in the *cafeteria.* (Wrong)
(D) A *patient* works in the *hospital.* (Wrong)

> PREFACE : BOOK ::
>
> (A) paragraph : page
>
> (B) act : play
>
> (C) overture : opera
>
> (D) postscript : letter
>
> (E) movement : symphony

A *preface* is a part of a *book.*
(A) A *paragraph* is part of a *page.* (?)
(B) An *act* is part of a *play.* (?)
(C) An *overture* is part of an *opera.* (?)
(D) A *postscript* is part of a *letter.* (?)
(E) A *movement* is part of a *symphony.* (?)

The initial summary of the relationship was not precise enough to eliminate any choices, so you must refine it:

A *preface* is the first part of a *book.*
(A) A *paragraph* is the first part of a *page.* (Wrong)
(B) An *act* is the first part of a *play.* (Wrong)
(C) An *overture* is the first part of an *opera.* (Correct)
(D) A *postscript* is the first part of a *letter.* (Wrong)
(E) A *movement* is the first part of a *symphony.* (Wrong)

Word order is very important in analogies.

An analogy is like a mathematical proportion in that the order of the elements makes a difference. For example, the following mathematical statement is true:

1 is to 2 as 3 is to 6.
That is:
$$\frac{1}{2} = \frac{3}{6}$$

However, it would be incorrect to say:

1 is to 2 as 6 is to 3.
For:
$$\frac{1}{2} \neq \frac{6}{3}$$

Consider the analogy:

GOOSE : BIRD :: ant : insect

This is a valid analogy, since a *goose* is a kind of *bird* and an *ant* is a kind of *insect*. However, suppose you were given the following word pairs:

GOOSE : BIRD :: insect : ant

Now the second pair no longer expresses the same relationship as the first pair, since an *insect* is not a kind of *ant*.

If your sentence changes the order of the capitalized words, then you must also change the order of the answer pairs. Sometimes it is easier to express the relationship between the capitalized words by putting them in a sentence that reverses their order. However, if you reverse the capitalized words, you must also remember to reverse the order of the words in the answer choices when you substitute them into your sentence. Here's how this works:

PRIDE : PEACOCK ::

(A) cheese : cow

(B) jockey : horse

(C) peace : dove

(D) hen : rooster

(E) honesty : redwood

A *peacock* is a symbol of *pride*.
(A) A *cow* is a symbol of *cheese*. (Wrong)
(B) A *horse* is a symbol of a *jockey*. (Wrong)
(C) A *dove* is a symbol of *peace*. (Correct)
(D) A *rooster* is a symbol of a *hen*. (Wrong)
(E) A *redwood* is a symbol of *honesty*. (Wrong)

Use the answer choices to determine parts of speech.

Often the hardest part of determining an analogy relationship is deciding what meaning a word has based on its part of speech. If you are uncertain of the part of speech of a capitalized word, frequently you can determine it from the answer choices. The parts of speech of the answer choices will always be the same as those of the capitalized words.

COOK : KITCHEN ::

(A) dine : victuals

(B) read : library

(C) invest : broker

(D) capitalize : letter

(E) announce : speaker

At first you might try to state the relationship between the capitalized words in this way:

A *cook* is found in the *kitchen*.

But the answer choices make no sense in this sentence because the first word of each answer choice is a verb. Since the first word of each answer choice is a verb, the first capitalized word must also be a verb:

You can *cook* in the *kitchen*.

And obviously the correct answer is (B):

You can *read* in the *library*.

Eliminate all choices for which you cannot state a relationship.

An answer choice cannot possibly be a correct answer if you cannot state a logical relationship between the two words. For example, try to state the relationship between the words in the following answer choice:

talkative : doctor

A doctor might be talkative, but then again a doctor might not be talkative. A talkative person might become a doctor, but that's not necessarily the case. Thus, there is no analogy connection between the two terms, and therefore this answer choice could never be correct.

The following lists show examples of possible and impossible analogy pairs.

Possible	Impossible
LAWYER : CLIENT	lawyer : sidewalk
GOOSE : FLOCK	goose : mammal
AIRPLANE : PROPELLER	airplane : mountain
TEACHER : CLASSROOM	teacher : happiness
TRIVIAL : IMPORTANCE	music : importance
LETTER : ALPHABET	hearing : alphabet
SAW : CARPENTER	plumber : carpenter
WEIGHT : OBESITY	retiree : obesity

This tip can actually help you even if you don't recognize either of the capitalized words.

XXXXXXXXXX : XXXXXXXXX ::

(A) impulsive : secretary

(B) entertaining : information

(C) tranquil : water

(D) overripe : apple

(E) athletic : marathoner

You can eliminate (A) through (D). None of those pairs can be related to each other in any meaningful way. Only (E) exhibits an analogy relationship: A *marathoner* is *athletic*. So even though you do not know the capitalized words, you can be confident that (E) is the right answer.

Learn the most common types of analogies used by the SAT.

The best strategy for attacking analogies is to state the relationship between the capitalized words. Certain relationships show up on the test very often.

"… is a kind of …"

Examples

SPARROW : BIRD	A sparrow is a kind of bird.
SNAKE : REPTILE	A snake is a kind of reptile.
ODE : POEM	An ode is a kind of poem.
SKYSCRAPER : BUILDING	A skyscraper is a kind of building.

"… is a part of …"

Examples

PETAL : FLOWER	A petal is a part of a flower.
SPOKE : WHEEL	A spoke is a part of a wheel.
NOTE : SCALE	A note is a part of a scale.
ACT : PLAY	An act is a part of a play.

"… is characteristic of …"

Examples

FEAR : COWARD	Fear is characteristic of a coward.
GENEROSITY : PHILANTHROPIST	Generosity is characteristic of a philanthropist.
HOPE : OPTIMIST	Hope is characteristic of an optimist.
BLAME : SCAPEGOAT	Blame is characteristic of a scapegoat.

"Lack of … is characteristic of …"

Examples

LOYALTY : TRAITOR	Lack of loyalty is characteristic of a traitor.
TRUTH : SLANDER	Lack of truth is characteristic of slander.
COMPANIONSHIP : HERMIT	Lack of companionship is characteristic of a hermit.
CONSCIOUSNESS : COMA	Lack of consciousness is characteristic of a coma.

"… is large (great) …"

Examples

CRATER : HOLE   A crater is a large hole.
DOWNPOUR : RAIN   A downpour is great rain.
INFERNO : FIRE   An inferno is a great fire.
RAGE : ANGER   Rage is great (intense) anger.

"… is the tool of …"

Examples

BRUSH : PAINTER   A brush is the tool of a painter.
CAMERA : PHOTOGRAPHER   A camera is the tool of a photographer.
GUN : HUNTER   A gun is the tool of a hunter.
AWL : CARPENTER   An awl is the tool of a carpenter.

"… is a place for …"

Examples

NEWSPAPER : EDITORIAL   A newspaper is a place for an editorial.
HOSPITAL : DOCTOR   A hospital is a place for a doctor.
SCHOOL : TEACHER   A school is a place for a teacher.
LIBRARY : BOOK   A library is a place for a book.

"… is an indication of …"

Examples

CRYING : SADNESS   Crying is an indication of sadness.
APPLAUSE : APPROVAL   Applause is an indication of approval.
GROAN : PAIN   A groan is an indication of pain.
SMILE : PLEASURE   A smile is an indication of pleasure.

PRE-TEST QUIZ

Select the best choice in each of the following questions, and circle the letter that appears before your answer. Then check the explanatory answers that follow.

1. MOUTH : ORIFICE ::
   (A) eye : sight
   (B) nose : odor
   (C) ear : protuberance
   (D) touch : feeling
   (E) taste : tongue

2. WORKER : BONUS ::
   (A) capitalist : principal
   (B) banker : interest
   (C) sports : winning
   (D) horse : spur
   (E) actor : applause

3. WIRE : FLEXIBLE ::
   (A) tire : brittle
   (B) beam : rigid
   (C) steel : rubbery
   (D) stone : yielding
   (E) muscle : watery

4. EATING : GOBBLE ::
   (A) speaking : jabber
   (B) drinking : guzzle
   (C) running : stumble
   (D) seeing : believing
   (E) going : ran

5. SIN : FORGIVE ::
   (A) error : mistake
   (B) reign : authority
   (C) debt : release
   (D) wrong : code
   (E) accident : intentional

6. INTERRUPT : HECKLE ::
   (A) disrupt : intrude
   (B) tease : hector
   (C) maintain : uphold
   (D) condemn : implore
   (E) speech : perform

7. ASTUTE : STUPID ::
   (A) scholar : idiotic
   (B) agile : clumsy
   (C) lonely : clown
   (D) dunce : ignorant
   (E) intelligent : smart

8. FRANGIBLE : BROKEN ::
   (A) smelly : offensive
   (B) candid : unwelcome
   (C) brittle : destroyed
   (D) fluid : liquefied
   (E) pliable : bent

9. PHARMACIST : DRUGS ::
   (A) psychiatrist : ideas
   (B) mentor : drills
   (C) mechanic : troubles
   (D) chef : foods
   (E) nurse : diseases

10. DECIBEL : SOUND ::
    (A) calorie : weight
    (B) volt : electricity
    (C) temperature : weather
    (D) color : light
    (E) area : distance

Explanatory Answers

1. **(C)** The *mouth* is an example of an *orifice* (opening) of the body; the *ear,* an example of a *protuberance* (an appendage or projecting part of an organism). This relationship does not hold with any of the remaining choices.

2. **(E)** The obvious relationship between *worker* and *bonus* is that a worker earns a bonus by his own effort. The only parallel choice is *actor : applause. Bankers* and *capitalists* do not earn interest or principal by their own efforts.

3. **(B)** The primary relationship is that the second word is a characteristic of the first word. A *beam* is *rigid* just as a *wire* is *flexible.*

4. **(B)** The primary relationship is present participle : synonymous verb. (A), (B), and (E) all fit. Choice (B) is best, because all four terms pertain to ingestion, and *gobbling* and *guzzling* are faster and less refined ways of *eating* and *drinking.*

5. **(C)** Here we have noun : verb. Only (A) and (C) are noun : verb pairs. But just as you can *forgive* a *sin,* you can *release* a *debt,* while you cannot *mistake* an *error.*

6. **(B)** *Heckling* is forceful and unpleasant *interrupting. Hectoring* is forceful and unpleasant *teasing,* though teasing has a playful feel to it that is entirely absent from hectoring.

7. **(B)** The primary relationship is adjective : antonym adjective. Only *agile* and *clumsy* are antonyms.

8. **(E)** *Frangible* means *breakable;* thus the original pair has the relationship of a potentiality and the realization of that potentiality. *Pliable* is bendable, and the realization of the potentiality is to be *bent.*

9. **(D)** Here, the first term produces something useful by putting together, or compounding, the "raw materials" expressed in the second term. (A) and (D) fit. (D) is the better choice because a *pharmacist* and a *chef* both deal in concrete substances.

10. **(B)** The obvious relationship is that the first term is a measure of the second term. Choice (B) fits. A *volt* is a measure of *electricity,* and the only other unit of measure mentioned, the *calorie,* measures heat, not *weight.*

LEVEL A ANALOGIES

Test 1   (Answers on Page 64)

Select the choice that is most parallel to the key word pair. Circle the letter that appears before your answer.

1. ABATE : WANE ::
   (A) lessen : wax
   (B) increase : wane
   (C) decrease : wax
   (D) slacken : wane
   (E) slacken : wax

2. BASIL : MARJORAM ::
   (A) pepper : corn
   (B) thyme : barleycorn
   (C) corn : peppercorn
   (D) curry powder : paprika
   (E) curry : comb

3. CABOOSE : BRAKEMAN ::
   (A) back : front
   (B) track : corral
   (C) track : coral
   (D) cowboy : train
   (E) bunkhouse : wrangler

4. DACHSHUND : ST. BERNARD ::
   (A) car : bicycle
   (B) house : tenement
   (C) table : chair
   (D) footstool : armchair
   (E) brandy : sausage

5. LEASH : DOG ::
   (A) tether : horse
   (B) cage : lion
   (C) lock : door
   (D) harness : parachute
   (E) bundle : child

6. SNAKE : SLITHER ::
   (A) feline : cat
   (B) canary : fly
   (C) spider : web
   (D) deer : antler
   (E) hawk : hunt

7. GASTROENTERITIS : CRAMPS ::
   (A) thunder : rain
   (B) rain : medicine man
   (C) allergy : rash
   (D) antihistamines : allergies
   (E) pain : relief

8. PITCHER : INFIELD ::
   (A) archer : bow
   (B) climber : mountain
   (C) goalie : goal
   (D) swimmer : race
   (E) player : net

9. IGLOO : TEPEE ::
   (A) ice : sod
   (B) chocks : skins
   (C) arctic : temperate
   (D) hides : snow
   (E) wampum : blubber

10. BOUQUET : FLOWER ::
    (A) key : door
    (B) air : balloon
    (C) skin : body
    (D) chain : link
    (E) rent : apartment

11. KEEL : SHIP ::

   (A) staircase : cellar

   (B) soul : body

   (C) sole : shoe

   (D) soul : psyche

   (E) engine : car

12. LETTER : WORD ::

   (A) club : people

   (B) homework : school

   (C) page : book

   (D) product : factory

   (E) galaxy : star

13. IMPEACH : DISMISS ::

   (A) arraign : convict

   (B) exonerate : charge

   (C) imprison : jail

   (D) plant : reap

   (E) pitted : discard

14. HOTEL : SHELTER ::

   (A) sofa : pillow

   (B) boat : transportation

   (C) train : recreation

   (D) restaurant : motel

   (E) home : recuperation

15. QUALMS : HESITATE ::

   (A) conscience : cooperate

   (B) guilt : snicker

   (C) courage : persevere

   (D) rage : amuse

   (E) beer : drink

Test 2   (Answers on Page 64)

Select the choice that is most parallel to the key word pair. Circle the letter that appears before your answer.

1. JUVENILE : SENESCENT ::

   (A) immature : impecunious

   (B) dying : living

   (C) growing : aging

   (D) happy : unconcerned

   (E) delinquent : overdue

2. ASSIST : SAVE ::

   (A) request : command

   (B) rely : descry

   (C) hurt : aid

   (D) declare : deny

   (E) want : deride

3. LANYARD : CANNON ::

   (A) trigger : pistol

   (B) handle : knife

   (C) blade : knife

   (D) butt : rifle

   (E) holster : derringer

4. ROCK : SLATE ::

   (A) wave : sea

   (B) boat : kayak

   (C) swimmer : male

   (D) lifeguard : beach

   (E) music : work

5. EXPLOSION : DEBRIS ::

   (A) fire : ashes

   (B) flood : water

   (C) famine : war

   (D) disease : germ

   (E) heat : wood

6. AGILE : ACROBAT ::

   (A) brassy : singer

   (B) loud : vendor

   (C) fine : weather

   (D) eloquent : orator

   (E) insincere : diplomat

7. BANANA : BUNCH ::

   (A) city : state

   (B) world : earth

   (C) president : nation

   (D) people : continent

   (E) apple : sauce

8. QUARRY : MARBLE ::

   (A) timber : forest

   (B) game : preserve

   (C) mine : coal

   (D) tungsten : wolframite

   (E) fire : fuel

9. RAM : LAMB ::

   (A) buck : doe

   (B) buck : dollar

   (C) bull : calf

   (D) ewe : sheep

   (E) male : female

10. SCRUPLES : CROOKED ::

    (A) fear : fearful

    (B) innocence : naïve

    (C) guilt : innocent

    (D) talent : proud

    (E) feathers : birdlike

11. TALISMAN : EVIL ::

    (A) horseshoe : amusement

    (B) amulet : bad luck

    (C) rabbit's foot : good luck

    (D) charm : joy

    (E) broken mirror : bad luck

12. LAW : CITIZEN ::

    (A) democracy : socialism

    (B) weapon : peace

    (C) reins : horse

    (D) gangster : police officer

    (E) novel : author

13. TOAD : TADPOLE ::

    (A) reptile : amphibian

    (B) water : land

    (C) tail : legs

    (D) lungs : gills

    (E) frog : flagpole

14. WAFT : ODOR ::

    (A) fry : plane

    (B) fly : train

    (C) honk : geese

    (D) ferry : troops

    (E) drag : sleigh

15. BOOK : PAGE ::

    (A) tunnel : car

    (B) passage : rite

    (C) work : desk

    (D) pen : pencil

    (E) violin : string

Test 3   (Answers on Page 64)

(Answers on Page 64)

Select the choice that is most parallel to the key word pair. Circle the letter that appears before your answer.

1. JOY : ECSTASY ::

   (A) admiration : love

   (B) weather : humidity

   (C) happiness : sorrow

   (D) life : hope

   (E) rage : dissatisfaction

2. VALVE : FLOW ::

   (A) water : dam

   (B) hose : gasoline

   (C) humerus : bone

   (D) throttle : speed

   (E) zoo : animals

3. LARCENY : GRAND ::

   (A) theft : daring

   (B) school : elementary

   (C) pepper : bitter

   (D) silence : peaceful

   (E) crime : senseless

4. BEAKER : FLASK ::

   (A) stainless steel : glass

   (B) glass : aluminum

   (C) mesh : plastic

   (D) test tube : condenser

   (E) water : alcohol

5. BIPED : QUADRUPED ::

   (A) bird : fish

   (B) mammal : reptile

   (C) man : dog

   (D) feet : appendages

   (E) cycle : tricycle

6. ANTISEPTIC : GERMS ::

   (A) bullet : death

   (B) mosquitoes : disease

   (C) lion : prey

   (D) doctor : medicine

   (E) sun : desert

7. CACHE : SUPPLIES ::

   (A) safe : cash

   (B) driveway : coach

   (C) honey : pot

   (D) receipt : check

   (E) nest : bird

8. WATTLE : TURKEY ::

   (A) feet : squid

   (B) scarf : hat

   (C) crown : king

   (D) core : apple

   (E) beard : man

9. CUMBER : HAMPER ::

   (A) cuke : clothes

   (B) green : laundry

   (C) prevent : abet

   (D) nuisance : obstruction

   (E) prevention : cure

10. TRACTOR : TRAILER ::

   (A) horse : cart

   (B) driver : motorcycle

   (C) car : engine

   (D) sled : dog

   (E) wagon : wheel

11. HORSE : RIDE ::

   (A) sharpener : sharpen

   (B) instrument : play

   (C) user : reuse

   (D) clothing : dress

   (E) gallop : trot

12. MYSTERY : CLUE ::

   (A) book : reader

   (B) fruit : bowl

   (C) door : key

   (D) detective : criminal

   (E) puzzle : enigma

13. EKE : LIVING ::

   (A) carve : turkey

   (B) turn : profit

   (C) wrest : profit

   (D) forage : crop

   (E) earn : wage

14. HAMMER : TOOL ::

   (A) tire : rubber

   (B) wagon : vehicle

   (C) nail : hangar

   (D) hide : drum

   (E) saw : tree

15. DECISION : DELIBERATION ::

   (A) gift : party

   (B) plea : request

   (C) fulfillment : wish

   (D) conference : constitution

   (E) condemnation : annulment

Test 4   (Answers on Page 64)

Select the choice that is most parallel to the key word pair. Circle the letter that appears before your answer.

1. FAUNA : FLORA ::

   (A) hide : hydra

   (B) mushrooms : verdure

   (C) starfish : starflower

   (D) peony : pony

   (E) botany : zoology

2. PENCIL : SHARPEN ::

   (A) wood : saw

   (B) carpenter : build

   (C) cloud : puff

   (D) well : fill

   (E) tree : swing

3. FISSION : FUSION ::

   (A) segregation : integration

   (B) hydrogen : uranium

   (C) miscellany : homogeneity

   (D) conservative : liberal

   (E) melting : splitting

4. GASTROPOD : SNAIL ::

   (A) arthropod : clam

   (B) utensil : strainer

   (C) mammal : reptile

   (D) screwdriver : tool

   (E) spider : moth

5. GENUS : SPECIES ::
   (A) state : counties
   (B) dog : fleas
   (C) rock star : admirers
   (D) phylum : Chordata
   (E) sentence : paragraphs

6. GERBIL : RODENT ::
   (A) rabbit : predator
   (B) cow : ruminant
   (C) student : school
   (D) fish : school
   (E) canine : dog

7. YOLK : PROTEIN ::
   (A) water : salt
   (B) news : media
   (C) fruit : sugar
   (D) lipid : fat
   (E) kidney : bile duct

8. FABLE : STORY ::
   (A) fiction : reality
   (B) bonnet : hat
   (C) literature : poetry
   (D) flower : stem
   (E) legend : fact

9. HERD : CATTLE ::
   (A) pride : lions
   (B) flock : mice
   (C) den : rabbits
   (D) ton : goods
   (E) pond : fish

10. ZEBRA : EQUINE ::
    (A) exaggeration : genuine
    (B) joke : inane
    (C) sheep : ovine
    (D) tooth : canine
    (E) fish : porcine

11. DUNCE : CLEVER ::
    (A) fool : ignorant
    (B) hero : fearful
    (C) helper : weak
    (D) worrier : poor
    (E) scholar : wise

12. ZOOLOGY : BOTANY ::
    (A) flora : fauna
    (B) fauna : chordata
    (C) phyla : species
    (D) fauna : flora
    (E) archaeology : paleontology

13. GRADUATE : DIPLOMA ::
    (A) victim : trauma
    (B) doctor : patient
    (C) retiree : plaque
    (D) baby : pacifier
    (E) lawyer : lawsuit

14. COLANDER : STRAIN ::
    (A) pickle : can
    (B) toast : butter
    (C) salad : dress
    (D) oven : roast
    (E) potato : slice

15. ENVY : GREEN ::
    (A) door : red
    (B) sadness : blue
    (C) shock : alert
    (D) hatred : purple
    (E) fun : amused

Test 5   (Answers on Page 64)

(Answers on Page 64)

Select the choice that is most parallel to the key word pair. Circle the letter that appears before your answer.

1. AFFLUENT : MONEY ::
   (A) charitable : stinginess
   (B) greedy : cruelty
   (C) free-flowing : barrier
   (D) venerated : respect
   (E) destitute : wealth

2. DOMINEERING : SADISTIC ::
   (A) sweet : sour
   (B) strong : weak
   (C) unpleasant : unkind
   (D) submissive : masochistic
   (E) lackluster : inspired

3. HOUSE : MANSION ::
   (A) barn : silo
   (B) horse : thoroughbred
   (C) garage : Porsche
   (D) chimney : fireplace
   (E) leopard : tiger

4. GRIMACE : DISTASTE ::
   (A) frown : pleasure
   (B) leer : dismay
   (C) grin : delight
   (D) sorrow : calmness
   (E) meat : wine

5. MORTICIAN : MORTUARY ::
   (A) pharmacy : doctor
   (B) technician : laboratory
   (C) veteran : veterinary clinic
   (D) analyst : couch
   (E) saint : sanctuary

6. SCHOOL : FISH ::
   (A) furniture : sofa
   (B) coffee : bean
   (C) cushion : floor
   (D) swing : tree
   (E) crayon : color

7. MILLIGRAM : DECILITER ::
   (A) mass : distance
   (B) weight : time
   (C) weight : volume
   (D) avoirdupois : pressure
   (E) pint : quart

8. MAMMOTH : BIG ::
   (A) emaciated : thin
   (B) sleek : lean
   (C) heavy : weighty
   (D) present : here
   (E) extinct : current

9. RETINUE : MONARCH ::
   (A) cortege : escort
   (B) princess : queen
   (C) moon : earth
   (D) second : first
   (E) senator : representative

10. NUT : SCREW ::
    (A) hat : head
    (B) acorn : driver
    (C) axle : wheel
    (D) wheel : axle
    (E) thread : pitch

11. UNUSUAL : EXTRAORDINARY ::

    (A) beautiful : pretty

    (B) further : farther

    (C) less : more

    (D) strange : bizarre

    (E) odd : similar

12. TWEEZERS : PLUCK ::

    (A) chicken : cook

    (B) axe : cut

    (C) saw : rebuild

    (D) razor : shave

    (E) motor : hum

13. OAK : ASH ::

    (A) olive : cherry

    (B) apple : carrot

    (C) cucumber : walnut

    (D) pecan : pie

    (E) acorn : corn

14. OPAQUE : TRANSLUCENT ::

    (A) mashed potatoes : roast beef

    (B) chowder : bouillon

    (C) invisible : insight

    (D) refraction : reflection

    (E) obtuse : acute

15. TREATY : PEACE ::

    (A) accord : discord

    (B) law : act

    (C) deed : ownership

    (D) disagreement : battle

    (E) fortune : cash

LEVEL B ANALOGIES

Test 1   (Answers on Page 64)

Select the choice that is most parallel to the key word pair. Circle the letter that appears before your answer.

1. CIRCLE : DIAMETER ::

    (A) square : diagonal

    (B) triangle : base

    (C) rectangle : four

    (D) line : point

    (E) arc : segment

2. FRANCE : SPAIN ::

    (A) Europe : Asia

    (B) Ireland : Canada

    (C) Italy : Austria

    (D) New York : Connecticut

    (E) Japan : Korea

3. CHEMIST : LABORATORY ::

    (A) teacher : office

    (B) artist : hospital

    (C) nurse : laundry

    (D) mechanic : garage

    (E) miner : tram

4. CAFFEINE : DROWSINESS ::

    (A) coffee : thirst

    (B) vaccine : disease

    (C) tea : wakefulness

    (D) calculation : solution

    (E) care : ability

5. BRANCH : TRUNK ::

   (A) leaf : stem

   (B) hair : scalp

   (C) wood : fire

   (D) leg : torso

   (E) part : piece

6. INTIMIDATE : FEAR ::

   (A) maintain : satisfaction

   (B) astonish : wonder

   (C) soothe : concern

   (D) feed : hunger

   (E) ridicule : awe

7. WRITING : PUBLICATION ::

   (A) reading : listening

   (B) selling : sale

   (C) painting : exhibition

   (D) fishing : catch

   (E) explaining : explanation

8. STOVE : KITCHEN ::

   (A) window : bedroom

   (B) sink : bathroom

   (C) television : living room

   (D) trunk : attic

   (E) door : garage

9. BRONCHUS : BRONCHIOLE ::

   (A) bronco : buster

   (B) artery : arteriole

   (C) vein : capillary

   (D) artery : artillery

   (E) artery : venule

10. SPEEDY : GREYHOUND ::

   (A) prepared : lamb

   (B) animate : animal

   (C) silent : tiger

   (D) sluggish : sloth

   (E) barking : dog

11. CATARACT : BLINDNESS ::

   (A) waterfall : nearsightedness

   (B) rapids : myopia

   (C) veil : face

   (D) measles : athlete's foot

   (E) burn : injury

12. CHRONOMETER : HOURGLASS ::

   (A) ship : land

   (B) schooner : spinnaker

   (C) ballpoint pen : quill pen

   (D) leviathan : whale

   (E) time : sand

13. CORNEA : EYEBALL ::

   (A) leg : arm

   (B) hand : finger

   (C) shadow : wall

   (D) seam : softball

   (E) casing : hot dog

14. CROISSANT : PASTRY ::

   (A) doughnut : bread

   (B) cake : layer

   (C) macaroon : cookie

   (D) roll : tart

   (E) pie : fruit

15. CELEBRATE : MARRIAGE ::

   (A) announce : event

   (B) report : injury

   (C) lament : bereavement

   (D) face : penalty

   (E) confess : sin

Test 2   (Answers on Page 65)

(Answers on Page 65)

Select the choice that is most parallel to the key word pair. Circle the letter that appears before your answer.

1. DEBACLE : LOSS ::
   - (A) embargo : union
   - (B) win : defeat
   - (C) sorrow : grief
   - (D) flood : fire
   - (E) conquest : success

2. DEFER : ENROLLMENT ::
   - (A) suspend : operations
   - (B) draft : exemption
   - (C) reveal : disclosure
   - (D) delay : clock
   - (E) hesitate : stutter

3. ARTICLES : JOURNAL ::
   - (A) stories : anthology
   - (B) sculptures : museum
   - (C) poems : poet
   - (D) lyrics : music
   - (E) dictionary : entries

4. SYMPATHY : CONDOLENCES ::
   - (A) hatred : friendship
   - (B) joy : congratulations
   - (C) happiness : mirth
   - (D) love : animosity
   - (E) jealousy : felicity

5. DYSLEXIA : READING ::
   - (A) dysentery : cramps
   - (B) dyspepsia : digestion
   - (C) dislocate : scapula
   - (D) psychosis : sight
   - (E) euphonia : sound

6. DRAKE : DUCKLING ::
   - (A) pony : foal
   - (B) pig : boar
   - (C) puppy : kitten
   - (D) doe : yearling
   - (E) bull : calf

7. MARGARINE : BUTTER ::
   - (A) cream : milk
   - (B) lace : cotton
   - (C) nylon : silk
   - (D) egg : chicken
   - (E) oil : animal fat

8. WOODSMAN : AXE ::
   - (A) mechanic : wrench
   - (B) carpenter : saw
   - (C) draftsman : ruler
   - (D) doctor : prescription
   - (E) lawyer : brief

9. FABLE : FICTION ::
   - (A) prose : poem
   - (B) lyric : song
   - (C) narrative : nonfiction
   - (D) ode : poetry
   - (E) poet : author

10. FALSEHOOD : WHOPPER ::
   - (A) glee : amusement
   - (B) wildness : tameness
   - (C) lie : truth
   - (D) liar : deceiver
   - (E) error : sin

11. HEPTATHLON : TRIATHLON ::

    (A) seven : three

    (B) decathlon : pentathlon

    (C) body builder : runner

    (D) athlete : worker

    (E) male : female

12. SINUOUS : SNAKE ::

    (A) furry : triangle

    (B) angular : polygon

    (C) steely : worm

    (D) evil : serpent

    (E) pliable : helix

13. NEGLIGENT : REQUIREMENT ::

    (A) careful : position

    (B) remiss : duty

    (C) cautious : injury

    (D) cogent : task

    (E) excuse : chore

14. ENDANGERED : EXTINCT ::

    (A) alarmed : frightened

    (B) impatient : annoyed

    (C) flammable : scorched

    (D) alive : vital

    (E) insurgent : resurgent

15. DISGRACE : DISLOYALTY ::

    (A) fame : heroism

    (B) castigation : praise

    (C) death : victory

    (D) approbation : consecration

    (E) shame : honor

Test 3   (Answers on Page 65)

Select the choice that is most parallel to the key word pair. Circle the letter that appears before your answer.

1. JOLLITY : CLOWN ::

    (A) agility : acrobat

    (B) mirth : juggler

    (C) amity : ringmaster

    (D) whip : lion tamer

    (E) tightrope : balancer

2. FRICTION : EVAPORATION ::

    (A) energy : weakness

    (B) frigidity : calories

    (C) heat : vapor

    (D) rubbing : sliding

    (E) frailty : strength

3. SATURNINE : MERCURIAL ::

    (A) planet : star

    (B) reluctant : loathe

    (C) redundant : wordy

    (D) proficient : inept

    (E) satisficd : lively

4. ORANGE : MARMALADE ::

    (A) potato : vegetable

    (B) jelly : jam

    (C) tomato : ketchup

    (D) cake : picnic

    (E) apple : seed

5. GOSLING : KID ::

   (A) goose : ram

   (B) duckling : foal

   (C) gander : billy goat

   (D) drake : nanny goat

   (E) duck : child

6. HEXAPOD : INSECT ::

   (A) cow : quadruped

   (B) quadruped : millipede

   (C) polypod : monopod

   (D) arthropod : dining table

   (E) tripod : milking stool

7. BANISH : TRAITOR ::

   (A) reward : betrayer

   (B) welcome : ally

   (C) avoid : truce

   (D) remove : result

   (E) believe : religion

8. HIND : STAG ::

   (A) buses : automobiles

   (B) buck : doe

   (C) doe : buck

   (D) bull : cow

   (E) cow : bull

9. HARE : HOUND ::

   (A) mouse : cat

   (B) lion : lamb

   (C) lion : tiger

   (D) dog : rabbit

   (E) gerbil : hamster

10. CIRCLE : SPHERE ::

    (A) square : cube

    (B) balloon : jet plane

    (C) heaven : hell

    (D) wheel : orange

    (E) earth : mountain

11. JACKHAMMER : FRACTURE ::

    (A) steamroller : smooth

    (B) eardrum : burst

    (C) bulldozer : carry

    (D) gravel : mix

    (E) taxi : drive

12. INDOLENT : LOAFER ::

    (A) soft : moccasin

    (B) tactful : diplomat

    (C) noisome : reveler

    (D) repulsive : salesperson

    (E) insolent : editor

13. SOLO : DUET ::

    (A) six : dozen

    (B) band : concert

    (C) flight : pilot

    (D) music : instrument

    (E) aria : music

14. LINOLEUM : FLOOR ::

    (A) pile : carpet

    (B) tile : roof

    (C) wall : wallpaper

    (D) glass : pane

    (E) wood : door

15. MOTORCYCLE : BICYCLE ::

    (A) wagon : car

    (B) snowmobile : sleigh

    (C) one : two

    (D) tire : wheel

    (E) train : engine

Test 4   (Answers on Page 65)

Select the choice that is most parallel to the key word pair. Circle the letter that appears before your answer.

1. BIGOTRY : HATRED ::
   (A) sweetness : bitterness
   (B) segregation : integration
   (C) fanaticism : intolerance
   (D) sugar : grain
   (E) benevolence : hostility

2. MOUNTAIN : TOPOGRAPHY ::
   (A) crystal : geology
   (B) writing : calligraphy
   (C) border : geography
   (D) medicine : biology
   (E) valley : agribiology

3. BOUNCE : TRAMPOLINE ::
   (A) fire : rifle
   (B) prepare : speech
   (C) revoke : amendment
   (D) bobble : ball
   (E) skate : pond

4. STARE : LEER ::
   (A) look : listen
   (B) chuckle : laugh
   (C) wink : blink
   (D) grin : smirk
   (E) stop : start

5. JESTER : KING ::
   (A) protestant : fragment
   (B) metropolitan : sugar
   (C) gorilla : existentialism
   (D) employee : employer
   (E) mortgagor : mortgagee

6. RECESSION : DEPRESSION ::
   (A) dementia : sanity
   (B) secession : loss
   (C) rise : fall
   (D) quarrel : battle
   (E) total : part

7. KILOTON : MILLIGRAM ::
   (A) horse : dog
   (B) heavy : short
   (C) macrocosm : microcosm
   (D) burden : buoy
   (E) minimum : maximum

8. KINSMAN : COUSIN ::
   (A) carnivore : zebra
   (B) omnivore : cow
   (C) herbivore : bull
   (D) herbivore : omnivore
   (E) amoeba : Protista

9. PUPPY : LITTER ::
   (A) dog : mess
   (B) skunk : odor
   (C) kitten : basket
   (D) food : picnic
   (E) grape : bunch

10. KITE : STRING ::
    (A) lasso : steer
    (B) rope : lariat
    (C) stallion : tether
    (D) anchor : buoy
    (E) flag : pole

11. PHYSICIAN : SYMPTOM ::

    (A) detective : clue

    (B) pharmacist : drug

    (C) magician : wand

    (D) actor : role

    (E) repairperson : manual

12. TUNNEL : TOLL ::

    (A) pipe : fee

    (B) subway : boat

    (C) cinema : ticket

    (D) gym : sneakers

    (E) laundry : pillowcase

13. TOKYO : ASIA ::

    (A) Paris : France

    (B) Albany : New York

    (C) Germany : Europe

    (D) Nairobi : Africa

    (E) New Mexico : Arizona

14. PARAGRAPH : WORD ::

    (A) number : code

    (B) money : cent

    (C) alphabet : letter

    (D) philosophy : model

    (E) action : plan

15. THROW : BALL ::

    (A) kill : bullet

    (B) shoot : pellet

    (C) question : answer

    (D) hit : run

    (E) swim : lake

Test 5   (Answers on Page 65)

Select the choice that is most parallel to the key word pair. Circle the letter that appears before your answer.

1. MANGER : CATTLE ::

    (A) sty : hogs

    (B) yard : chickens

    (C) table : chairs

    (D) trough : pigs

    (E) hopper : corn

2. ROTOR : ROTATE ::

    (A) motor : mutate

    (B) color : collate

    (C) record : skip

    (D) top : spin

    (E) rock : roll

3. MICROBIOLOGY : BACTERIA ::

    (A) entomology : wasps

    (B) etymology : giraffes

    (C) psychology : psychics

    (D) parasitology : politicians

    (E) cosmology : cosmetics

4. MILLIPEDE : CENTIPEDE ::

    (A) insect : bug

    (B) millimeter : centimeter

    (C) leg : arm

    (D) arthropod : crustacean

    (E) stampede : cattle

5. MOTH : CLOTHING ::

    (A) egg : larva

    (B) suit : dress

    (C) hole : repair

    (D) stigma : reputation

    (E) fame : reward

6. NADIR : ZENITH ::

    (A) apex : posterior

    (B) bottom : heart

    (C) sole : scalp

    (D) peak : abyss

    (E) most : least

7. NAUSEA : STOMACH ::

    (A) molar : toothache

    (B) unity : strength

    (C) migraine : head

    (D) sinusitis : leg

    (E) ecstasy : excitement

8. NEO- : ARCHEO- ::

    (A) expert : amateur

    (B) stone age : iron age

    (C) old : new

    (D) new : old

    (E) recent : original

9. TABLE : TABLECLOTH ::

    (A) couch : slipcover

    (B) bed : pillow

    (C) picture : wall

    (D) lawn : front yard

    (E) wall : roof

10. CLOSING : OPENING ::

    (A) dusk : dawn

    (B) black : white

    (C) vanish : disappear

    (D) senescent : senile

    (E) efflorescent : deliquescent

11. DOUBLEHEADER : TRIDENT ::

    (A) twins : troika

    (B) ballgame : three-bagger

    (C) chewing gum : toothpaste

    (D) freak : zoo

    (E) legend : myth

12. INFLEXIBLE : STEEL ::

    (A) iron : will

    (B) depressed : patient

    (C) manic : down

    (D) colorful : diamond

    (E) malleable : gold

13. OCCIDENT : WESTERN ::

    (A) east : southeastern

    (B) orient : exotic

    (C) north : polar

    (D) west : mountainous

    (E) inlet : interior

14. INTRUSION : RUDE ::

    (A) detachment : forceful

    (B) cruise : pleasant

    (C) compliment : kind

    (D) adventure : exciting

    (E) trial : extended

15. BUZZ : BEE ::

    (A) ring : explosion

    (B) clang : alarm

    (C) chirp : cricket

    (D) echo : sound

    (E) rumble : earthquake

LEVEL C ANALOGIES

Test 1   (Answers on Page 65)

Select the choice that is most parallel to the key word pair. Circle the letter that appears before your answer.

1. TROT : GALLOP ::
   (A) jog : walk
   (B) swim : run
   (C) paddle : row
   (D) pace : step
   (E) lope : scurry

2. TRELLIS : PROP ::
   (A) ladder : climb
   (B) pillar : buttress
   (C) flowerpot : plant
   (D) seed : sow
   (E) buoy : moor

3. CROWN : ROYAL ::
   (A) gun : imperial
   (B) cola : sweet
   (C) crucifix : religious
   (D) wrap : ermine
   (E) staff : general

4. ISLAND : OCEAN ::
   (A) hill : stream
   (B) forest : valley
   (C) oasis : desert
   (D) tree : field
   (E) house : lawn

5. MATHEMATICS : NUMEROLOGY ::
   (A) biology : botany
   (B) psychology : physiology
   (C) anatomy : medicine
   (D) astronomy : astrology
   (E) magic : science

6. BUCOLIC : URBAN ::
   (A) dense : sparse
   (B) rural : ephemeral
   (C) elastic : plastic
   (D) rustic : toxic
   (E) misty : smoggy

7. DISLIKABLE : ABHORRENT ::
   (A) trustworthy : helpful
   (B) difficult : arduous
   (C) silly : young
   (D) tender : hard
   (E) ugly : beautiful

8. WOOD : CORD ::
   (A) tree : pasture
   (B) nature : industry
   (C) milk : quart
   (D) leaf : cow
   (E) fire : string

9. DROUGHT : THIRST ::
   (A) blizzard : snow blindness
   (B) food : hunger
   (C) music : sorrow
   (D) heat : light
   (E) aridity : dryness

10. MINARET : MOSQUE ::
    (A) religion : laity
    (B) steeple : church
    (C) chapel : altar
    (D) tower : turret
    (E) tent : house

11. WHEAT : CHAFF ::

   (A) wine : dregs

   (B) bread : roll

   (C) laughter : raillery

   (D) oat : oatmeal

   (E) whiskey : vodka

12. DEVIOUS : SPY ::

   (A) productive : farmer

   (B) orthodox : heretic

   (C) balanced : reporter

   (D) normal : psychologist

   (E) practical : nurse

13. EBB : WAX ::

   (A) rise : flow

   (B) increase : ascend

   (C) abate : recede

   (D) slacken : grow

   (E) fill : replenish

14. DRAMA : DIRECTOR ::

   (A) class : principal

   (B) magazine : editor

   (C) actor : playwright

   (D) tragedy : producer

   (E) leader : group

15. COMMONPLACE : CLICHE ::

   (A) serious : play

   (B) annoying : pun

   (C) appreciated : gift

   (D) terse : maxim

   (E) ordinary : miracle

Test 2   (Answers on Page 65)

Select the choice that is most parallel to the key word pair. Circle the letter that appears before your answer.

1. PLEASED : THRILLED ::

   (A) tipsy : drunk

   (B) sensible : lively

   (C) intelligent : dumb

   (D) liberal : tolerant

   (E) happy : despairing

2. GROVE : WILLOW ::

   (A) stack : novel

   (B) fence : shrub

   (C) pine : stand

   (D) thicket : blackberry

   (E) glen : birch

3. MORAL : SIN ::

   (A) civil : court

   (B) popular : law

   (C) legal : crime

   (D) silent : priest

   (E) social : philosopher

4. ELLIPSE : CURVE ::

   (A) stutter : speech

   (B) triangle : base

   (C) revolution : distance

   (D) square : polygon

   (E) sun : moon

5. SUGAR : SACCHARIN ::

   (A) candy : cake

   (B) butter : margarine

   (C) cane : stalk

   (D) spice : pepper

   (E) vitamin : nutrient

6. REQUEST : DEMAND ::

   (A) reply : respond

   (B) regard : reject

   (C) inquire : require

   (D) wish : crave

   (E) accept : question

7. PHOTOGRAPH : ALBUM ::

   (A) skillet : stove

   (B) money : wallet

   (C) porcelain : whatnot

   (D) chair : veranda

   (E) receptacle : recipient

8. WATER : FAUCET ::

   (A) fuel : throttle

   (B) H_2O : O

   (C) kitchen : sink

   (D) steam : solid

   (E) vapor : tub

9. HOLOCAUST : FIRE ::

   (A) drum : water

   (B) hanging : noose

   (C) murder : knife

   (D) flame : candle

   (E) trial : jury

10. OSCILLATE : PENDULUM ::

    (A) obligate : promise

    (B) catch : fish

    (C) turn : car

    (D) spin : gyroscope

    (E) learn : student

11. HERB : DILL ::

    (A) plantain : berry

    (B) legume : tuber

    (C) conifer : fir

    (D) fruit : vegetable

    (E) tree : bark

12. INTESTINE : DIGESTIVE ::

    (A) biceps : neurological

    (B) cerebellum : skeletal

    (C) pores : excretory

    (D) lungs : circulatory

    (E) aorta : alimentary

13. FLASK : BOTTLE ::

    (A) whiskey : food

    (B) metal : glass

    (C) pamphlet : book

    (D) quart : pint

    (E) stopper : sink

14. MONEY : AVARICE ::

    (A) taxes : greed

    (B) property : insolence

    (C) dollar sign : capitalism

    (D) food : voracity

    (E) wages : overtime

15. HAIR : BALDNESS ::

    (A) wig : head

    (B) egg : eggshell

    (C) rain : drought

    (D) skin : scar

    (E) mammal : bird

Test 3   (Answers on Page 65)

Select the choice that is most parallel to the key word pair. Circle the letter that appears before your answer.

1. BOAT : SHIP ::
    (A) book : tome
    (B) canoe : paddle
    (C) oar : water
    (D) aft : stern
    (E) river : ocean

2. SCYTHE : DEATH ::
    (A) fall : winter
    (B) knife : murder
    (C) heart : love
    (D) harvest : crops
    (E) flag : war

3. KENNEL : DOG ::
    (A) fennel : channel
    (B) stall : horse
    (C) hangar : vehicle
    (D) nest : stork
    (E) cubby : cub

4. CARNIVORE : ANIMALS ::
    (A) omnivore : omelets
    (B) vegetarian : vegetables
    (C) trace : minerals
    (D) herbivore : health
    (E) predator : plants

5. LIBEL : SLANDER ::
    (A) chair : office
    (B) telephone : dictaphone
    (C) computer : input
    (D) copier : plagiarist
    (E) typewriter : microphone

6. ENTRY : DICTIONARY ::
    (A) pedal : bike
    (B) wheel : car
    (C) note : score
    (D) car : sedan
    (E) fold : fan

7. MAUVE : COLOR ::
    (A) basil : spice
    (B) art : photography
    (C) form : function
    (D) tan : brown
    (E) gold : sunset

8. MUFFLE : SILENCE ::
    (A) cover : clang
    (B) sound : hear
    (C) cry : guffaw
    (D) stymie : defeat
    (E) snuggle : confront

9. WHALE : FISH ::
    (A) poodle : dog
    (B) fly : insect
    (C) bat : bird
    (D) clue : trance
    (E) mako : shark

10. VERB : ACTION ::
    (A) grammar : word
    (B) speech : discourse
    (C) adverb : adjective
    (D) pronoun : person
    (E) proverb : reaction

11. EPOXY : AFFIX ::

   (A) crowbar : pry
   (B) glue : freshen
   (C) tongs : secure
   (D) proxy : fix
   (E) stone : lift

12. DISCIPLINE : ORDER ::

   (A) military : rank
   (B) authority : follower
   (C) parent : child
   (D) training : preparation
   (E) form : formlessness

13. SUFFICIENT : OVERABUNDANT ::

   (A) few : many
   (B) scarce : absent
   (C) insufficient : abundant
   (D) empty : full
   (E) left : sinister

14. WATERMARK : PAPER ::

   (A) buoy : stamp
   (B) birthmark : person
   (C) tide : character
   (D) line : signal
   (E) date : certificate

15. BRIGHT : BRILLIANT ::

   (A) color : red
   (B) yellow : sparkly
   (C) contented : overjoyed
   (D) light : fire
   (E) sun : star

Test 4   (Answers on Page 65)

Select the choice that is most parallel to the key word pair. Circle the letter that appears before your answer.

1. PLUTOCRAT : WEALTH ::

   (A) autocrat : industry
   (B) theocrat : religion
   (C) oligarch : ruler
   (D) technocrat : popularity
   (E) republican : conservation

2. NEWS REPORT : DESCRIPTIVE ::

   (A) weather report : unpredictable
   (B) editorial : one-sided
   (C) feature story : newsworthy
   (D) commercial : prescriptive
   (E) fact : fiction

3. PROPHYLACTIC : PREVENT ::

   (A) toothbrush : clean
   (B) aspirin : throb
   (C) therapeutic : cure
   (D) surgery : cut
   (E) alcohol : harm

4. RIGGING : ROPE ::

   (A) barrels : brass
   (B) figurehead : beam
   (C) sails : canvas
   (D) ship : steam
   (E) portage : weight

5. MATRICULATE : GRADUATION ::

    (A) grow : harvest

    (B) enlist : discharge

    (C) boil : canning

    (D) endow : bestowal

    (E) register : election

6. WATER : HYDRAULIC ::

    (A) energy : atomic

    (B) power : electric

    (C) air : pneumatic

    (D) pressure : compressed

    (E) gas : politic

7. EGRET : PLUMAGE ::

    (A) sheep : fur

    (B) zebra : stripe

    (C) ostrich : egg

    (D) beaver : pelt

    (E) seal : tusk

8. STABLE : HORSE ::

    (A) barn : silo

    (B) sty : hog

    (C) fold : ram

    (D) hen : coop

    (E) shed : tools

9. PETAL : BLOSSOM ::

    (A) cone : pine tree

    (B) vane : windmill

    (C) flower : shrub

    (D) pane : window

    (E) clock : digit

10. ROLE : ACTOR ::

    (A) aria : soprano

    (B) private : soldier

    (C) composition : singer

    (D) position : ballplayer

    (E) hierarchy : bureaucrat

11. *ILIAD* : EPIC ::

    (A) *Hamlet* : tragedy

    (B) Dickens : novel

    (C) *Cinderella* : plot

    (D) *Macbeth* : prosody

    (E) sonnet : narration

12. SILO : FODDER ::

    (A) barn : corn

    (B) farm : crops

    (C) tractor : fuel

    (D) cask : wine

    (E) vine : grapes

13. KILT : SARI ::

    (A) gown : robe

    (B) senator : fakir

    (C) man : woman

    (D) tartan : plaid

    (E) skirt : blouse

14. PROW : SHIP ::

    (A) caboose : train

    (B) nose : airplane

    (C) bird : beak

    (D) wheel : car

    (E) tail : cat

15. TRESS : HAIR ::

    (A) pat : butter

    (B) slice : lox

    (C) flock : geese

    (D) land : cotton

    (E) skein : wool

Test 5   (Answers on Page 66)

Select the choice that is most parallel to the key word pair. Circle the letter that appears before your answer.

1. BLUSH : ABASHED ::

   (A) shrug : annoyed

   (B) blanch : appalled

   (C) wink : amused

   (D) blink : disheartened

   (E) flush : irate

2. MAXIMUM : MINIMUM ::

   (A) pessimist : misogynist

   (B) minimum : optimum

   (C) best : good

   (D) most : least

   (E) nadir : apogee

3. SENSATION : ANESTHETIC ::

   (A) breath : lung

   (B) drug : reaction

   (C) satisfaction : disappointment

   (D) poison : antidote

   (E) senses : beauty

4. URSINE : BEAR ::

   (A) vulpine : wolf

   (B) buffoon : clown

   (C) celestial : earth

   (D) arboreal : primate

   (E) feline : cat

5. DISEMBARK : SHIP ::

   (A) board : train

   (B) dismount : horse

   (C) intern : jail

   (D) discharge : navy

   (E) enter : plane

6. PROTEIN : MEAT ::

   (A) butter : cream

   (B) energy : sugar

   (C) cyclamates : diet

   (D) starch : potatoes

   (E) muscle : strength

7. NECK : NAPE ::

   (A) foot : heel

   (B) head : forehead

   (C) arm : wrist

   (D) stomach : back

   (E) mouth : throat

8. BEAN : CHOCOLATE ::

   (A) leaf : tea

   (B) berry : strawberry

   (C) cola : nectar

   (D) banana : plantain

   (E) juice : cherry

9. DINOSAUR : CROCODILE ::

   (A) zebra : horse

   (B) woolly mammoth : elephant

   (C) exotic : mundane

   (D) deer : elk

   (E) lemming : hyena

10. WOOF : TRANSVERSE ::

    (A) warp : longitudinal

    (B) cluck : reverse

    (C) downtown : crosstown

    (D) wool : warm

    (E) dog : perverse

11. XYLOPHONE : PERCUSSION ::

    (A) wood : brass

    (B) cylinder : planar

    (C) bassoon : wind

    (D) bass : treble

    (E) string : cello

12. STALLION : GELDING ::

    (A) mare : filly

    (B) buck : deer

    (C) pig : boar

    (D) bull : steer

    (E) trotter : pacer

13. GRIPPING : PLIERS ::

    (A) chisel : gouging

    (B) breaking : hammer

    (C) elevating : jack

    (D) killing : knife

    (E) glue : attaching

14. RADIUS : CIRCLE ::

    (A) rubber : tire

    (B) spoke : wheel

    (C) equator : earth

    (D) cord : circumference

    (E) center : naval

15. ZODIAC : SIGN ::

    (A) auto : wheel

    (B) year : month

    (C) hand : finger

    (D) team : tackle

    (E) country : land

LEVEL D ANALOGIES

Test 1   (Answers on Page 66)

Select the choice that is most parallel to the key word pair. Circle the letter that appears before your answer.

1. AXIOM : TRANSITIVITY ::

    (A) feeling : sensitivity

    (B) theorem : Pythagorean

    (C) longevity : exercise

    (D) commutativity : association

    (E) proof : acceptance

2. ALLAY : FEARS ::

    (A) alloy : metals

    (B) bandage : stomach

    (C) quell : enemy

    (D) pacify : infant

    (E) placate : relaxation

3. ALCOVE : ROOM ::

    (A) roof : house

    (B) county : nation

    (C) censure : excommunication

    (D) cave : mountain

    (E) recess : school

4. JUPITER : ZEUS ::

    (A) god : goddess

    (B) planet : star

    (C) war : peace

    (D) Mars : Ares

    (E) Saturn : Pluto

5. MISDEMEANOR : FELONY ::

(A) pilfer : steal

(B) thief : burglar

(C) murder : manslaughter

(D) cracked : smashed

(E) accident : oversight

6. EROSION : FLOODING ::

(A) timber : fire

(B) population : explosion

(C) extinction : death

(D) pollution : corrosion

(E) movement : agility

7. HYGROMETER : HUMIDITY ::

(A) thermometer : temperature

(B) valve : pressure

(C) rate : speed

(D) barometer : weather

(E) tide : mist

8. DRIP : DROP ::

(A) pop : bubble

(B) hip : hop

(C) ship : shop

(D) rain : snow

(E) shock : show

9. CULL : INFERIOR ::

(A) reject : regular

(B) select : choice

(C) affect : voice

(D) predict : abnormal

(E) benefit : imperfect

10. CANTICLE : SONG ::

(A) major : minor

(B) celery : olives

(C) medal : wreath

(D) broadloom : carpet

(E) shoe : necklace

11. CLUTCH : CHICKS ::

(A) herd : animals

(B) pride : pigeons

(C) den : foxes

(D) spell : witches

(E) covey : quail

12. HIGHWAY : ROAD MAP ::

(A) sky : chart

(B) wall : painting

(C) hallway : blueprint

(D) avenue : bus stop

(E) planet : topographic map

13. DYNAST : REGAL ::

(A) lord : masterful

(B) serf : lowly

(C) king : courtly

(D) royalty : gentle

(E) vassal : popular

14. BOLD : COWED ::

(A) daring : intrepid

(B) demanding : satisfied

(C) loving : selfish

(D) good : delicious

(E) thriving : hearty

15. PINT : CREAM ::

(A) metric ton : automobile

(B) bushel : fuel

(C) yard : fabric

(D) milligram : flour

(E) dram : cider

Test 2   (Answers on Page 66)

1. EXPOSITORY : ARTICLE ::
   (A) epistolary : conjunction
   (B) explanatory : news
   (C) narrative : story
   (D) lyrical : music
   (E) persuasive : poem

2. GOLD : PROSPECTOR ::
   (A) medicine : doctor
   (B) prayer : preacher
   (C) wood : carpenter
   (D) clues : detective
   (E) coal : fire

3. DEXTROSE : SUGAR ::
   (A) sucrose : sweetener
   (B) corn : maize
   (C) fat : lipid
   (D) enzyme : protein
   (E) heart attack : embolism

4. SWARM : APIARY ::
   (A) eagles : aerie
   (B) ants : anthill
   (C) herd : field
   (D) flock : aviary
   (E) family : home

5. LATCH : GATE ::
   (A) lock : key
   (B) hasp : jar
   (C) knob : door
   (D) lever : stone
   (E) buckle : belt

6. STYLUS : INCISE ::
   (A) stiletto : sharpen
   (B) penknife : whittle
   (C) hammer : pound
   (D) bread : knead
   (E) axe : hone

7. COCKPIT : INTERIOR ::
   (A) aileron : exterior
   (B) propeller : rolling
   (C) elevator : supportive
   (D) tail : yawing
   (E) rudder : pitching

8. VICAR : CLERGY ::
   (A) president : legislature
   (B) dragoon : military
   (C) Catholic : Protestant
   (D) rabbi : synagogue
   (E) rancher : farm

9. GARNER : WEALTH ::
   (A) assemble : glue
   (B) make : honey
   (C) collate : pages
   (D) achieve : intelligence
   (E) plant : sheaves

10. GIGATON : MEGATON ::
    (A) megacycle : kilocycle
    (B) deciliter : liter
    (C) milligram : centigram
    (D) microsecond : millisecond
    (E) decivolt : dekavolt

11. GOURMAND : UNDISCRIMINATING ::

(A) wisdom : epicurean

(B) spaghetti : edible

(C) atrophy : empathetic

(D) good : plenty

(E) gourmet : selective

12. COUPLET : POEM ::

(A) page : poster

(B) sentence : paragraph

(C) number : alphabet

(D) epic : poetry

(E) sonnet : poem

13. CLIMBER : PEAK ::

(A) hunter : game

(B) rifle : bull's-eye

(C) runner : mile

(D) boxer : glove

(E) victory : jockey

14. OIL : WELL ::

(A) water : faucet

(B) iron : ore

(C) silver : mine

(D) gas : pump

(E) steel : factory

15. PIGMENTS : PALETTE ::

(A) pigs : farm

(B) trees : nursery

(C) chalk : chalkboard

(D) paints : easel

(E) painter : artist

Test 3   (Answers on Page 66)

Select the choice that is most parallel to the key word pair. Circle the letter that appears before your answer.

1. SIEVE : FILTER ::

(A) colander : drain

(B) water : drip

(C) cigar : smoke

(D) gold : pan

(E) mesh : clean

2. INDUBITABLE : CONTRADICT ::

(A) unhappy : cry

(B) immovable : budge

(C) unlikely : like

(D) false : deny

(E) breakable : smash

3. STALLION : ROOSTER ::

(A) buck : doe

(B) mare : hen

(C) horse : poultry

(D) foal : calf

(E) mouse : rodent

4. JUDO : WEAPONS ::

(A) bridge : aces

(B) football : helmets

(C) auto : horses

(D) golf : clubs

(E) soccer : hands

5. JUDICIAL : ENFORCE ::

   (A) administrative : veto

   (B) legislative : enact

   (C) elected : appoint

   (D) bench : try

   (E) federal : elect

6. RUDDER : SHIP ::

   (A) wheel : car

   (B) motor : truck

   (C) row : boat

   (D) kite : string

   (E) track : train

7. KARATE : FOOT ::

   (A) judo : chop

   (B) bridge : hand

   (C) fencing : foil

   (D) boxing : glove

   (E) baseball : bat

8. LEECH : PARASITE ::

   (A) tree : host

   (B) surgeon : butcher

   (C) worm : turner

   (D) pomegranate : citrus

   (E) mushroom : saprophyte

9. LEAVENING : FERMENTATION ::

   (A) argument : fight

   (B) snow : precipitation

   (C) rain : condensation

   (D) sleet : hail

   (E) sleeping : eating

10. AMUSING : HILARIOUS ::

    (A) grave : disgusting

    (B) unwise : irrational

    (C) grotesque : odd

    (D) funny : happy

    (E) glad : mocking

11. LIST : ITEM ::

    (A) portrait : person

    (B) constitution : article

    (C) computer : disk

    (D) trial : motion

    (E) tree : bark

12. READ : BOOK ::

    (A) taste : fruit

    (B) attend : movie

    (C) smell : odor

    (D) listen : tape

    (E) speak : words

13. PREMIERE : MOVIE ::

    (A) unveiling : statue

    (B) premier : president

    (C) debutante : teenager

    (D) ruler : subject

    (E) show : play

14. PARROT : TROPICS ::

    (A) dog : house

    (B) elephant : India

    (C) roadrunner : desert

    (D) lion : zoo

    (E) zebra : Africa

15. MEDIAN : MIDDLE ::

    (A) center : radius

    (B) angle : measurement

    (C) fashion : mode

    (D) mode : mean

    (E) mean : average

Test 4   (Answers on Page 66)

Select the choice that is most parallel to the key word pair. Circle the letter that appears before your answer.

1. BONES : LIGAMENT ::
   (A) breakage : elasticity
   (B) muscle : tendon
   (C) fat : cell
   (D) knuckle : finger
   (E) leg : arm

2. DOWN : FLUFFY ::
   (A) elevator : fast
   (B) language : fluent
   (C) satin : smooth
   (D) coat : warm
   (E) board : level

3. BURL : TREE ::
   (A) wart : toad
   (B) bronze : copper
   (C) plank : wood
   (D) glass : sand
   (E) pebble : rock

4. YEAST : LEAVEN ::
   (A) soda : bubble
   (B) iodine : antiseptic
   (C) aspirin : medicine
   (D) flour : dough
   (E) bread : roll

5. LIST : CAPSIZE ::
   (A) fall : rise
   (B) careen : crash
   (C) trouble : irk
   (D) lose : discover
   (E) pretend : realize

6. PERIMETER : POLYGON ::
   (A) circumference : circle
   (B) hypotenuse : triangle
   (C) side : square
   (D) degree : angle
   (E) angle : rectangle

7. OMEGA : ENDING ::
   (A) fraternity : sorority
   (B) epsilon : femur
   (C) alpha : beginning
   (D) gamma : ray
   (E) river : delta

8. EXPURGATE : PASSAGES ::
   (A) defoliate : leaves
   (B) cancel : checks
   (C) incorporate : ideas
   (D) invade : privacy
   (E) admit : dissent

9. GERM : DISEASE ::
   (A) trichinosis : pork
   (B) men : women
   (C) doctor : medicine
   (D) war : destruction
   (E) nurse : illness

10. QUASH : MOTION ::
    (A) squeeze : melon
    (B) destroy : building
    (C) quell : riot
    (D) impel : engine
    (E) conduct : voltage

11. QUEUE : PEOPLE ::

    (A) gaggle : geese

    (B) pile : pails

    (C) stack : hay

    (D) string : pearls

    (E) file : letters

12. RECRUIT : ENLIST ::

    (A) embalmer : putrefy

    (B) hireling : fire

    (C) heir : disinherit

    (D) army : leave

    (E) employee : apply

13. CONTROL : ORDER ::

    (A) joke : clown

    (B) teacher : pupil

    (C) disorder : climax

    (D) anarchy : chaos

    (E) impulsive : deliberate

14. REMORSE : RUE ::

    (A) pain : cough

    (B) pleasure : enjoy

    (C) sense : commiserate

    (D) senility : age

    (E) rationality : cogitate

15. RETARDANT : FIRE ::

    (A) repellant : infestation

    (B) fertilizer : crop

    (C) disease : vaccination

    (D) accelerant : fumes

    (E) depressant : mood

Test 5   (Answers on Page 66)

Select the choice that is most parallel to the key word pair. Circle the letter that appears before your answer.

1. SEWER : SEAM ::

    (A) tailor : thimble

    (B) surgeon : scalpel

    (C) electrician : splice

    (D) seed : spore

    (E) court : plaintiff

2. APOLOGY : ACCEPT ::

    (A) face : feature

    (B) forgiveness : beg

    (C) promise : break

    (D) issue : force

    (E) leverage : earn

3. WOOD : CARVE ::

    (A) trees : sway

    (B) paper : burn

    (C) clay : mold

    (D) pipe : blow

    (E) furnace : melt

4. SPIRE : TOWER ::

    (A) crest : mountain

    (B) frog : pond

    (C) city : state

    (D) man : hat

    (E) church : roof

5. SOLECISM : GRAMMAR ::

   (A) separation : marriage

   (B) foul : game

   (C) incest : family

   (D) race : stumble

   (E) apostasy : dogma

6. VALANCE : ROD ::

   (A) pendant : chain

   (B) curtain : ruffle

   (C) tie : pleat

   (D) body : cravat

   (E) choker : necklace

7. TELEMETRY : DISTANT ::

   (A) geology : earthshaking

   (B) optometry : real

   (C) micrometry : tiny

   (D) vision : near

   (E) astronomy : invisible

8. NATION : BORDER GUARDS ::

   (A) state : toll

   (B) property : fence

   (C) mountain : hollow

   (D) planet : satellite

   (E) delta : river

9. TOLERATE : PREJUDICE ::

   (A) survive : food

   (B) swim : cramps

   (C) kill : knife

   (D) estimate : computer

   (E) respect : wife

10. SOLDIER : REGIMENT ::

    (A) navy : army

    (B) lake : river

    (C) star : constellation

    (D) amphibian : frog

    (E) nurse : doctor

11. GRAVEL : CONCRETE ::

    (A) eggs : soufflé

    (B) rocks : stones

    (C) shovel : mixer

    (D) car : truck

    (E) aggregate : congregate

12. APOGEE : ORBIT ::

    (A) pedigree : dog

    (B) detergent : laundry

    (C) apex : mountain

    (D) radius : circle

    (E) perigee : planet

13. WHEELBARROW : TRANSPORT ::

    (A) wagon : pull

    (B) shovel : handle

    (C) axe : hone

    (D) stump : excavate

    (E) lever : lift

14. ASYLUM : REFUGEE ::

    (A) flight : escapee

    (B) destination : traveler

    (C) lunatic : insanity

    (D) accident : injury

    (E) hospital : inmate

15. WORRIED : HYSTERICAL ::

    (A) hot : cold

    (B) happy : ecstatic

    (C) lonely : crowded

    (D) happy : serious

    (E) anxious : speechless

Analogies

Answer Key

For explanations see page 67.

LEVEL A

TEST 1

1. D	4. D	7. C	10. D	13. A
2. D	5. A	8. C	11. C	14. B
3. E	6. B	9. C	12. C	15. C

TEST 2

1. C	4. B	7. A	10. C	13. D
2. A	5. A	8. C	11. B	14. D
3. A	6. D	9. C	12. C	15. E

TEST 3

1. A	4. D	7. A	10. A	13. C
2. D	5. C	8. E	11. B	14. B
3. B	6. C	9. D	12. C	15. C

TEST 4

1. C	4. B	7. C	10. C	13. C
2. A	5. A	8. B	11. B	14. D
3. A	6. B	9. A	12. D	15. B

TEST 5

1. D	4. C	7. C	10. D	13. A
2. D	5. B	8. A	11. D	14. B
3. B	6. A	9. C	12. D	15. C

LEVEL B

TEST 1

1. A	4. B	7. C	10. D	13. E
2. C	5. D	8. B	11. E	14. C
3. D	6. B	9. B	12. C	15. C

TEST 2

1. E	4. B	7. C	10. E	13. B
2. A	5. B	8. B	11. A	14. C
3. A	6. E	9. D	12. B	15. A

TEST 3

1. A	4. C	7. B	10. A	13. A
2. C	5. B	8. C	11. A	14. B
3. D	6. E	9. A	12. B	15. B

TEST 4

1. C	4. D	7. C	10. C	13. D
2. C	5. D	8. C	11. A	14. C
3. E	6. D	9. E	12. C	15. B

TEST 5

1. D	4. B	7. C	10. A	13. C
2. D	5. D	8. D	11. A	14. C
3. A	6. C	9. A	12. E	15. C

LEVEL C

TEST 1

1. E	4. C	7. B	10. B	13. D
2. B	5. D	8. C	11. A	14. B
3. C	6. E	9. A	12. A	15. D

TEST 2

1. A	4. D	7. C	10. D	13. C
2. D	5. B	8. A	11. C	14. D
3. C	6. D	9. B	12. C	15. C

TEST 3

1. A	4. B	7. A	10. D	13. B
2. C	5. E	8. D	11. A	14. B
3. B	6. C	9. C	12. D	15. C

TEST 4

1. B	4. C	7. D	10. D	13. C
2. D	5. B	8. B	11. A	14. B
3. C	6. C	9. B	12. D	15. E

TEST 5

1. E	4. E	7. A	10. A	13. C
2. D	5. B	8. A	11. C	14. B
3. D	6. D	9. B	12. D	15. B

LEVEL D

TEST 1

1. B	4. D	7. A	10. D	13. B
2. C	5. D	8. A	11. E	14. B
3. D	6. D	9. B	12. C	15. C

TEST 2

1. C	4. D	7. A	10. A	13. A
2. D	5. E	8. B	11. E	14. C
3. C	6. B	9. C	12. B	15. B

TEST 3

1. A	4. E	7. C	10. B	13. A
2. B	5. B	8. E	11. B	14. C
3. B	6. A	9. A	12. D	15. E

TEST 4

1. B	4. B	7. C	10. C	13. D
2. C	5. B	8. A	11. D	14. B
3. A	6. A	9. D	12. E	15. A

TEST 5

1. C	4. A	7. C	10. C	13. E
2. B	5. B	8. B	11. A	14. B
3. C	6. A	9. B	12. C	15. B

Explanatory Answers

LEVEL A

TEST 1

1. **(D)** To *abate* is to become less strong, less forceful. *Slacken* and *wane* are both synonyms for *abate,* so their relationships are equal.

2. **(D)** Both *basil* and *marjoram* are mild greenish herbs. Of all the choices, only (D) contains items that are similar—*curry powder* and *paprika,* which are pungent reddish spices.

3. **(E)** Both *caboose* and *bunkhouse* are places associated with a particular occupation—in this case, railroads and ranching. A *brakeman* and a *wrangler* work for the railroad and ranch, respectively.

4. **(D)** *Dachshund* and *St. Bernard* are both dogs, one small, the other large. Of all the choices, only *footstool* and *armchair,* both pieces of furniture, share the same relationship.

5. **(A)** A *dog* is put on a *leash* to keep it in place. A *horse* is put on a *tether* for the same reason.

6. **(B)** A *snake* moves by *slithering;* a *canary* moves by *flying.*

7. **(C)** *Gastroenteritis* is a physical ailment that can cause *cramps.* This causal relationship is matched in (C)— an *allergy* causes a *rash.*

8. **(C)** In baseball, the *pitcher* works in the *infield* of the playing field. In hockey, the *goalie* covers the *goal* area of the hockey rink.

9. **(C)** An *igloo* is a dwelling built by Native Americans living in the *arctic* zones. A *tepee* is a dwelling built by Native Americans living in the *temperate* zones.

10. **(D)** A *flower* is part of a *bouquet;* a *link* is part of a *chain.*

11. **(C)** The *keel* is the bottom of a *ship.* Although an *engine* is part of a *car,* it is not the bottom or underside. Therefore, (C) is correct: the *sole* is the bottom of a *shoe.*

12. **(C)** *Letters* make up a *word; pages* make up a *book.*

13. **(A)** To *impeach* is to charge or challenge; if the impeachment proceedings are successful, the charged person is *dismissed.* To *arraign* is to call into court as a result of accusation; if the accusation is proved correct, the arraigned person is *convicted.*

14. **(B)** A *hotel* is a kind of *shelter;* a *boat* is a kind of *transportation.*

15. **(C)** *Qualms* can cause one to *hesitate; courage* can lead one to *persevere.*

TEST 2

1. **(C)** *Juvenile* and *senescent* mean young and old respectively. *Growing* and *aging* mean the same thing.

2. **(A)** When you *assist,* you help; when you *save,* you help a great deal. When you *request,* you ask; when you *command,* you are very strong in what you ask for.

3. **(A)** A *lanyard* is a cord pulled to set off a *cannon.* Although all of the paired choices contain words pertaining to weapons, only (A) is correct; a *trigger* is pulled to set off a *pistol.*

4. **(B)** *Slate* is a type of *rock;* a *kayak* is a type of *boat.*

5. **(A)** The remains after an *explosion* are *debris;* the remains after a *fire* are *ashes.*

6. **(D)** An *acrobat* must be *agile;* an *orator, eloquent.*

7. **(A)** A *banana* is one of several bananas in a *bunch;* a *city* is one of several cities in a *state.*

8. **(C)** A *quarry* is where *marble* is extracted. A *mine* is where *coal* is extracted.

9. **(C)** A *ram* is a full-grown male sheep; a *lamb* is a young sheep of either sex. A *bull* is a full-grown male bovine; a *calf* is a young bovine of either sex.

10. **(C)** A *crooked* person does not have *scruples;* an *innocent* person does not have *guilt.*

11. **(B)** A *talisman* is worn to ward off *evil.* Similarly, an *amulet* is worn to ward off *bad luck.*

12. **(C)** *Law* controls the *citizen; reins* control the *horse.*

13. **(D)** A *toad* has *lungs;* a *tadpole* has *gills.*

14. **(D)** When an *odor wafts* through the air, it is carried through the air. The only pair that implies this relationship of carrying, of movement, is (D), *ferry* and *troops.*

15. **(E)** A *page* is an essential part of a *book;* a *string* is an essential part of a *violin.*

TEST 3

1. **(A)** *Joy* is a milder term than *ecstasy; admiration* is a milder term than *love.*

2. **(D)** A *valve* regulates the *flow* of a fluid; a *throttle* regulates the *speed* of a vehicle.

3. **(B)** A level of *larceny* is *grand larceny;* a level of *school* is *elementary school.*

4. **(D)** A *beaker* and a *flask* are equipment used by scientists. Although many of the paired choices involve substances used by scientists, only *test tube* and *condenser* are equipment.

5. **(C)** A *biped* has two legs, a *quadruped,* four. Of all the choices, *man* is two-legged, *dog* is four-legged.

6. **(C)** An *antiseptic* kills *germs;* a *lion* kills his *prey.*

7. **(A)** You hide your provisions, or *supplies,* in a hole, or *cache.* You hide your *cash* in a *safe.*

8. **(E)** A *beard* hangs from a *man* as a *wattle* hangs from a *turkey.*

9. **(D)** To *cumber* or *hamper* someone's efforts is to block them, make them difficult, *hamper* being a stronger term. A *nuisance* would cumber, and an *obstruction* would hamper.

10. **(A)** The *tractor* of a large truck pulls the *trailer,* and a *horse* pulls a *cart. Dogs* pull *sleds,* but (D) is incorrect because the pair is not in the same order as the original pair.

11. **(B)** You ride a *horse;* you play an *instrument.*

12. **(C)** You use a *clue* to unlock a *mystery;* you use a *key* to unlock a *door.*

13. **(C)** To *eke* out a *living* is to do so with great difficulty and sacrifice. Carving a turkey is not difficult, nor is earning a wage or turning a profit. But to *wrest* a *profit* implies great difficulty and hardship.

14. **(B)** A *hammer* is a *tool;* a *wagon* is a *vehicle.*

15. **(C)** *Deliberation* is a likely preliminary to making a *decision;* a *wish* is preliminary to the *fulfillment* of that wish.

TEST 4

1. **(C)** *Fauna* is animal life; *flora* is plant life. Of all the pairs, only *starfish,* an aquatic animal, and *starflower,* a flower, follow this pattern.

2. **(A)** You *sharpen* a *pencil* and *saw wood.*

3. **(A)** Nuclear *fission* is the splitting of atoms; nuclear *fusion* is the joining together of atoms. This relationship of splitting and joining is best reflected in *segregation,* the setting apart or separation of groups, and *integration,* the blending or joining of groups.

4. **(B)** A *snail* is a kind of *gastropod.* This pattern, large group : member of group, is best exemplified in *utensil* and *strainer.*

5. **(A)** Again, the relationship here is large group—*genus*—and member of group—*species.* Of all the choices, *state* and *counties* follows this pattern best.

6. **(B)** A *gerbil* is a kind of *rodent.* This is the reverse pattern of the previous two questions—here we have the specific member, then the name of the group to which it belongs. Of the choices, (B) is best—a *cow* is a kind of *ruminant,* a cud-chewing animal.

7. **(C)** *Yolk* contains *protein* as *fruit* contains *sugar.*

8. **(B)** A *fable* is a type of *story;* a *bonnet* is a type of *hat.*

9. **(A)** A *herd* is a large group of *cattle.* The only pair that gives the correct collective term for a large group of animals is (A), a *pride* of *lions.*

10. **(C)** A *zebra* is *equine;* a *sheep* is *ovine.*

11. **(B)** A *dunce* is not *clever;* a *hero* is not *fearful.*

12. **(D)** *Zoology* is a branch of biology dealing with *fauna* or animals; *botany* is a branch of biology concerned with *flora* or plant life.

13. **(C)** Just as a *graduate* is awarded a *diploma* in recognition of time and work spent achieving a goal, so a *retiree* is often awarded a *plaque.*

14. **(D)** A *colander* is used to *strain;* an *oven* is used to *roast.*

15. **(B)** Both of these colors are associated with emotions—*green* with *envy* and *blue* with *sadness.*

TEST 5

1. **(D)** A person becomes *affluent* by garnering *money;* a person becomes *venerated* by garnering *respect.*

2. **(D)** A person who is too *domineering* may become *sadistic;* a person who is too *submissive* may verge on being *masochistic.*

3. **(B)** A *mansion* is a fine *house;* a *thoroughbred* is a fine *horse.*

4. **(C)** Someone who feels *distaste* may *grimace;* someone who feels *delight* may *grin.*

5. **(B)** A *mortician* works in a *mortuary,* and a *technician* works in a *laboratory.*

6. **(A)** *School,* in a specialized sense, is the collective noun used to describe a large group of *fish.* The only pair to parallel this relationship is *furniture* and *sofa.*

7. **(C)** A *milligram* is a metric unit describing the weight of a solid. A *deciliter* is a metric unit describing the volume or quantity of a liquid. Therefore, *weight : volume* is the correct choice.

8. **(A)** *Mammoth* is an extreme form of *big.* The only pair to exemplify this pattern is (A): *emaciated* is an extreme form of *thin.*

9. **(C)** A *retinue* attends a person of rank such as a *monarch;* the *moon* is a satellite attending upon and revolving around the *earth.*

10. **(D)** A *nut* is a metal piece that fits onto a metal *screw.* Although a hat fits onto a head, (D) is a better choice, as both *wheel* and *axle* are metal, too.

11. **(D)** Consider the placement of each of these words in the analogy and the degree to which each pair is a synonym pair. *Extraordinary* refers to something very *unusual,* and it is the second word in the pair. *Bizarre* refers to something very *strange,* and it is also the second word in the pair.

12. **(D)** You can use *tweezers* to *pluck* hair. Of the other possible tool : action relationships, only (D), *razor : shave,* relates to hair.

13. **(A)** *Oak* and *ash* are both trees; *olive* and *cherry* are both fruit-bearing trees.

14. **(B)** An *opaque* substance allows no light to get through; a *translucent* substance is clear and allows light to pass. Of all the pairs, only (B) repeats this pattern: *chowder* and *bouillon.*

15. **(C)** A *treaty* is a tangible representation of *peace,* just as a *deed* is a tangible representation of *ownership.*

LEVEL B

TEST 1

1. **(A)** A *circle's diameter* bisects the circle. The *diagonal* of a *square* bisects the square.

2. **(C)** *France* and *Spain* are countries, but that does not limit your choices enough. Only (C), *Italy* and *Austria,* are countries that also share a border.

3. **(D)** A *chemist* works in a *laboratory,* just as a *mechanic* works in a *garage.* None of the other choices connect a worker with the correct workplace.

4. **(B)** *Caffeine* is a substance taken to prevent *drowsiness.* A *vaccine* is a substance taken to prevent *disease.*

5. **(D)** A *branch* is an appendage to the *trunk* of a tree, and a *leg* is an appendage to the *torso* of a person's body.

6. **(B)** To *intimidate* is to inspire *fear;* to *astonish* is to inspire *wonder.*

7. **(C)** *Publication* is the for-an-audience result of *writing; exhibition* is the public result of *painting.*

8. **(B)** A *stove* is an indispensable fixture in a *kitchen;* a *sink* is a basic piece of equipment in a *bathroom.*

9. **(B)** A *bronchiole* is a branch of a *bronchus,* which is a bronchial tube. An *arteriole* is a small terminal twig of an *artery.* The vessels in (E) are not connected; in (C), the *capillary* does not branch off a *vein.*

10. **(D)** A *greyhound* is proverbially *speedy;* on the other hand, a *sloth* is proverbially *sluggish.*

11. **(E)** A *cataract* can cause *blindness;* a *burn* can cause an *injury.*

12. **(C)** A *chronometer* is a more advanced instrument for measuring time than an *hourglass;* a *quill* is an early type of *pen.*

13. **(E)** The *cornea* is the transparent part of the coat of the *eyeball* that covers the iris and pupil; a *casing* is a transparent covering of a *hot dog.*

14. **(C)** A *croissant* is a kind of *pastry.* A *macaroon* is a kind of *cookie.*

15. **(C)** You happily *celebrate* a *marriage;* you sorrowfully *lament* a *bereavement.*

TEST 2

1. **(E)** A great *loss* might be a *debacle;* a great *success* might be a *conquest.*

2. **(A)** *Defer, suspend,* and *delay* all refer to postponement of action. You can *defer enrollment,* but you *suspend operations.*

3. **(A)** As several *articles* make up a *journal,* so several *stories* make up an *anthology.*

4. **(B)** When you feel *sympathy* for a person, you might offer your *condolences.* When you feel *joy,* you offer *congratulations.*

5. **(B)** *Dyslexia* is a disturbance in the ability to read; *dyspepsia* is indigestion. These two conditions directly affect the processes of *reading* and *digestion,* respectively.

6. **(E)** *Drake* and *duckling* are the male and young forms of ducks. *Bull* and *calf* are the male and young forms of cattle.

7. **(C)** *Margarine* is a manufactured substitute for *butter; nylon* is a manufactured substitute for *silk.*

8. **(B)** A *woodsman* cuts with an *axe;* a *carpenter* cuts with a *saw.*

9. **(D)** A *fable* is a form of *fiction,* just as an *ode* is a form of *poetry.* Some narratives are nonfiction (C), but many are not.

10. **(E)** A *whopper* is a big *falsehood;* a *sin* is a big *error.*

11. **(A)** The prefixes *hept-* and *tri-* mean *seven* and *three,* respectively. A *heptathlon* is an athletic contest featuring *seven* events; a *triathlon* features *three* events.

12. **(B)** *Sinuous* means "bending and curving"; *angular* means "having one or more angles." A *snake* is *sinuous;* a *polygon* is *angular.*

13. **(B)** A person may be *negligent* in meeting a *requirement;* he or she may similarly be *remiss* in performing a *duty.*

14. **(C)** If care is not taken, an *endangered* species may become *extinct,* as a *flammable* object may become *scorched.*

15. **(A)** *Disgrace* often follows an act of *disloyalty; fame* often follows an act of *heroism.*

TEST 3

1. **(A)** *Jollity,* or cheerfulness, is a quality you would expect to see in a *clown,* much as you'd expect *agility* from an *acrobat.*

2. **(C)** *Friction* produces *heat; evaporation* produces *vapor.*

3. **(D)** *Saturnine* (sluggish) and *mercurial* (volatile) are antonyms. Only *proficient* (skilled) and *inept* (clumsy) are related in the same way.

4. **(C)** *Marmalade* is made of *oranges; ketchup* is made of tomatoes.

5. **(B)** A *gosling* is a young goose; a *kid* is a young goat. A *duckling* is a young duck; a *foal,* a young horse.

6. **(E)** Both *hexapod* and *tripod* contain a prefix that is a number and a suffix that means foot. *Hexapod* means *insect;* a *milking stool* is usually a *tripod.*

7. **(B)** A *traitor* is *banished* (sent away); an *ally* is *welcomed* (brought in).

8. **(C)** A *hind* and a *doe* are female deer; a *stag* and a *buck* are male deer.

9. **(A)** A *hound* chases a *hare;* a *cat* chases a *mouse.*

10. **(A)** A *circle* is a round plane figure; a *sphere* is a round solid figure. A *square* is a rectangular plane figure; a *cube* is a rectangular solid figure.

11. **(A)** A *jackhammer* is used to break up, or *fracture,* old pavement. A *steamroller* is used to *smooth* new pavement.

12. **(B)** *Loafer* is used here in its "lazy person" connotation. One expects such a person to be *indolent,* just as one expects a *diplomat* to be *tactful.*

13. **(A)** The word *solo* implies one person, while the word *duet* implies two, or twice as many as *solo.* A *dozen* is twice as many as *six.*

14. **(B)** *Linoleum* is used to cover a *floor; tile* is used to cover a *roof.* The act of covering is essential to this analogy.

15. **(B)** A *motorcycle* could be considered a motorized *bicycle,* and a *snowmobile* is a kind of motorized *sleigh.*

TEST 4

1. **(C)** *Bigotry* breeds *hatred; fanaticism* breeds *intolerance.*

2. **(C)** A *mountain* is the feature of the *topography* of an area, and a *border* is a feature of the *geography* of an area.

3. **(E)** One *bounces* on a *trampoline;* one *skates* on a *pond.*

4. **(D)** A *leer* is an unpleasant *stare;* a *smirk* is an unpleasant *grin.*

5. **(D)** A *jester* can be an *employee* of a *king,* who would be his *employer.*

6. **(D)** Just as a bad *recession* may lead to a *depression,* a bad *quarrel* may lead to a *battle.*

7. **(C)** *Kiloton* and *macrocosm* express the idea of immensity; *milligram* and *microcosm* share the notion of minuteness.

8. **(C)** A *cousin* is a *kinsman;* a *bull* is an *herbivore,* a plant-eating animal.

9. **(E)** Several *puppies* can make up a *litter;* several *grapes* can make up a *bunch.*

10. **(C)** A *kite* is held by a *string* to prevent its flying off; a *stallion* is fastened with a *tether* (as a rope or chain) so that it can range only within a set radius.

11. **(A)** A *physician* diagnoses based on a *symptom* much as a *detective* solves a case based on a *clue.*

12. **(C)** Paying a *toll* might get you into a *tunnel;* buying a *ticket* is required to get you into a *cinema.*

13. **(D)** *Tokyo* is a city in *Asia,* a continent, and *Nairobi* is a city on the continent of *Africa.*

14. **(C)** A *paragraph* is composed of *words,* and an *alphabet* is made up of *letters.*

15. **(B)** One *throws* a *ball* and one *shoots* a *pellet.*

TEST 5

1. **(D)** *Cattle* eat out of a *manger,* which is an open box designed to hold feed or fodder for livestock; *pigs* eat out of a *trough.*

2. **(D)** To move like a *rotor* is to *rotate.* To move like a *top* is to *spin.*

3. **(A)** *Microbiology* is a branch of biology dealing especially with microscopic forms of life, of which *bacteria* are one. *Entomology* is a branch of zoology that deals with insects, of which *wasps* are one.

4. **(B)** The prefix *mille* means thousand, and the prefix *cent* means hundred.

5. **(D)** A *moth* will injure *clothing;* a *stigma* will injure a *reputation.*

6. **(C)** *Nadir* and *zenith* express the lowest and the highest point, respectively; *sole* and *scalp* are the lowest and highest points on a person's body.

7. **(C)** *Nausea* is an illness centered in the *stomach; migraine* is a pain in the *head.*

8. **(D)** The prefixes *neo-* and *archeo-* mean *new* and *old,* respectively.

9. **(A)** A *table* can be covered with a *tablecloth;* a *couch,* with a *slipcover.*

10. **(A)** The *closing* of day is *dusk;* the *opening* of day is *dawn.*

11. **(A)** A *doubleheader* has two parts; a *trident* has three teeth. *Twins* are two of a kind; a *troika* is a vehicle drawn by three horses.

12. **(E)** *Steel* is *inflexible; gold* is *malleable* (easy to shape or form).

13. **(C)** The adjective that applies to the *Occident* (a portion of the globe) is *western.* The adjective for the *north* is *polar.*

14. **(C)** A person's *intrusion* might be considered *rude;* whereas a *compliment* would be considered *kind.* Although a cruise may be pleasant (B), and an adventure may be exciting (D), neither of these choices contain the notion of a person's action and its description.

15. **(C)** A *bee* and a *cricket* are insects associated with specific onomatopoetic sounds: *buzz* and *chirp.*

LEVEL C

TEST 1

1. **(E)** A *gallop* is faster than a *trot*. Only *scurry* and *lope* have a similar speed differential.

2. **(B)** A *trellis* may be used to *prop* a rosebush as a *pillar* is used to *buttress* a structure.

3. **(C)** A *crown* is a *royal* symbol; a *crucifix* is a *religious* symbol.

4. **(C)** An *island* is surrounded by the *ocean;* an *oasis* is surrounded by the *desert.*

5. **(D)** *Mathematics* is the science of numbers, and *numerology* is the occult study of numbers; *astronomy* is the science of celestial bodies, and *astrology* is the occult study of celestial bodies.

6. **(E)** *Bucolic* relates to rural life and suggests the natural; *urban* implies the manufactured. *Mist* is a natural occurrence; *smog* is fog made foul by smoke and chemical fumes.

7. **(B)** To be *abhorrent* is to be extremely *dislikable;* to be *arduous* is to be extremely *difficult.*

8. **(C)** *Wood* may be measured by the *cord; milk* may be measured by the *quart.*

9. **(A)** One result of a *drought* is *thirst;* a possible result of a *blizzard* is *snow blindness.*

10. **(B)** A *minaret* is a high tower attached to a *mosque;* a *steeple* is a high structure rising above a *church.*

11. **(A)** *Chaff* is the worthless husks of grain left after the threshing of *wheat; dregs* are the worthless residue created by the process of making *wine.*

12. **(A)** A *spy* needs to be *devious* to succeed; a *farmer* must be *productive.*

13. **(D)** *Ebb* and *wax* are opposite motions, as are *slacken* and *grow; ebb* and *slacken* connote recession, while *wax* and *grow* connote expansion.

14. **(B)** A *director* is responsible for the production of a *drama;* an *editor* is responsible for the production of a *magazine.*

15. **(D)** A *cliché* is *commonplace;* a *maxim* is *terse.*

TEST 2

1. **(A)** To be *thrilled* is to be extremely *pleased;* to be *drunk* is to be extremely *tipsy.*

2. **(D)** A collection of *willow* trees may make up a *grove;* a collection of *blackberry* bushes may make up a *thicket.*

3. **(C)** A *sin* is not *moral;* a *crime* is not *legal.*

4. **(D)** An *ellipse* is a kind of *curved figure;* a *square* is a kind of *polygon.*

5. **(B)** *Saccharin* is a manufactured substitute for *sugar; margarine,* made from vegetable oils and milk, is a substitute for *butter.*

6. **(D)** To *demand* is to *request* in a strong manner; to *crave* is to *wish* in a strong manner.

7. **(C)** You may use an *album* to display a *photograph* or a *whatnot* to showcase *porcelain.*

8. **(A)** A *faucet* controls the flow of *water;* a *throttle* controls the flow of *fuel.*

9. **(B)** A *holocaust* is thorough destruction, especially when caused by *fire;* a *hanging* is death caused by a *noose* breaking the person's neck.

10. **(D)** A *pendulum oscillates,* that is, swings backward and forward; a *gyroscope spins.*

11. **(C)** *Dill* is one kind of *herb; fir* is one kind of *conifer,* or cone-producing tree.

12. **(C)** The *intestine* is part of the *digestive* system; *pores* are part of the *excretory* system.

13. **(C)** A *flask* is a small *bottle;* a *pamphlet* is a small *book.*

14. **(D)** Some people have an extreme desire (*avarice*) for *money;* some have an extreme desire (*voracity*) for *food.*

15. **(C)** Loss of *hair* creates *baldness*. Lack of *rain* creates *drought*.

TEST 3

1. **(A)** A *ship* is a large *boat;* a *tome* is a large *book.*

2. **(C)** A *scythe* symbolizes *death;* a *heart* symbolizes *love.*

3. **(B)** A *kennel* is a human-made shelter for dogs; a *stall* is usually employed to house *horses.*

4. **(B)** A *carnivore* eats *animals;* a *vegetarian* eats *vegetables.*

5. **(E)** A *libel* is invariably a written defamation of character; a *slander* is a false and defamatory oral statement about a person. A *typewriter* is used for writing; a *microphone* is used for speaking.

6. **(C)** An *entry* is the smallest unit in a *dictionary,* and a *note* is the smallest unit in a musical *score.*

7. **(A)** *Mauve* is a *color,* and *basil* is a *spice.*

8. **(D)** To *muffle* something is almost to *silence* it. To *stymie* something is almost to *defeat* it.

9. **(C)** A *whale* is an aquatic mammal that superficially resembles a *fish*. A *bat* is a nocturnal flying mammal that resembles a *bird.*

10. **(D)** A *verb* can name an *action* as a *pronoun* can name a *person.*

11. **(A)** As *epoxy* may be used to *affix* or attach objects, a *crowbar* may be used to *pry* them apart.

12. **(D)** *Discipline* brings about *order; training* brings about *preparation.*

13. **(B)** Something that is *overabundant* is more than *sufficient*. Something that is *absent* is more than *scarce.*

14. **(B)** *Paper* is sometimes identified by a *watermark;* a *person,* by a *birthmark.*

15. **(C)** A person who is extremely *bright* is *brilliant*. A person who is extremely *contented* is *overjoyed.*

TEST 4

1. **(B)** A *plutocrat* is a ruler distinguished by *wealth;* a *theocrat,* by *religion.*

2. **(D)** A *news report* is *descriptive* of an event, but a *commercial* is *prescriptive,* recommending rather than describing.

3. **(C)** *Prophylactic* means "tending to *prevent*"; *therapeutic* means "tending to *cure.*"

4. **(C)** *Rigging* on a ship is mosty *rope,* and *sails* are traditionally made of *canvas.*

5. **(B)** *Matriculation,* or enrollment, is the beginning of a process whose end is *graduation*. *Enlistment* and *discharge* are a similar beginning and ending, referring to military service.

6. **(C)** *Hydraulic* describes something that is operated by means of *water; pneumatic* describes something that is operated by means of *air.*

7. **(D)** An *egret* (a bird) is hunted for its *plumage,* or feathers. A *beaver* is hunted for its *pelt,* or skin.

8. **(B)** A *horse* is usually kept and fed in a *stable;* a *hog* is usually kept and fed in a *sty.*

9. **(B)** A *blossom* is made up of *petals* as a *windmill* is made up of *vanes,* which catch the wind. A window is made up of panes (D), but the similarity in configuration between flower petals and windmill vanes makes (B) the better choice.

10. **(D)** The *actor* plays a *role,* as a *ballplayer* plays a *position.*

11. **(A)** *Hamlet* is an example of a *tragedy* just as the *Iliad* is an example of an *epic.*

12. **(D)** *Fodder* or silage for animals is stored in a *silo; wine* is stored in a *cask.*

13. **(C)** A *kilt* is a traditional skirt worn by a *man* in Scotland; a *sari* is a traditional garment worn by a *woman* in India.

14. **(B)** The *prow* is the forward part of the *ship;* the *nose* is the forward part of the *airplane.*

15. **(E)** A *tress* is a lock of hair, especially the long unbound hair of a woman; a *skein* is a loosely coiled length of yarn or thread wound on a real. Hence, one can speak of a *tress* of *hair* and a *skein* of *wool.*

TEST 5

1. **(E)** One is likely to *blush* when one is embarrassed, or *abashed.* Similar reddening of the skin is called a *flush* when one is angry, or *irate.*

2. **(D)** *Maximum* and *minimum* mark extremes, as do *most* and *least.*

3. **(D)** One can counteract a *sensation* with an *anesthetic,* and a *poison* with an *antidote.*

4. **(E)** *Ursine* refers to a *bear* or the bear family; *feline* refers to a *cat* or the cat family.

5. **(B)** One leaves a *ship* by *disembarking* and a *horse* by *dismounting.*

6. **(D)** *Meat* contains *protein; potatoes* contain *starch.*

7. **(A)** The *nape* is the back of the *neck,* and the *heel* is the back of the *foot.*

8. **(A)** *Chocolate* is derived from a *bean,* and *tea* is derived from a *leaf.*

9. **(B)** The *dinosaur* is an extinct relative of the *crocodile;* the *woolly mammoth* is an extinct relative of the *elephant.*

10. **(A)** The *warp* is a series of yarns extended lengthwise in a loom and crossed by the *woof;* hence, the *warp* is the *longitudinal* segment and the *woof* is the *transverse.*

11. **(C)** A *xylophone* is a *percussion* instrument, and a *bassoon* is a *wind* instrument.

12. **(D)** A *stallion* is an adult male horse; a *gelding* is specifically a castrated horse. A *bull* is an adult male bovine animal; a *steer* is a bovine animal castrated before sexual maturity.

13. **(C)** *Pliers* are tools designed for *gripping,* and a *jack* is a tool for *elevating.*

14. **(B)** A *radius* extends from the center of a *circle* to its edge, as a spoke extends from the center of a *wheel* to its edge.

15. **(B)** The zodiac has twelve *signs;* the *year* has twelve *months.*

LEVEL D

TEST 1

1. **(B)** *Transitivity* is an *axiom;* the *Pythagorean* theorem is a *theorem* in geometry.

2. **(C)** To *allay fears* is to alleviate or subdue them; to *quell* the *enemy* would be to reduce the enemy to submission.

3. **(D)** An *alcove* is a small recessed section of a *room;* a *cave* is a recessed chamber in a *mountain.*

4. **(D)** *Jupiter* and *Mars* are the Roman names for the Greek gods *Zeus* and *Ares.*

5. **(D)** A *misdemeanor,* though serious, is not as serious as a *felony.* Though something that is *cracked* is damaged, it is not so seriously damaged as a *smashed* object.

6. **(D)** *Erosion* can cause *flooding* as topsoil no longer exists to hold water; certain kinds of *pollution* may, over time, cause *corrosion* as material is eaten away by chemicals.

7. **(A)** A *hygrometer* is used to measure *humidity,* and a *thermometer, temperature.*

8. **(A)** A *drop*—for example, a drop of water—may *drip;* a *bubble* may *pop.*

9. **(B)** To *cull* is to remove what is *inferior* or worthless. To *select* is to pick out the *choice,* the best.

10. **(D)** A *canticle* is a kind of religious *song;* a *broadloom* is a kind of *carpet.*

11. **(E)** A brood or family of *chicks* is a *clutch;* a small flock of *quail* is a *covey.*

12. **(C)** An architect's *blueprint* would show the location of a *hallway* much as a *road map* shows the location of a *highway.*

13. **(B)** A *dynast* is a ruler; a *serf* is a peasant. Only *regal* and *lowly* repeat this contrast.

14. **(B)** Someone who is *bold* is not easily *cowed;* someone who is *demanding* is not easily *satisfied.*

15. **(C)** *Cream* may be sold by the *pint.* The other combinations of goods and measurements are unlikely, except for (C).

TEST 2

1. **(C)** An *article* is one form of *expository* writing; a *story* is one form of *narrative* writing.

2. **(D)** A *prospector* looks for *gold,* and a *detective* looks for *clues.*

3. **(C)** *Dextrose* is one kind of *sugar; fat* is one kind of *lipid.*

4. **(D)** You would expect to see a *swarm* of bees in an *apiary,* or collection of hives. You would expect to see a *flock* of birds in an *aviary.*

5. **(E)** A *latch* may fasten a *gate* as a *buckle* fastens a *belt.*

6. **(B)** Cutting motions have different names, depending on the tool used. A *stylus* is used to *incise,* and a *penknife* may be used to *whittle.*

7. **(A)** The *cockpit* is an *interior* section of an airplane; *ailerons* are on an airplane's *exterior,* on its wings.

8. **(B)** A *vicar* is a member of the *clergy;* a *dragoon* is a member of the *military.*

9. **(C)** One would *garner* (gather) *wealth;* one would *collate* (assemble) *pages.*

10. **(A)** A *gigaton,* which is a billion tons, is a thousand times larger than a *megaton,* a million tons. A *megacycle,* a million cycles, is a thousand times larger than a *kilocycle,* which is a thousand cycles.

11. **(E)** A *gourmand* is *undiscriminating* in his love of food. A *gourmet* is *selective* in his choice of food.

12. **(B)** A *couplet* may be part of a *poem,* and a *sentence* may be art of a *paragraph.*

13. **(A)** a *climber* seeks to reach the *peak;* a *hunter* seeks *game.*

14. **(C)** *Oil* is extracted from the earth by means of a *well; silver,* by means of a *mine.*

15. **(B)** A *palette* holds a variety of *pigments.* A *nursery* contains a variety of *trees.*

TEST 3

1. **(A)** A *colander* is used to *drain* food; a *sieve* is used to *filter.*

2. **(B)** If something is *indubitable,* you cannot *contradict* it. If something is *immovable,* you cannot *budge* it.

3. **(B)** A *stallion* and a *rooster* are two different animals of the same sex, as are a *mare* and a *hen.*

4. **(E)** In *judo,* no *weapons* are used; in *soccer,* except for the goalie, players may not use their *hands.*

5. **(B)** A *judicial* function is to *enforce* laws; a *legislative* function is to *enact* laws.

6. **(A)** A *rudder* is used in directing a *ship;* a *wheel* is used in directing a *car.*

7. **(C)** In *karate,* the *foot* is used as a weapon; in *fencing,* the *foil* is a weapon.

8. **(E)** A *leech* is a *parasite;* a *mushroom* is a *saprophyte,* which is an organism, especially a plant, living on dead or decaying matter.

9. **(A)** *Leavening* is a process using a leaven (such as yeast) to produce *fermentation.* An *argument* can produce a *fight.*

10. **(B)** A greatly *amusing* action can be *hilarious.* A very *unwise* action can be *irrational.*

11. **(B)** As an *item* is an entry on a *list,* an *article* is a unit of a *constitution.*

12. **(D)** We assimilate a *book* through *reading* and a *tape* through *listening.*

13. **(A)** The first public showing of a *movie* is its *premiere;* similarly, the first public showing of a *statue* is its *unveiling.*

14. **(C)** A *parrot* is a bird found in the climatic region known as the *tropics.* Only (C), *roadrunner* and *desert,* parallels this analogy.

15. **(E)** The *median* is the *middle,* having an equal number of items above and below it; the *mean* is the *average.*

TEST 4

1. **(B)** *Muscles* are connected to bone by *tendons,* just as *bones* are connected to bones by *ligaments.*

2. **(C)** *Fluffiness* may be considered a quality of *down; smoothness* is a quality of *satin.*

3. **(A)** A *burl* is an outgrowth of a *tree,* and a *wart* is an outgrowth of an *toad.*

4. **(B)** *Yeast* is used as a *leaven,* and *iodine,* as an *antiseptic.* These functions are more specific than *aspirin's* function as a *medicine.*

5. **(B)** When a boat is *listing,* it threatens to *capsize;* when a car *careens* out of control, it may *crash.*

6. **(A)** The distance around a *polygon* is its *perimeter;* the distance around a *circle* is its *circumference.*

7. **(C)** *Alpha* and *omega* are the *beginning* and *ending* of the Greek alphabet.

8. **(A)** *Passages* can be eliminated by *expurgation,* and *leaves,* by *defoliation.*

9. **(D)** A *germ* often causes *disease;* a *war* often causes *destruction.*

10. **(C)** To *quash* a *motion* (a proposal advanced at a meeting) is to nullify it; to *quell* a *riot* is to crush it.

11. **(D)** *People* form in a *queue* like *pearls* on a *string.*

12. **(E)** Someone can *enlist* in order to become a *recruit* in the military. In the workforce, someone can *apply* to become an *employee.*

13. **(D)** *Control* results in *order; anarchy* results in *chaos.*

14. **(B)** To *rue* is to feel *remorse;* to *enjoy* is to feel *pleasure.*

15. **(A)** A *retardant* protects from *fire* as a *repellant* protects from *infestation* by insects.

TEST 5

1. **(C)** A *sewer* uses a *seam* to connect pieces of fabric. An *electrician* uses a *splice* to connect pieces of wire.

2. **(B)** You can *accept* someone else's *apology;* you can *beg* someone else's *forgiveness.*

3. **(C)** One can create something by *carving wood;* one can create something by *molding clay.*

4. **(A)** A *spire* surmounts a *tower.* A *crest* is the highest point of a *mountain.*

5. **(B)** A *solecism* is a violation of the rules of *grammar;* a *foul* is a violation of the rules of a *game.*

6. **(A)** A *valance* (a short decorative drapery) hangs from a curtain *rod.* A *pendant* hangs from a *chain* around a person's neck.

7. **(C)** *Telemetry* is concerned with the *distant* and *micrometry* with the *tiny.*

8. **(B)** *Border guards* protect the boundary of a *nation;* a *fence* protects the boundary of a *property.*

9. **(B)** *Prejudice* can interfere with one's ability to *tolerate; cramps* can interfere with one's ability to *swim.*

10. **(C)** A *soldier* is part of a *regiment;* a *star* is part of a *constellation.*

11. **(A)** *Gravel* is an ingredient in *concrete*. *Eggs* are an ingredient in a *soufflé*.

12. **(C)** The *apogee* is the outer limit of an *orbit*. The *apex* is the upper limit of a *mountain*.

13. **(E)** A *lever* helps you *lift* objects, and a *wheelbarrow* allows you to *transport* them easily.

14. **(B)** A *refugee* seeks *asylum;* a *traveler* seeks a *destination*.

15. **(B)** One who is greatly *worried* may be *hysterical;* one who is extremely *happy* may be *ecstatic*.

Sentence Completions

WHAT IS A SENTENCE COMPLETION QUESTION?

In each SAT sentence completion question, you are given a sentence containing one or more blanks. A number of words, or pairs of words, are suggested to fill the blank spaces. You must select the word or pair of words that best completes the meaning of the sentence as a whole.

> Through his ---- he managed to cheat his partners out of their earnings.
>
> (A) inefficiency
>
> (B) ineptness
>
> (C) machinations
>
> (D) regime
>
> (E) dealings

(C) You should ask, "Through *what* (noun) does one cheat?" You should be able to answer, "Through unfair play, conspiracy, evil planning, or the like." A look at the five possibilities reveals *machinations* as the only possible choice.

> Normally a(n) ---- of dependability, he had let his colleagues down; now he could not face their ----.
>
> (A) pillar .. smirks
>
> (B) besmircher .. titillation
>
> (C) paragon .. wrath
>
> (D) bastion .. adulation
>
> (E) anathema .. debts

(C) Despite being a *what* (noun) of dependability did he let his colleagues down so badly that he couldn't face them? *Paragon, bastion,* and *pillar*—all symbols of strength or virtue—would work; *besmircher* ("one who dirties") and *anathema* ("curse") would not. Using any of the three, focus now on the fact that he had "let them down." What do people show when they are severely disappointed? Certainly not *smirks* ("crooked smiles") or *adulation* ("praise")! *Wrath,* however, is a perfect fit.

HOW TO ANSWER SENTENCE COMPLETION QUESTIONS

READ THE SENTENCE THROUGH FOR SENSE AND TRY TO ANTICIPATE WHAT WORD WOULD BEST FILL THE BLANK. THEN LOOK FOR THAT WORD IN THE ANSWER CHOICES.

> Alan waited ---- for his turn, relaxing in an easy chair with his eyes closed.
>
> (A) impatiently
>
> (B) eagerly
>
> (C) warily
>
> (D) calmly
>
> (E) tensely

When you read the sentence, you might have anticipated that a word like *patiently* could be used in the blank. *Patiently* does not appear as an answer choice, but there is one choice that is close to that meaning: *calmly.* None of the other choices has a meaning that is appropriate in the context of the sentence.

This sentence was a fairly easy one. And some of those you encounter on your SAT will be easy. Others, however, will be more difficult. These will require that you analyze the logical structure of the sentence to see what is required.

DETERMINE WHETHER THE MISSING WORD MUST CONTRAST WITH OR SUPPORT ANOTHER IDEA IN THE SENTENCE.

Although this method will not solve every sentence completion item on the SAT, it is a fairly useful and easy-to-use tool. The idea is that the logic of a sentence requires a certain result, as in the following example.

> The service at the restaurant was usually very attentive, but on this one occasion the waiter seemed to ---- the diners.
>
> (A) applaud
>
> (B) urge
>
> (C) ignore
>
> (D) restrain
>
> (E) fulfill

The *but* in this sentence sets up a contrasting idea. The word that fills the blank must contrast with the idea of "very attentive." So the best answer is (C).

> If Peter continues to skip classes and continues to fail to complete homework assignments, he will soon find that he has been ---- the university.
>
> (A) dismissed from

(B) invited to

(C) trapped in

(D) warned about

(E) reminded of

The logical structure of this sentence requires a completion that shows the logical conclusion of "skipping classes and not completing assignments." The best answer, therefore, is (A).

WORDS SUCH AS ALTHOUGH, THOUGH, NOT, BUT, AND HOWEVER SIGNAL CONTRAST.

If you spot any of these words in a sentence completion question, you know that you should look for an answer that contrasts with an idea in the sentence.

Although the movie was panned by all the major critics, audiences around the country seemed to find it ----.

(A) reprehensible

(B) worthless

(C) subdued

(D) iconoclastic

(E) entertaining

The correct answer here is (E). The *although* signals a reversal of the *panning* or disapproval of the critics: The critics disliked the movie but the audiences like it.

The restaurant itself was beautiful and the service excellent, but the food was ----.

(A) outstanding

(B) morose

(C) conclusive

(D) inedible

(E) filling

Here the *but* signals a contrast between the positive ideas of *beautiful* and *excellent* and an adjective with negative connotations that describes the food. What is a good way of describing bad food? (D) gives the correct answer.

WORDS SUCH AS SO, FOR, BECAUSE, THEREFORE, AND AS A RESULT SIGNAL IDEAS THAT SUPPORT EACH OTHER.

If you spot one of these words in a sentence completion question, you know that you should look for an answer that supports an idea in the sentence.

> Millicent was extremely ---- to be given the award, for she had worked very hard for it.
>
> (A) pleased
>
> (B) open-minded
>
> (C) embarrassed
>
> (D) interested
>
> (E) fruitful

Here the word that fills in the blank must be something that is consistent with the idea of "working very hard" for something. Had you worked very hard for something, what would be your attitude toward it? You would be proud, or happy, or satisfied. So you can see that (A) gives the best completion.

> Throughout his young life, John excelled in sports, and as a result he decided he wanted to become a professional ----.
>
> (A) chemist
>
> (B) athlete
>
> (C) accountant
>
> (D) sales representative
>
> (E) student

This is a rather simple example of how the logic of a sentence dictates your choice. The phrase "as a result" tells you that John's decision was the logical outcome of his excellence in sports. What is the logical outcome of excellence in sports? A career as a professional athlete.

SOMETIMES THE BLANK REQUIRES A WORD THAT RESTATES AN IDEA ALREADY MENTIONED IN THE SENTENCE.

> Joan was so abrupt with clients that her supervisor eventually put a letter in her file citing her ----.
>
> (A) enthusiasm
>
> (B) rudeness
>
> (C) lethargy
>
> (D) diligence
>
> (E) patience

Here the correct answer is (B). Notice that the idea of "rudeness" restates the idea of "abruptness."

SOMETIMES THE BLANK REQUIRES A WORD THAT SUMMARIZES AN IDEA ALREADY MENTIONED IN THE SENTENCE.

> After seeing shocking films of animals maimed and tortured by traps of hunters, Marie concluded that purchasing a new fur coat would be ----.
>
> (A) mandatory
>
> (B) subliminal
>
> (C) glamorous
>
> (D) immoral
>
> (E) redundant

Here the word that fills the blank must be an adjective that describes a reaction to the shocking hurting of animals. The choice that best describes such an act would be *immoral.*

IF YOU HAVE TO GUESS, FIRST ELIMINATE ALL CHOICES THAT MAKE NO SENSE.

Many wrong answer choices, when inserted into a blank, create a meaningless phrase. Suppose, for example, that you have a sentence completion item that includes as a subpart the element "---- task." Some English words would suitably modify the word *task.* You might have an easy task, a simple task, a difficult task, an arduous task, or even a monstrous task. You could not, however, have a blushing task, an alert task, a famished task, a determined task, or an excitable task. These are words that just cannot be used to modify the word *task.* Therefore, even if you don't understand the overall logic of a sentence, you should be able to eliminate one or more choices that contain words that are unsuitable.

> Professor Martin spent his entire career as a teacher trying to ---- his students to appreciate the beauty of poetry.
>
> (A) alienate
>
> (B) disrupt
>
> (C) encourage
>
> (D) repeal
>
> (E) define

Test each for its suitability in the subpart "---- his students." Using just this part of the sentence, you should be able to eliminate (B), (D), and (E). As for (B), you can disrupt a class or a meeting, but you cannot disrupt a student; as for (D), you can repeal an act or a law, but you cannot repeal a student; and as for (E) you can define the word *student,* but you cannot define a student. Having eliminated three choices, you can make your guess. The correct answer is (C).

IF YOU HAVE TO GUESS, AS A LAST RESORT, SELECT A DIFFICULT VOCABULARY WORD.

SAT sentence completion items are arranged in order of increasing difficulty. What makes one item more difficult than another? Sometimes it is the logic of the sentence, but other times it is the vocabulary. And for a question to be difficult because it uses difficult vocabulary, the correct answer must be a difficult vocabulary word.

Here is an example of a problem using difficult vocabulary:

> Because the speaker had a reputation for ----, the chairperson warned him to be succinct.
>
> (A) bravery
>
> (B) creativity
>
> (C) lassitude
>
> (D) piety
>
> (E) loquaciousness

Assume that this item is one of the last in a series of sentence completions. Given its position, you know that it is supposed to be a difficult question (remember the order of increasing difficulty). And what makes it difficult is that many test-takers won't know the meaning of the correct answer. Since (A), (B), and (D) are likely to be familiar to most test-takers, none of them is a likely candidate for a correct answer. Having eliminated those three, you would guess either (C) or (E), one of the two difficult vocabulary words. The correct answer is (E); *loquaciousness* means "talkativeness."

PRE-TEST QUIZ

Circle the letter that appears before your answer.

1. The film was completely devoid of plot or character development; it was merely a ---- of striking images.

   (A) renouncement

   (B) montage

   (C) calumny

   (D) carnage

   (E) premonition

2. She delivered her speech with great ----, gesturing flamboyantly with her hands and smiling broadly from her opening remarks through her conclusion.

   (A) candor

   (B) consternation

   (C) acerbity

   (D) verve

   (E) innuendo

3. As a result of a(n) ---- with her landlord, she was evicted.

   (A) contusion
   (B) alternative
   (C) conflagration
   (D) altercation
   (E) aggression

4. It was not possible to set a monetary value on the legal services she provided, so, the grateful town had a gold medal struck as a(n) ----.

   (A) affirmation
   (B) eulogy
   (C) exultation
   (D) elegy
   (E) honorarium

5. No elected official who remains ---- can play a major role in public life; compromise is the life-blood of politics.

   (A) obdurate
   (B) dogmatic
   (C) pragmatic
   (D) irrefutable
   (E) inflexible

6. Contrary to popular opinion, bats are not generally aggressive and rabid; most are shy and ----.

   (A) turgid
   (B) disfigured
   (C) punctual
   (D) innocuous
   (E) depraved

7. The ballet company demonstrated its ---- by putting both classical and modern works in the repertoire.

   (A) versatility
   (B) mollification
   (C) treachery
   (D) dignity
   (E) obtrusiveness

8. Though the concert had been enjoyable, it was overly ---- and the three encores seemed ----.

   (A) extensive .. garrulous
   (B) protracted .. gratuitous
   (C) inaudible .. superfluous
   (D) sublime .. fortuitous
   (E) contracted .. lengthy

9. A good trial lawyer will argue only what is central to an issue, eliminating ---- information or anything else that might ---- the client.

   (A) seminal .. amuse
   (B) extraneous .. jeopardize
   (C) erratic .. enhance
   (D) prodigious .. extol
   (E) reprehensible .. initiate

10. Peter, ---- by the repeated rejections of his novel, ---- to submit his manuscript to other publishers.

    (A) encouraged .. declined
    (B) elated .. planned
    (C) undaunted .. continued
    (D) inspired .. complied
    (E) undeterred .. refused

Explanatory Answers

1. **(B)** A film that has no plot or character development is simply a collection, or *montage,* of images.

2. **(D)** Putting together the gestures and smile yields an impression of enthusiam. *Verve,* a synonym for *spirit,* is the right choice.

3. **(D)** Eviction is a drastic measure, usually the result of nonpayment of rent or some other negative occurrence. The only possible choice that fits the logic of the sentence is *altercation* (heated argument).

4. **(E)** The context indicates some sort of payment for services but also shows that the amount of remuneration could not be calculated in monetary terms. The correct choice, *honorarium,* according to *Webster's,* is "a payment as to a professional person for services on which no fee is set or legally obtainable."

5. **(E)** The context indicates that whoever does not compromise has no future in politics. The missing word, then, must mean "*not* amenable to compromise." All choices except (D) describe varying degrees of stubbornness, but only *inflexible* means a complete refusal to compromise.

6. **(D)** The sentence starts with *contrary,* a "thought reverser." So we know that bats are something that is the opposite of *aggressive* and *rabid. Innocuous,* or harmless, is the opposite of *rabid* and goes nicely with *shy.*

7. **(A)** This is basically a vocabulary question. You need to know what noun means "the ability to do more than one thing well." Only *versatility* completes the sentence correctly.

8. **(B)** The *though* sets up a contrast. The concert was enjoyable, but it suffered from some defect. Additionally, the two blanks themselves are parallel, for they complete similar thoughts. Only the words in choice (B) satisfy this condition. The concert was *protracted* (too long), and the encores were *gratuitous* (uncalled for).

9. **(B)** The first blank calls for a word indicating information that a trial lawyer would eliminate because it is not central to an issue. The only possible choice is *extraneous.* Likewise, a good lawyer would not mention anything that might *jeopardize* (endanger) a client.

10. **(C)** Even though Peter's novel was rejected by many publishers, he was *undaunted* (not discouraged) and *continued* to submit it to others.

LEVEL A SENTENCE COMPLETIONS

Test 1 (Answers on Page 121)

Select the word or word pair that best completes each sentence. Circle the letter that appears before your answer.

1. Although her lips wore a smile, her eyes wore a ----.
   - (A) veil
   - (B) laugh
   - (C) shadow
   - (D) frown
   - (E) stare

2. Martha's ---- handling of the steaks caused us to amend our plans for dinner and eat out.
   - (A) ingenious
   - (B) ingenuous
   - (C) disingenuous
   - (D) inverted
   - (E) inept

3. The stigma attached to this job makes it ---- even at a(n) ---- salary.
   - (A) enticing .. fabulous
   - (B) unattractive .. attractive
   - (C) attractive .. attractive
   - (D) sybaritic .. meager
   - (E) uninviting .. nominal

4. One man's meat is another man's ----.
   - (A) dairy
   - (B) flesh
   - (C) poison
   - (D) meeting
   - (E) prerogative

5. Joseph's ---- handling of the Thompson account made him the laughingstock of the industry.
   - (A) proper
   - (B) dishonest
   - (C) maudlin
   - (D) humorous
   - (E) incompetent

6. By shrewdly shifting district lines, a party boss can ---- any voting bloc out of ----.
   - (A) talk .. registering
   - (B) gerrymander .. existence
   - (C) shift .. precinct
   - (D) cheat .. majority
   - (E) gerrymander .. hand

7. The prisoner was in a state of great ---- after three months in solitary confinement with no bathing.
   - (A) lassitude
   - (B) decrepitude
   - (C) solitude
   - (D) rectitude
   - (E) fortitude

8. He was the chief ---- of his uncle's will. After taxes, he was left with an inheritance of $20,000,000.
   - (A) exemption
   - (B) pensioner
   - (C) beneficiary
   - (D) contestant
   - (E) winner

9. Don't be ----; I don't have time to split hairs.
   (A) spurious
   (B) childish
   (C) picayune
   (D) erudite
   (E) absurd

10. When his temperature climbed above 104 degrees, he became ----.
   (A) tepid
   (B) discordant
   (C) deceased
   (D) delirious
   (E) presumptuous

11. To climb at another's expense is to ---- yourself morally.
   (A) upbraid
   (B) elevate
   (C) energize
   (D) enervate
   (E) abase

12. We waited patiently for the storm to slacken; it ---- refused to ----.
   (A) persistently .. strengthen
   (B) stoutly .. abate
   (C) wanly .. sublimate
   (D) sternly .. mitigate
   (E) consistently .. perambulate

13. The prince decided to ---- when he found that he couldn't have his love and his throne at the same time; it was 1937.
   (A) prevaricate
   (B) ablute
   (C) alter
   (D) abrogate
   (E) abdicate

14. Although he was not ever at the scene of the crime, his complicity was uncovered; he had ---- and ---- in the robbery by acting as a fence.
   (A) stolen .. sold
   (B) assisted .. testified
   (C) witnessed .. participated
   (D) aided .. abetted
   (E) financed .. mastermind

15. In view of the extenuating circumstances and the defendant's youth, the judge recommended ----.
   (A) conviction
   (B) a defense
   (C) a mistrial
   (D) leniency
   (E) hanging

Test 2   (Answers on Page 121)

Select the word or word pair that best completes each sentence. Circle the letter that appears before your answer.

1. A person who will not take "no" for an answer may sometimes be classified as a ----.
   (A) salesman
   (B) persistent
   (C) zealot
   (D) heretic
   (E) notary

2. The children were told that they should be ---- of strangers offering candy.
   (A) weary
   (B) wary
   (C) envious
   (D) considerate
   (E) happy

3. Politicians are not coerced into taxing the public; they do it of their own ----.

   (A) reputation

   (B) appraisal

   (C) graft

   (D) expediency

   (E) volition

4. Elder statesmen used to be ---- for their wisdom when respect for age was an integral part of the value structure.

   (A) known

   (B) venerated

   (C) exiled

   (D) abused

   (E) used

5. The 45-minute sermon is a potent ----; it is an absolute cure for ----.

   (A) astringent .. drowsiness

   (B) aphrodisiac .. celibacy

   (C) soporific .. insomnia

   (D) therapeutic .. malaise

   (E) trial .. lassitude

6. His cynicism was ----; it was written all over him.

   (A) affected

   (B) covert

   (C) infamous

   (D) manifest

   (E) famous

7. Suffering from ----, she was forced to spend most of her time indoors.

   (A) claustrophobia

   (B) anemia

   (C) agoraphobia

   (D) ambivalence

   (E) xenophobia

8. We were not allowed to ---- our appetite until we had tidied up our living quarters.

   (A) fill

   (B) whet

   (C) sate

   (D) flag

   (E) address

9. If you don't badger the child, he may do what you want him to do without ----.

   (A) pleasure

   (B) pain

   (C) pressure

   (D) volition

   (E) waste

10. You must see the head of the agency; I am not ---- to give out that information.

    (A) nervous

    (B) authorized

    (C) programmed

    (D) happy

    (E) avid

11. The magazine is considered a ---- of literary good taste; the stories it publishes are genteel and refined.

    (A) cabal

    (B) credential

    (C) potential

    (D) bastion

    (E) maelstrom

12. The ship was in a(n) ---- position; having lost its rudder it was subject to the ---- of the prevailing winds.

    (A) inexcusable .. direction

    (B) unintended .. riptides

    (C) untenable .. vagaries

    (D) dangerous .. breezes

    (E) favored .. weaknesses

13. ---- shadows played over her face as the branches above her danced in the sunlight.

    (A) Transient

    (B) Prolonged

    (C) Swarthy

    (D) Clandestine

    (E) Sedentary

14. Alchemists expended their energies in an attempt to ---- base elements into gold.

    (A) transfer

    (B) raise

    (C) translate

    (D) commute

    (E) transmute

15. Publication of the article was timed to ---- with the professor's fiftieth birthday.

    (A) coincide

    (B) adapt

    (C) amalgamate

    (D) terminate

    (E) interfere

Test 3   (Answers on Page 121)

Select the word or word pair that best completes each sentence. Circle the letter that appears before your answer.

1. The chariot ---- around the curve completely out of control when Thessalius dropped the reins.

    (A) trotted

    (B) competed

    (C) careened

    (D) fell

    (E) caromed

2. Don't ----; stick to the ---- of the issue so that we can take it to a vote.

    (A) prevaricate .. jist

    (B) stammer .. meat

    (C) procrastinate .. promptness

    (D) delay .. urgency

    (E) digress .. crux

3. The more the search proved fruitless, the more ---- the parents of the missing child became.

    (A) disconsolate

    (B) dislocated

    (C) disappointed

    (D) disheveled

    (E) disinfected

4. When the unpopular war began, only a few citizens enlisted; the rest had to be ----.

    (A) shot

    (B) processed

    (C) pacified

    (D) reassured

    (E) conscripted

5. The ---- fumes from the refinery poisoned the air, causing many people to fall ill.

    (A) superfluous

    (B) peremptory

    (C) noxious

    (D) lugubrious

    (E) intransigent

6. The upset furniture and broken window silently ---- to the fact that the apartment had been robbed.

    (A) witnessed

    (B) confirmed

    (C) attested

    (D) admitted

    (E) alleged

7. Although the warrior could cope with blows from swords, he was ---- to gunshots; his armor was not ---- to them.

   (A) reachable .. proof

   (B) vulnerable .. susceptible

   (C) vulnerable .. impervious

   (D) invulnerable .. susceptible

   (E) invulnerable .. impervious

8. When she addressed the reporters, her beauty, bearing, and elegant garb were belied by the ---- words she uttered.

   (A) untrue

   (B) uncouth

   (C) unemotional

   (D) unfettered

   (E) unequivocal

'9. "A stitch in time saves nine" and other such ---- expressions made his speeches insufferable.

   (A) tried

   (B) cryptic

   (C) redundant

   (D) trite

   (E) true

10. The new regulations turned out to be ----, not permissive.

    (A) impermissive

    (B) liberal

    (C) stringent

    (D) uniform

    (E) unrestrictive

11. They prefer to hire someone fluent in Spanish, since the neighborhood where the clinic is located is ---- Hispanic.

    (A) imponderably

    (B) sparsely

    (C) consistently

    (D) predominantly

    (E) not at all

12. A dark, cloudy sky is a ---- of a storm.

    (A) remnant

    (B) precursor

    (C) belier

    (D) proof

    (E) constellation

13. The Freedom of Information Act gives private citizens ---- government files.

    (A) access to

    (B) excess of

    (C) redress of

    (D) release from

    (E) no rights to

14. His remarks were so ---- we could not decide which of the possible meanings was correct.

    (A) ambiguous

    (B) facetious

    (C) improper

    (D) congruent

    (E) quiet

15. His performance was ----; it made a fool of him.

    (A) auspicious

    (B) ludicrous

    (C) luscious

    (D) interlocutory

    (E) internecine

Test 4   (Answers on Page 121)

Select the word or word pair that best completes each sentence. Circle the letter that appears before your answer.

1. A person who commits a wrong may be required to ---- his property as a penalty.

   (A) confiscate

   (B) destroy

   (C) forfeit

   (D) assess

   (E) sell

2. When the desk was placed facing the window, she found herself ---- from her work by the activity in the street.

   (A) distraught

   (B) destroyed

   (C) distracted

   (D) decimated

   (E) diminished

3. He said he didn't get the job done because he was incapacitated; in truth, he was ----.

   (A) indigent

   (B) indolent

   (C) indulgent

   (D) insipid

   (E) inculpable

4. The "police" turned out to be clowns; it was all a ----.

   (A) stickup

   (B) mystery

   (C) mixup

   (D) fracas

   (E) hoax

5. The authorities declared an ---- on incoming freight because of the trucking strike.

   (A) impression

   (B) immolation

   (C) embargo

   (D) alert

   (E) opprobrium

6. The grade was steep and the load heavy; we had to ---- the oxen in order to arrive home on time.

   (A) rest

   (B) eat

   (C) feed

   (D) goad

   (E) slaughter

7. He was proved guilty; his alibi had been a complete ----.

   (A) attestation

   (B) fabrication

   (C) intonation

   (D) litany

   (E) cementation

8. He claimed to be deathly ill, although he looked perfectly ---- and ---- to us.

   (A) fine .. fettle

   (B) sane .. sound

   (C) hale .. hearty

   (D) hectic .. healthy

   (E) sound .. decrepit

9. Although she had ---- about the weather, she had no ---- about her ability to navigate through it.

   (A) doubts .. confidence

   (B) confidence .. qualms

   (C) qualms .. confidence

   (D) misgivings .. qualms

   (E) reports .. foresight

10. The police department will not accept for ---- a report of a person missing if his residence is outside the city.

   (A) foreclosure

   (B) convenience

   (C) investigation

   (D) control

   (E) guidance

11. Rabbits, elephants, deer, and sheep are ----; they eat only plants.

    (A) omnivorous

    (B) herbivorous

    (C) carnivorous

    (D) ruminants

    (E) pachyderms

12. Foreman and Ali were fighting tooth and nail when suddenly, in the thick of the ----, the bell rang.

    (A) night

    (B) day

    (C) thievery

    (D) fray

    (E) ring

13. The judge ---- the union from blocking the accesses.

    (A) suspended

    (B) ordered

    (C) forbade

    (D) unfrocked

    (E) enjoined

14. The ---- on the letter showed it had been mailed in North Dakota two weeks previously.

    (A) address

    (B) stamp

    (C) postmark

    (D) envelope

    (E) printing

15. It is easy to see the difference between the two photographs when they are placed in ----.

    (A) disarray

    (B) juxtaposition

    (C) composition

    (D) jeopardy

    (E) collaboration

Test 5   (Answers on Page 121)

Select the word or word pair that best completes each sentence. Circle the letter that appears before your answer.

1. We are indeed sorry to hear of your mother's passing; please accept our sincerest ----.

   (A) adulations

   (B) congratulations

   (C) condolences

   (D) concatenations

   (E) contortions

2. While on a diet I remained lean, but once off it I became ----.

   (A) adept

   (B) remiss

   (C) corpulent

   (D) corporeal

   (E) corporal

3. With his gutter language and vile manner he was positively ----.

(A) urbane

(B) banal

(C) rural

(D) liberal

(E) boorish

4. The voters show their ---- by staying away from the polls.

(A) interest

(B) usury

(C) apathy

(D) serendipity

(E) registration

5. Being less than perfectly prepared, I took my exams with ----.

(A) aplomb

(B) confidence

(C) trepidation

(D) indifference

(E) skepticism

6. During colonial winters in America there was a ---- in every ----.

(A) fire .. hearth

(B) stoker .. pot

(C) flintlock .. chimney

(D) tepee .. stockade

(E) blizzard .. storm

7. The good-humored joke ---- the tension in the room.

(A) enervated

(B) allocated

(C) dispelled

(D) cited

(E) berated

8. When the bomb exploded in front of the building, it destroyed the whole ----.

(A) cellar

(B) pontoon

(C) facade

(D) facet

(E) cupola

9. He is expected to testify that he saw the ---- thief fleeing the scene of the crime.

(A) convicted

(B) delinquent

(C) alleged

(D) offensive

(E) innocent

10. A child who has not slept well will be anything but ----.

(A) intractable

(B) docile

(C) equine

(D) bovine

(E) ill-tempered

11. What we thought was a ---- volcano suddenly erupted.

(A) deceased

(B) dactylic

(C) dormant

(D) disruptive

(E) discontinued

12. Cigarette smoking is ---- to your health.

(A) disengaging

(B) deleterious

(C) delectable

(D) irrespective

(E) irrelevant

13. My uncle hardly ever needed a telephone; his voice was ---- from a distance of half a mile.

   (A) inaudible
   (B) audible
   (C) suspicious
   (D) visible
   (E) copious

14. Her parents never had to ---- her for being ----.

   (A) chide .. industrious
   (B) ride .. superfluous
   (C) chide .. indolent
   (D) punish .. independent
   (E) commend .. intransigent

15. The current use of "----" in place of "fat" is a euphemism.

   (A) overwrought
   (B) portly
   (C) insipid
   (D) obstreperous
   (E) pugilistic

LEVEL B SENTENCE COMPLETIONS

Test 1 (Answers on Page 121)

Select the word or word pair that best completes each sentence. Circle the letter that appears before your answer.

1. An accident report should be written as soon as possible after the necessary ---- has been obtained.

   (A) bystander
   (B) formulation
   (C) information
   (D) charter
   (E) specimen

2. A change in environment is very likely to ---- a change in one's work habits.

   (A) affect
   (B) inflict
   (C) effect
   (D) prosper
   (E) rupture

3. With typical diplomatic maneuvering, the State Department used every known ---- to avoid expressing the avowed policy in ---- language.

   (A) trick .. diplomatic
   (B) page .. gobbledygook
   (C) circumlocution .. concise
   (D) summary .. plain
   (E) formula .. cryptic

4. The astute attorney asked many ---- questions of the witness in an attempt to ---- the truth.

   (A) pretentious .. prolong
   (B) loquacious .. placate
   (C) nebulous .. mitigate
   (D) probing .. elicit
   (E) spurious .. verify

5. The main reason for the loss of the Alamo was the ---- of Santa Ana's forces.

   (A) decline

   (B) felicitation

   (C) preponderance

   (D) isolation

   (E) absence

6. A cloudy suspension may be described as ----.

   (A) turbid

   (B) precipitous

   (C) suspicious

   (D) auspicious

   (E) temporary

7. The flamenco dancer stood still, ready to perform, his arms ----.

   (A) blazing

   (B) akimbo

   (C) flailing

   (D) deadlocked

   (E) askew

8. The celebrity sued the magazine, claiming that the article ---- his character.

   (A) demoted

   (B) deplored

   (C) defamed

   (D) implicated

   (E) whitewashed

9. To be a "joiner" is to be ----.

   (A) gregarious

   (B) popular

   (C) hilarious

   (D) woodworking

   (E) singular

10. As a result of constant and unrelenting eating, he changed from slightly overweight to ----.

    (A) overrun

    (B) parsimonious

    (C) oblate

    (D) obese

    (E) lilliputian

11. When you have ---- your palate with pickles, you want no more.

    (A) scarred

    (B) satiated

    (C) imbibed

    (D) covered

    (E) palavered

12. To protect the respondents' privacy, names and Social Security numbers are ---- the questionnaires before the results are tabulated.

    (A) referred to

    (B) deleted from

    (C) retained in

    (D) appended to

    (E) computerized in

13. TASS was the ---- for Telegrafnoe Agentsvo Sovietskovo Soyuza.

    (A) homonym

    (B) acronym

    (C) heteronym

    (D) antonym

    (E) pseudonym

14. After the deluge, flood waters ---- the town.

    (A) imperiled

    (B) redeemed

    (C) impugned

    (D) regaled

    (E) traduced

15. To put off until tomorrow what you should do today is to ----.

    (A) prorate

    (B) procrastinate

    (C) preface

    (D) proscribe

    (E) promulgate

Test 2   (Answers on Page 122)

Select the word or word pair that best completes each sentence. Circle the letter that appears before your answer.

1. New York's climate is not very ----; its winters give you colds, and its summers can cause heat prostration.
   (A) sanitary
   (B) volatile
   (C) salubrious
   (D) healthy
   (E) pathogenic

2. One who ---- another is laughing *at* him, not *with* him.
   (A) derides
   (B) defiles
   (C) irks
   (D) buffoons
   (E) harasses

3. To give in to the terrorists' demands would be a betrayal of our responsibilities; such ---- would only encourage others to adopt similar ways to gain their ends.
   (A) defeats
   (B) appeasement
   (C) appeals
   (D) subterfuge
   (E) treaties

4. It is hard to believe that the Trojans could have been so easily deceived by the ---- of the wooden horse.
   (A) tragedy
   (B) stratagem
   (C) strategy
   (D) prolixity
   (E) fetlocks

5. She pretended to be nonchalant but her movements betrayed signs of ----.
   (A) greed
   (B) weariness
   (C) worry
   (D) boredom
   (E) evil

6. We can easily forgo a ---- we have never had, but once obtained it often is looked upon as being ----.
   (A) requirement .. unusual
   (B) gift .. useless
   (C) bonus .. unearned
   (D) luxury .. essential
   (E) necessity .. important

7. ---- means an injustice so ---- that it is wicked.
   (A) Iniquity .. gross
   (B) Lobotomy .. inane
   (C) Perjury .. mendacious
   (D) Lobotomy .. pernicious
   (E) Bias .. slanted

8. The navy scoured the area for over a month, but the ---- search turned up no clues.
   (A) temporary
   (B) cursory
   (C) fruitful
   (D) painstaking
   (E) present

9. The ---- assumed for the sake of discussion was that business would improve for the next five years.
   (A) labyrinth
   (B) hypothesis
   (C) outlay
   (D) itinerary
   (E) assumption

10. I wish you wouldn't be so ----; you make faces at everything I say.

    (A) supercilious

    (B) insubordinate

    (C) disconsolate

    (D) superficial

    (E) banal

11. I felt as ---- as a fifth wheel.

    (A) rolled

    (B) round

    (C) superfluous

    (D) axillary

    (E) rotational

12. If we were to ---- our democracy with a ----, there would be no way, short of civil war, to reverse the change.

    (A) contrast .. parliament

    (B) substitute .. constitutional monarchy

    (C) supplant .. dictatorship

    (D) reinforce .. three-party system

    (E) automate .. technocracy

13. A(n) ---- look came into the poodle's eye as a dachshund wandered onto its territory.

    (A) feline

    (B) bellicose

    (C) onerous

    (D) canine

    (E) felonious

14. A few of the critics ---- the play, but in general they either disregarded or ridiculed it.

    (A) mocked

    (B) discredited

    (C) criticized

    (D) denounced

    (E) appreciated

15. The annual ---- in his school attendance always coincided with the first week of fishing season.

    (A) sequence

    (B) hiatus

    (C) accrual

    (D) increment

    (E) motivation

Test 3   (Answers on Page 122)

Select the word or word pair that best completes each sentence. Circle the letter that appears before your answer.

1. During the Revolutionary War, Hessian troops fought on the British side not as allies, but as ----. They were paid in money, not glory.

    (A) assistants

    (B) orderlies

    (C) valets

    (D) infantry

    (E) mercenaries

2. On and on they came, countless as the blades of grass in a field, a ---- of them.

    (A) myriad

    (B) dryad

    (C) dozen

    (D) multitudinous

    (E) multiplicity

3. If you find peeling potatoes to be ----, perhaps you'd prefer to scrub the floors?

    (A) preferable

    (B) onerous

    (C) infectious

    (D) relevant

    (E) passé

4. The offenders then prostrated themselves and ---- for mercy.

(A) entreated

(B) applauded

(C) begged

(D) imprecated

(E) deprecated

5. His rebelliousness was ----; it was written all over him.

(A) exterior

(B) covert

(C) implicit

(D) contumacious

(E) manifest

6. A system of education should be ---- by the ---- of students it turns out, for quality is preferred to quantity.

(A) controlled .. intelligence

(B) justified .. number

(C) examined .. wealth

(D) judged .. caliber

(E) condemned .. ability

7. Giving preference to his brother's son for that office smacks of ---- to me!

(A) chauvinism

(B) sycophancy

(C) nepotism

(D) nihilism

(E) pleonasm

8. We seldom feel ---- when we are allowed to speak freely, but any ---- of our free speech brings anger.

(A) angry .. defense

(B) blessed .. restriction

(C) scholarly .. understanding

(D) enslaved .. misuse

(E) upset .. explanation

9. Although the wind was quite dependable in those waters, the schooner had an inboard engine as a ---- just in case.

(A) relief

(B) substitute

(C) ballast

(D) generator

(E) subsidiary

10. Being perfectly prepared, I took my exams with ----.

(A) aplomb

(B) pugnacity

(C) trepidation

(D) indifference

(E) resentment

11. Her speech was too ----; its meaning escaped me completely.

(A) protracted

(B) concise

(C) sordid

(D) circumspect

(E) abstruse

12. The "life" of some subatomic particles is so ---- it has to be measured in nanoseconds.

(A) contrived

(B) finite

(C) ephemeral

(D) circumscribed

(E) macroscopic

13. When income taxes are repealed, the ---- will have arrived.

(A) apocalypse

(B) holocaust

(C) millstone

(D) milestone

(E) millennium

14. Government often seems to regard money as the route to social salvation: a ---- for all the troubles of humanity.

    (A) provocation

    (B) panacea

    (C) standard

    (D) nucleus

    (E) resource

15. You'll ---- the day you voted for Zilch; he'll break every promise he's made to you.

    (A) regard

    (B) eschew

    (C) obliterate

    (D) rue

    (E) darken

Test 4   (Answers on Page 122)

> Select the word or word pair that best completes each sentence. Circle the letter that appears before your answer.

1. If he hasn't yet learned the importance of speaking well of others, he must be quite ----.

    (A) loquacious

    (B) oblique

    (C) mathematical

    (D) arcane

    (E) obtuse

2. Louis XIV was the ---- of ---- elegance; he wore a different outfit for practically every hour of the day.

    (A) paragon .. peripatetic

    (B) epitome .. sartorial

    (C) acme .. epicurean

    (D) architect .. gastronomic

    (E) root .. European

3. Favoring one child over another will only intensify ---- rivalry.

    (A) fraternal

    (B) sororal

    (C) parental

    (D) maternal

    (E) sibling

4. The man ---- the speaker at the meeting by shouting false accusations.

    (A) corrected

    (B) interfered

    (C) disconcerted

    (D) collapsed

    (E) acknowledged

5. The literal meaning of *astronaut* is "----."

    (A) space jockey

    (B) cosmic navigator

    (C) star sailor

    (D) space pilot

    (E) sky pilot

6. If you ---- your energy wisely you will never lack for it; if you ---- it, you'll remain poor.

    (A) burn .. cauterize

    (B) use .. dissipate

    (C) husband .. economize

    (D) expend .. spend

    (E) economize .. alter

7. The only fair way to choose who will have to work over the holiday is to pick someone ---- by drawing lots.
   (A) covertly
   (B) conspicuously
   (C) randomly
   (D) painstakingly
   (E) senior

8. Richelieu achieved eminence under Louis XIII; few cardinals since have been so politically ----.
   (A) retiring
   (B) unassuming
   (C) prominent
   (D) hesitant
   (E) wavering

9. People started calling him a ----; he had broken a law.
   (A) conspirator
   (B) transgressor
   (C) transient
   (D) bystander
   (E) paragon

10. "---- and ----," he said with a smile as he met his class for the new term.
    (A) Warm .. welcome
    (B) Pupils .. colleagues
    (C) Friends .. countrymen
    (D) Hail .. farewell
    (E) Greetings .. salutations

11. I'm glad to see you have ----; patience is a virtue!
    (A) arrived
    (B) decided
    (C) distemper
    (D) time
    (E) forbearance

12. As the fog came ----, visibility dropped to five feet.
    (A) often
    (B) silently
    (C) nigh
    (D) damp
    (E) unopposed

13. A(n) ---- jogger, she could do 15 miles a day.
    (A) reluctant
    (B) indefatigable
    (C) outfitted
    (D) aged
    (E) distant

14. The ---- speech, given on the spur of the moment, received as much publicity as a carefully planned announcement.
    (A) affable
    (B) resilient
    (C) indigenous
    (D) impromptu
    (E) pernicious

15. A week of sun and exercise had a ---- effect; the dark circles under her eyes were ---- and her skin took on a rosy glow.
    (A) peremptory .. reinstated
    (B) salutary .. obliterated
    (C) sentient .. proscribed
    (D) contentious .. deluded
    (E) fulsome .. censured

Test 5   (Answers on Page 122)

Select the word or word pair that best completes each sentence. Circle the letter that appears before your answer.

1. Although she is reputed to be aloof, her manner that day was so ---- that everyone felt perfectly at ease.

   (A) reluctant

   (B) gracious

   (C) malign

   (D) plausible

   (E) arrogant

2. Speeding may be a ----, but fleeing from the scene of a crime is a ----.

   (A) mistake .. nuisance

   (B) faux pas .. crime

   (C) misdemeanor .. felony

   (D) felony .. misdemeanor

   (E) homicide .. fratricide

3. Among his ---- was the skill of escaping from any type of handcuffs.

   (A) strengths

   (B) crafts

   (C) habits

   (D) repertories

   (E) disadvantages

4. His remarks were too ---- to be taken seriously.

   (A) insipid

   (B) crucial

   (C) timely

   (D) pointed

   (E) germane

5. Familiar with the countryside, they were able to ---- the soldiers who pursued them.

   (A) upbraid

   (B) restrain

   (C) elude

   (D) abet

   (E) eschew

6. A(n) ---- lawyer will help her client ---- the law.

   (A) efficient .. abrogate

   (B) honest .. bend

   (C) unscrupulous .. evade

   (D) clever .. elect

   (E) forthright .. obfuscate

7. Your banker may look at you ---- if you admit to not wanting to save money.

   (A) respectfully

   (B) only

   (C) askance

   (D) directly

   (E) subvertly

8. The gossip-hungry readers combed through the article for every ---- detail.

   (A) lurid

   (B) common

   (C) nagging

   (D) recurring

   (E) earthy

9. Worshipping her every move, he was her most ---- admirer.

   (A) beneficent

   (B) fatuous

   (C) ardent

   (D) sophisticated

   (E) urbane

10. She was stubbornly persistent; nothing or nobody could ---- her from her self-appointed mission.

    (A) prevent

    (B) slow

    (C) arrest

    (D) pervade

    (E) dissuade

11. To be ---- was her lot; she was destined never to earn enough money to support herself.

    (A) important

    (B) impulsive

    (C) impecunious

    (D) innocuous

    (E) intemperate

12. There was a ---- of food on the table, and no one could finish the meal.

    (A) surfeit

    (B) diatribe

    (C) rancor

    (D) vestige

    (E) remnant

13. Thanks to the state ----, the Arts Center is able to offer the finest in music at prices affordable to all.

    (A) developments

    (B) subsidies

    (C) conventions

    (D) revivals

    (E) clearances

14. The general couldn't attend, but he sent his ----.

    (A) commandant

    (B) commander

    (C) adjutant

    (D) superior

    (E) successor

15. You can depend on a malingerer to ---- his or her duty.

    (A) perform

    (B) pursue

    (C) shirk

    (D) lack

    (E) subordinate

LEVEL C SENTENCE COMPLETIONS

Test 1 (Answers on Page 122)

Select the word or word pair that best completes each sentence. Circle the letter that appears before your answer.

1. Her selection was kept in ---- pending receipt of response from her references.

    (A) purgatory

    (B) abeyance

    (C) obeisance

    (D) refrigeration

    (E) back

2. Scattered around the dead dragon were mementos of the ----: heads, arms, and torsos of its hapless victims.

    (A) contest

    (B) relics

    (C) prom

    (D) carnage

    (E) feast

3. The small, prestigious school had very ----
   requirements for admission.

   (A) insidious

   (B) stringent

   (C) strident

   (D) invidious

   (E) salutary

4. Gold is one of the most ---- elements; it can be
   hammered into sheets thinner than a human
   hair.

   (A) brittle

   (B) adamantine

   (C) soft

   (D) malleable

   (E) plastic

5. To call a man a coward is to cast ---- on his
   virility.

   (A) unkindness

   (B) aspersion

   (C) cloud

   (D) prevarication

   (E) guilt

6. Noah Webster was famous as a ----; his dictionaries abounded in the English-speaking world.

   (A) lexicographer

   (B) cartographer

   (C) holographer

   (D) dictographer

   (E) publisher

7. I don't have time to ---- with you; I'm here on
   business.

   (A) caucus

   (B) palaver

   (C) brainstorm

   (D) consort

   (E) plunder

8. Propaganda is a(n) ---- of the truth; it is a mixture
   of half-truths and half-lies calculated to deceive
   people.

   (A) revision

   (B) perversion

   (C) inversion

   (D) invasion

   (E) dispersion

9. The ---- conflicts of the civil war have cost
   untold thousands of lives.

   (A) piercing

   (B) hallucinatory

   (C) international

   (D) infinite

   (E) internecine

10. He had a(n) ---- knowledge of photography; he
    had learned it entirely by experiment, trial, and
    error.

    (A) esoteric

    (B) intimate

    (C) sketchy

    (D) thorough

    (E) empirical

11. ---- in his income caused both feast and famine.

    (A) Reduction

    (B) Accretion

    (C) Taxes

    (D) Fluctuation

    (E) Amortization

12. The general ---- his order; he had the traitor shot
    instead of ----.

    (A) reinforced .. hung

    (B) confirmed .. roasted

    (C) rescinded .. hung

    (D) countermanded .. hanged

    (E) reviewed .. canonized

13. Close examination of the ---- and ---- of the island revealed that no new variety of plant or animal had been admitted for at least fifty years.

    (A) rocks .. minerals

    (B) tracks .. trees

    (C) shoreline .. contours

    (D) flora .. fauna

    (E) crustaceans .. mollusks

14. The missionary was determined to ---- the islanders; her aim in life was to bring them into the faith.

    (A) educate

    (B) civilize

    (C) proselytize

    (D) protect

    (E) sterilize

15. The impact of the situation failed to touch him; he remained ---- as a stone.

    (A) oppressive

    (B) reticent

    (C) immaculate

    (D) impassive

    (E) diffident

Test 2   (Answers on Page 122)

Select the word or word pair that best completes each sentence. Circle the letter that appears before your answer.

1. If parole boards functioned properly, there would be less ----; more parolees would remain out of jail permanently.

    (A) criminals

    (B) graft

    (C) plea bargaining

    (D) recidivism

    (E) chauvinism

2. Failure to use the Salk vaccine caused a ---- of polio in isolated communities; many fell ill with it.

    (A) renascence

    (B) recrudescence

    (C) renaissance

    (D) redevelopment

    (E) revival

3. His uncle was the town drunk; the old ---- had never had a sober day in his life.

    (A) lecher

    (B) pensioner

    (C) voyeur

    (D) reprobate

    (E) sadist

4. Never did I see a more ---- crowd than at Neumann's funeral; there wasn't a dry eye in the chapel.

    (A) bellicose

    (B) adipose

    (C) lachrymose

    (D) comatose

    (E) sucrose

5. The Sunday sermon was, as usual, ----; the minister used 4,000 words where 400 would have sufficed.

   (A) finite

   (B) prolix

   (C) prolific

   (D) propounded

   (E) pontifical

6. The battle finally became a ----; neither side could win.

   (A) truce

   (B) stalemate

   (C) fiasco

   (D) rout

   (E) debacle

7. With her tarot cards she made a(n) ---- prediction, but it was so veiled in secrecy and mystery that I couldn't fathom it.

   (A) illicit

   (B) sibylline

   (C) aquiline

   (D) asinine

   (E) bovine

8. No one knows more about the special program than she does; she has been its director since its ----.

   (A) operation

   (B) inception

   (C) culmination

   (D) fulfillment

   (E) disbandment

9. He was ---- as an administrator, forever arguing with the staff.

   (A) unkind

   (B) contentious

   (C) restive

   (D) restless

   (E) accepted

10. The desire for peace should not be equated with ----, for ---- peace can be maintained only by brave people.

    (A) intelligence .. ignoble

    (B) bravery .. stable

    (C) cowardice .. lasting

    (D) pacification .. transitory

    (E) neutrality .. apathetic

11. The couple had been meeting secretly for years at the hotel, but their ---- were rumored among their friends.

    (A) solipsisms

    (B) trysts

    (C) fidelities

    (D) disputes

    (E) gambits

12. That judge is ---- enough to accept a bribe any time.

    (A) obsequious

    (B) venal

    (C) servile

    (D) vilifying

    (E) sanctimonious

13. Don't get involved with ---- politicians; you'll get caught in a(n) ---- from which you'll never extricate yourself.

    (A) promiscuous .. orgy

    (B) sleazy .. quagmire

    (C) spurious .. counterfeit

    (D) felonious .. prison

    (E) venal .. anathema

14. Algebra I is a ---- for Algebra II; it must be taken first.

    (A) corequisite

    (B) precursor

    (C) prerequisite

    (D) sinecure

    (E) substitute

15. Most of today's students leave school not a(n) ---- wiser.

    (A) atom
    (B) parsec
    (C) inch
    (D) whit
    (E) omega

Test 3   (Answers on Page 122)

Select the word or word pair that best completes each sentence. Circle the letter that appears before your answer.

1. The solution was ----; both parties could live with it.
    (A) friable
    (B) tenable
    (C) reprehensible
    (D) trenchant
    (E) frangible

2. Benedictine was a ---- treat for the count and countess; they enjoyed a glass of it every evening after dinner.
    (A) postponed
    (B) postposition
    (C) posted
    (D) postprandial
    (E) posterior

3. He was considered a(n) ---- on things Russian; he claimed to have read every article written about Russia in the past two years.
    (A) eclectic
    (B) eremite
    (C) authority
    (D) teacher
    (E) source

4. He was ---- as an elder statesman; his colleagues held him in highest esteem.
    (A) venereal
    (B) venerated
    (C) venial
    (D) valetudinarian
    (E) valedictory

5. The ---- of such crimes between midnight and 6 A.M. has been reduced 30% since April.
    (A) threat
    (B) circumstance
    (C) incidence
    (D) graph
    (E) fantasy

6. When she was pursued by the press, the film star sought ---- in her palatial home.
    (A) refuge
    (B) repute
    (C) reserve
    (D) renown
    (E) reference

7. Do not ---- me for giving John a zero in Science; it is my ---- to do so.

   (A) chide .. privilege

   (B) thank .. trouble

   (C) fire .. pleasure

   (D) castigate .. prerogative

   (E) distrust .. honor

8. He couldn't tell the truth if he wanted to; he was a(n) ---- liar.

   (A) misguided

   (B) resiliant

   (C) prevaricating

   (D) exorbitant

   (E) psychopathic

9. Their flight to escape persecution was a necessary ----; had they remained they would have been killed.

   (A) escapade

   (B) adventure

   (C) diaspora

   (D) hegira

   (E) genesis

10. Snakebites are not ---- fatal, but they can sometimes cause death if not treated immediately.

    (A) occasionally

    (B) inevitably

    (C) ever

    (D) never

    (E) undubitably

11. The typhoon had ripped every shred of green from the palm tree; it didn't have a ---- left.

    (A) seed

    (B) stalk

    (C) blade

    (D) blossom

    (E) frond

12. A police officer's ---- job is to prevent crime.

    (A) primary

    (B) compendious

    (C) only

    (D) infrequent

    (E) ostentatious

13. The rocking of the boat made him feel ----; he soon felt the onset of an attack of ----.

    (A) oily .. anger

    (B) bionic .. acrimony

    (C) languid .. panic

    (D) queasy .. nausea

    (E) callow .. remorse

14. The soup was served in an antique china ----, which all admired.

    (A) saucer

    (B) platter

    (C) pot

    (D) compote

    (E) tureen

15. The mosque, from the air, appeared to bristle, with its six ---- pointing toward the heavens.

    (A) gibbets

    (B) minarets

    (C) jihads

    (D) staffs

    (E) halberds

Test 4   (Answers on Page 122)

(Answers on Page 122)

Select the word or word pair that best completes each sentence. Circle the letter that appears before your answer.

1. I could not bear the woodpecker's ---- rhythm; the endless choppy beat aggravated my headache.

    (A) melodic

    (B) staccato

    (C) harmonic

    (D) crescendo

    (E) stentorian

2. She accepted his proposal with alarming ----; she had the "yes" out of her mouth before he finished popping the question.

    (A) joy

    (B) verve

    (C) reserve

    (D) celerity

    (E) acerbity

3. His first novel was ----; in other words, it was dull as well as a waste of time to read.

    (A) topical

    (B) jejune

    (C) historical

    (D) platonic

    (E) narcissistic

4. Despite the judge's ---- to stick to the truth, the defendant perjured herself in her testimony.

    (A) adjuration

    (B) adjudication

    (C) avowal

    (D) determination

    (E) blandishment

5. After the chemical spill we had to drink bottled water; the well water was no longer ----.

    (A) risible

    (B) potable

    (C) supine

    (D) viable

    (E) tenable

6. An item cannot be sent by first-class mail if it ---- 70 pounds.

    (A) exceeds

    (B) is under

    (C) has over

    (D) holds

    (E) equals

7. The company received a ---- from the government to develop new sources of energy.

    (A) reward

    (B) compendium

    (C) subsidy

    (D) memorandum

    (E) salary

8. Because of her long experience in office management, it was ---- that she was the best person for the job.

    (A) revealed

    (B) assigned

    (C) proved

    (D) assumed

    (E) promulgated

9. For many years slums have been recognized for breeding disease, juvenile delinquency, and crime, which ---- not only the welfare of people who live there but also the structure of society as a whole.

    (A) rebuild

    (B) bolster

    (C) undermine

    (D) disengage

    (E) weld

10. The water just below the falls was sweet, but where it entered the estuary it became ----.

    (A) murky

    (B) brackish

    (C) alkaline

    (D) radioactive

    (E) potable

11. ---- countries almost never seek military conquest; aggression does not seem to be characteristics of self-governing societies.

    (A) Democratic

    (B) Despotic

    (C) Agrarian

    (D) Autocratic

    (E) Plebeian

12. He expressed his displeasure to the mayor in ugly and threatening terms; as a result he was charged with sending a ---- communication to a public official.

    (A) pornographic

    (B) lascivious

    (C) holographic

    (D) minatory

    (E) proscribed

13. You might say that a pupil has ---- to the mind of his teacher; after all, he has the privilege of picking his brain.

    (A) resistance

    (B) access

    (C) congruence

    (D) proclivity

    (E) deference

14. As the ----, I have a right to change my own will.

    (A) witness

    (B) peculator

    (C) testator

    (D) testifier

    (E) deceased

15. ---- breathing annoys me; I can't stand snoring.

    (A) Sternal

    (B) Stertorous

    (C) Soporific

    (D) Sublimate

    (E) Salutatorian

Test 5   (Answers on Page 123)

Select the word or word pair that best completes each sentence. Circle the letter that appears before your answer.

1. Commencing with radio in 1928, Buck Rogers was the ---- of all the space jockeys who followed.

    (A) pariah

    (B) prototype

    (C) pilot

    (D) pioneer

    (E) pacemaker

2. Her admirers were ----; her novels were translated into thirty-six languages.

    (A) frenetic

    (B) arcane

    (C) hascent

    (D) legion

    (E) erudite

3. Many of the other crew members panicked when the ship ran aground, but she remained ----.

(A) truculent

(B) credulous

(C) amenable

(D) imperturbable

(E) incongruent

4. Until recently, *Ars Amatoria* was not studied in high school; the authorities thought it too ----; its more explicit love scenes, ----.

(A) pornographic .. deleted

(B) erotic .. taboo

(C) revealing .. eliminated

(D) pastoral .. rustic

(E) traumatic .. depicted

5. His book on smoking was more ---- than ----; it was too "how to" and not enough fire and brimstone.

(A) inspiring .. instructive

(B) pedagogic .. academic

(C) didactic .. inspirational

(D) prescriptive .. descriptive

(E) autobiographical .. graphic

6. Juliet, although only 14, was able to dismiss her ---- at will, so as to be alone with Romeo.

(A) stevedore

(B) students

(C) confidante

(D) paramour

(E) duenna

7. The old ---- had the temper of a she-bear and the vocabulary of a sailor; she was formidable.

(A) misogynist

(B) sinner

(C) knave

(D) termagant

(E) tar

8. Don't name Herbert as your ----; I wouldn't trust him with money!

(A) villain

(B) friend

(C) corespondent

(D) fiduciary

(E) domicile

9. His net worth was ----; there was no way of computing how much money he had.

(A) unlimited

(B) imponderable

(C) imposing

(D) waning

(E) assumed

10. The 10 years of ---- didn't mellow him; they made him bitter enough to use his freedom for seeking revenge.

(A) penance

(B) incarceration

(C) penitence

(D) extortion

(E) pillage

11. Among the workers there was complete agreement; on the other hand, there was constant bickering on the part of the ----.

(A) workforce

(B) antagonists

(C) enemy

(D) disenfranchised

(E) managers

12. Few people are more ---- than some city dwellers I know; they think the world begins and ends within city limits.

(A) cosmopolitan

(B) circumspect

(C) provident

(D) provincial

(E) bucolic

13. In city politics a(n) ---- voice will get you further than an honest heart; loudness is more likely to achieve results than ----.

    (A) earnest .. enthusiasm

    (B) sonorous .. candor

    (C) talented .. action

    (D) silky .. shenanigans

    (E) resounding .. promises

14. If we do identify with an unlikable, evil character in a novel, we probably do so unconsciously, allowing the darker side of our nature to explore evil ----.

    (A) consciously

    (B) deliberately

    (C) vicariously

    (D) conscientiously

    (E) unconsciously

15. The defendant could almost feel the ---- of the hostile crowd.

    (A) eyes

    (B) sympathy

    (C) animus

    (D) detritus

    (E) incubus

LEVEL D SENTENCE COMPLETIONS

Test 1   (Answers on Page 123)

Select the word or word pair that best completes each sentence. Circle the letter that appears before your answer.

1. Beverly Sills, the opera singer, was given the ---- "Bubbles" because of her sparkling personality.

   (A) honorific

   (B) soubrette

   (C) sobriquet

   (D) briquette

   (E) role

2. We usually buy flowers for ---- reasons; there is really nothing of the ---- in the purchase.

   (A) morganatic .. utilitarian

   (B) ulterior .. impractical

   (C) aesthetic .. practical

   (D) lugubrious .. elation

   (E) festive .. funereal

3. Despite the flawless ---- I was unable to read the letter; it was written in Hungarian.

   (A) grammar

   (B) spelling

   (C) rhetoric

   (D) meter

   (E) calligraphy

4. The beggar smiled ---- as he threw back the nickel, saying, "Here! You must need it more than I do."

   (A) sweetly

   (B) blindly

   (C) intermittently

   (D) sardonically

   (E) infinitely

5. Most people eat to live; a(n) ---- lives to eat.

   (A) aesthete

   (B) spartan

   (C) trencherman

   (D) gourd

   (E) alimentarian

6. Get those ---- out of my sight; I won't tolerate a bunch of tattered beggars in front of my restaurant!

   (A) muffins

   (B) ragamuffins

   (C) felons

   (D) miscreants

   (E) poltroons

7. The governor changed her mind at the last minute and granted a pardon; had she remained ----, an innocent person would have died.

   (A) committed

   (B) uncommitted

   (C) governor

   (D) exacerbated

   (E) adamant

8. Augmentation of the deficit caused much ---- for the general manager from the board of directors.

   (A) adulation

   (B) commendation

   (C) approbation

   (D) reprobation

   (E) felicitation

9. The press secretary had more ---- than a Philadelphia lawyer; he could never be pinned down to a substantive answer.

   (A) lubricity

   (B) complicity

   (C) duplicity

   (D) lucidity

   (E) temerity

10. The shark's ---- hold on life is unrivaled; it can remain viable even after half a day out of water.

    (A) constant

    (B) tenacious

    (C) relative

    (D) tenuous

    (E) transient

11. His ---- smile indicated to me that he was guilty as sin, but I would be absolutely unable to prove it in court.

    (A) sardonic

    (B) sympathetic

    (C) affable

    (D) schizophrenic

    (E) paranoiac

12. Fountains are ---- in Rome; you can hardly turn a corner without spotting one.

    (A) vicarious

    (B) ubiquitous

    (C) meticulous

    (D) vacuous

    (E) insidious

13. I will grant them ---- when they can govern themselves.

    (A) federation

    (B) release

    (C) autonomy

    (D) autocracy

    (E) hegemony

14. There was a three-year ---- in her education; she missed second, third, and fourth grades because of illness.

    (A) vacation

    (B) surplus

    (C) deficiency

    (D) hiatus

    (E) relapse

15. Beneath the thin ---- of civilization lies the ---- in humans, feral and vicious.

   (A) layer .. psyche

   (B) history .. superego

   (C) veneer .. beast

   (D) protection .. subconscious

   (E) frosting .. id

Test 2   (Answers on Page 123)

Select the word or word pair that best completes each sentence. Circle the letter that appears before your answer.

1. You cannot be present in fifth-century Britain, but you can experience it ---- by reading Joy Chant's *The High Kings*.

   (A) directly

   (B) reminiscently

   (C) vicariously

   (D) subliminally

   (E) infinitely

2. If my house were to ---- yours, you'd be complaining constantly about my stereo.

   (A) face

   (B) approach

   (C) affront

   (D) abut

   (E) equal

3. Catherine, a passionate woman, agreed to marry a rich, ---- neighbor even though she loved a(n) ----, uneducated orphan.

   (A) sophisticated .. orphaned

   (B) indigent .. impoverished

   (C) opulent .. unschooled

   (D) affluent .. untutored

   (E) educated .. poor

4. An erstwhile friendly argument degenerated into a(n) ---- that led to blows.

   (A) debacle

   (B) altercation

   (C) litigation

   (D) fisticuffs

   (E) rhubarb

5. Don't deal with that ----; he's no more a doctor than Satan is a saint!

   (A) devil

   (B) cherub

   (C) seraph

   (D) quack

   (E) sage

6. Those were ---- days; we didn't have a worry in the world!

   (A) fraternal

   (B) prewar

   (C) early

   (D) halcyon

   (E) spartan

7. Physics was Einstein's ----; he did not claim to be a great mathematician.

   (A) bugaboo

   (B) forte

   (C) hobby

   (D) avocation

   (E) Waterloo

8. There should be no ---- between them; neither has done anything to make the other bitter.

   (A) matrimony

   (B) acrimony

   (C) alimony

   (D) testimony

   (E) litigation

9. As much as we tried to throw him off balance, he remained ----.

   (A) equilibrated

   (B) offset

   (C) immaculate

   (D) imperturbable

   (E) disproportionate

10. I wish they wouldn't go around attempting to ---- my people, who are happy with the religion they have.

   (A) persecute

   (B) orient

   (C) proselytize

   (D) baptize

   (E) secularize

11. Art was merely his ----; although he could paint and did, he remained best known for his political prowess.

   (A) profession

   (B) calling

   (C) weakness

   (D) preference

   (E) avocation

12. The villagers had nothing but ---- for their lord; he protected them from bandits and shared his land with them.

   (A) mitigation

   (B) adulation

   (C) tribulation

   (D) trepidation

   (E) consternation

13. Even a trip to the ---- would not take him far enough away from me; the world is not big enough for both of us!

   (A) continent

   (B) pole

   (C) antipode

   (D) tropics

   (E) arctic

14. There had been no ----; the cards were honestly dealt, and I lost the hand.

   (A) diamonds

   (B) chicanery

   (C) knaves

   (D) elation

   (E) contusion

15. There was a(n) ---- in the party; one group decided to back Smith and the other, Garcia.

   (A) hiatus

   (B) concordat

   (C) entente

   (D) ambiguity

   (E) schism

Test 3   (Answers on Page 123)

Select the word or word pair that best completes each sentence. Circle the letter that appears before your answer.

1. Dreyfus was ---- after Zola presented proof of his innocence.

   (A) indicted

   (B) proliferated

   (C) exonerated

   (D) exasperated

   (E) prolific

2. You would not be so ---- if you worked out at the gym; you have loose fat all over!

   (A) flaccid

   (B) placid

   (C) pliant

   (D) complacent

   (E) gaunt

3. She was known for her ----; no one was more ---- than she.

   (A) communism .. conservative

   (B) economy .. profligate

   (C) virtue .. wanton

   (D) conservatism .. leftist

   (E) altruism .. selfless

4. Being a stickler for punctuality is just one of my ----; you'll have to accept this little fault as part of me.

   (A) aversions

   (B) peccadillos

   (C) armadillos

   (D) perversions

   (E) weaknesses

5. A few ---- lectures would be greatly appreciated; any change from your usual long-windedness would be welcome.

   (A) prolix

   (B) pithy

   (C) abrogated

   (D) protracted

   (E) verbose

6. Ancient Greek authors believed that literature should contain a perfect balance between the social and the personal, objectivity and ----, ---- and emotion.

   (A) selectivity .. passion

   (B) subjectivity .. reason

   (C) subjection .. rationality

   (D) passion .. socialism

   (E) personality .. sociability

7. I think this is gobbledygook. Can you ---- it?

   (A) smell

   (B) taste

   (C) touch

   (D) sense

   (E) understand

8. The IRS is doing its best to make a ---- of me; it takes every cent I have!

   (A) millionaire

   (B) mendicant

   (C) mentor

   (D) manager

   (E) manatee

9. Fiedler always conducted with great ----; his brilliance was unrivaled for over fifty years.

   (A) eclat

   (B) elan

   (C) elite

   (D) eclair

   (E) encomium

10. Whenever I got home late I was greeted with a ---- from both parents on the dangers of the night; it would last for hours.

   (A) monologue

   (B) screed

   (C) chat

   (D) brevet

   (E) premonition

11. The ancient tomb was a shambles, all dug up and pillaged; some ---- had got there before us.

   (A) relatives

   (B) undertakers

   (C) ghouls

   (D) morticians

   (E) bureaucrats

12. Your ---- is inopportune; I am not in the mood for riddles at this time.

   (A) opposition

   (B) leniency

   (C) conundrum

   (D) lemma

   (E) equation

13. He took such a(n) ---- position that nothing could change it.

   (A) tenable

   (B) inalienable

   (C) entrenched

   (D) fractious

   (E) refectory

14. The ---- committed by the invading troops was complete; not a single house or a blade of grass remained standing.

   (A) defoliation

   (B) spoliation

   (C) depravity

   (D) postmortem

   (E) asceticism

15. His troubles were not ----; they were more of the spirit.

   (A) illusory

   (B) clerical

   (C) lay

   (D) personal

   (E) somatic

Test 4   (Answers on Page 123)

Select the word or word pair that best completes each sentence. Circle the letter before your answer.

1. If you act ---- at their party, you won't be asked back; they don't want spiteful and irritating people at their affairs.

   (A) contrite

   (B) passionate

   (C) frenetic

   (D) frantic

   (E) splenetic

2. The ---- from the factory stack was ----; the thick, black smoke was evil-smelling and noxious.

   (A) outflow .. aromatic

   (B) overflow .. salubrious

   (C) view .. provoking

   (D) effluvium .. noisome

   (E) effluent .. redolent

3. The ---- of a Stradivarius violin is unique; no known technology can duplicate its tone.

   (A) string

   (B) pitch

   (C) timbre

   (D) wood

   (E) bridge

4. The candidate's ---- was carefully planned; she traveled to six cities and spoke at nine rallies.

   (A) pogrom

   (B) itinerary

   (C) adjournment

   (D) apparition

   (E) diet

5. The cavern was so ---- that the children huddled together in terror around the feeble torches.

   (A) stalactic

   (B) ferocious

   (C) tenebrous

   (D) cold

   (E) located

6. Their ---- abated as the causes of the bitterness began to disappear, one by one.

   (A) storm

   (B) banter

   (C) forensics

   (D) apathy

   (E) acerbity

7. To put off until tomorrow what you should do today is to ----.

   (A) prorate

   (B) procrastinate

   (C) premeditate

   (D) proscribe

   (E) prevaricate

8. The novel was advertised as a ---- romance of unbridled passions and burning desire.

   (A) gossamer

   (B) torrid

   (C) dulcet

   (D) gelid

   (E) pristine

9. Her fortune was now secured; nobody could ---- it from her.

   (A) preempt

   (B) litigate

   (C) wrest

   (D) coax

   (E) embezzle

10. The sails, touched by the westerly ----, slowly drew the ship landward.

    (A) storm

    (B) nimbuses

    (C) sirocco

    (D) zephyrs

    (E) gales

11. The old ---- had a bad word for everyone in her company; she was the consummate shrew.

    (A) virago

    (B) imago

    (C) bear

    (D) senator

    (E) codger

12. If he continues to ---- liquor at this rate, he will end up as an alcoholic.

    (A) buy

    (B) imbibe

    (C) secrete

    (D) accumulate

    (E) cache

13. The professor was in high ----; someone had put glue on his seat, and now he couldn't rise!

    (A) mass

    (B) gear

    (C) anxiety

    (D) dudgeon

    (E) humor

14. The soldiers ---- their spears; the enemy troops, feeling the threat, backed away.

    (A) threw

    (B) showed

    (C) sharpened

    (D) burnished

    (E) brandished

15. Let's keep away from the populated part of the ----; the smaller islands are more attractive and unspoiled.

    (A) commonwealth

    (B) sound

    (C) archipelago

    (D) bay

    (E) peninsula

Test 5 (Answers on Page 123)

Select the word or word pair that best completes each sentence. Circle the letter that appears before your answer.

1. The farce was so ---- I couldn't stop laughing.
   (A) dispirited
   (B) obscure
   (C) pitiful
   (D) titillating
   (E) mirthless

2. His writing was replete with ---- like "miserably wretched" or "an original prototype."
   (A) hyperboles
   (B) apologies
   (C) tautologies
   (D) metonymies
   (E) synecdoches

3. In the face of an uncooperative Congress, the President may find himself ---- to accomplish the political program to which he is committed.
   (A) impotent
   (B) equipped
   (C) neutral
   (D) contingent
   (E) potent

4. The treaty cannot go into effect until it has been ---- by the Senate.
   (A) considered
   (B) debated
   (C) ratified
   (D) tabled
   (E) voted on

5. The financially strapped city managed to get a ---- on repaying the principal of its municipal bonds; the grace time saved it from bankruptcy.
   (A) lien
   (B) foreclosure
   (C) moratorium
   (D) crematorium
   (E) cancellation

6. The living room was a ---- of furniture ranging from 18th century to glass-and-steel modern.
   (A) museum
   (B) potpourri
   (C) plethora
   (D) prolix
   (E) diaspora

7. His behavior was strictly ----; he was acting like a child.
   (A) kittenish
   (B) playful
   (C) puerile
   (D) febrile
   (E) senile

8. Out of sheer ---- she kept putting money into a business that had proved a lost cause.
   (A) wealth
   (B) adversity
   (C) valiance
   (D) perversity
   (E) pragmatism

9. After the quarrel he sent flowers as a ---- gesture.
   (A) rueful
   (B) conciliatory
   (C) sartorial
   (D) stringent
   (E) benevolent

10. Getting a 90 in the history test ---- him with confidence.
    (A) titillated
    (B) reviled
    (C) inflated
    (D) imbued
    (E) reimbursed

11. It would be ---- to ask for a raise now; the boss is in no mood to grant us a boon.

    (A) propitious

    (B) improper

    (C) impetuous

    (D) impolitic

    (E) fortuitous

12. Do not undertake a daily program of ---- exercise such as jogging without first having a physical checkup.

    (A) light

    (B) spurious

    (C) hazardous

    (D) strenuous

    (E) token

13. The police received a(n) ---- call giving them valuable information that led to an arrest. The caller refused to give his name out of fear of reprisals.

    (A) anonymous

    (B) asinine

    (C) private

    (D) candid

    (E) obscene

14. It is not the function of a newspaper to reflect on ---- but simply to record ----, leaving ethical judgments to the individual reader.

    (A) causes .. opinions

    (B) morality .. events

    (C) deeds .. values

    (D) accuracy .. stories

    (E) validity .. hearsay

15. Your teacher can't control everything; she's not ----.

    (A) omnipresent

    (B) germane

    (C) ambivalent

    (D) redundant

    (E) omnipotent

Answer Key

For explanations see page 124.

LEVEL A

TEST 1

1. D	4. C	7. B	10. D	13. E
2. E	5. E	8. C	11. E	14. D
3. B	6. B	9. C	12. B	15. D

TEST 2

1. C	4. B	7. C	10. B	13. A
2. B	5. C	8. C	11. D	14. E
3. E	6. D	9. C	12. C	15. A

TEST 3

1. C	4. E	7. C	10. C	13. A
2. E	5. C	8. B	11. D	14. A
3. A	6. C	9. D	12. B	15. B

TEST 4

1. C	4. E	7. B	10. C	13. E
2. C	5. C	8. C	11. B	14. C
3. B	6. D	9. D	12. D	15. B

TEST 5

1. C	4. C	7. C	10. B	13. B
2. C	5. C	8. C	11. C	14. C
3. E	6. A	9. C	12. B	15. B

LEVEL B

TEST 1

1. C	4. D	7. B	10. D	13. B
2. C	5. C	8. C	11. B	14. A
3. C	6. A	9. A	12. B	15. B

TEST 2

1. C	4. B	7. A	10. A	13. B
2. A	5. C	8. D	11. C	14. E
3. B	6. D	9. B	12. C	15. B

TEST 3

1. E	4. C	7. C	10. A	13. E
2. A	5. E	8. B	11. E	14. B
3. B	6. D	9. E	12. C	15. D

TEST 4

1. E	4. C	7. C	10. E	13. B
2. B	5. C	8. C	11. E	14. D
3. E	6. B	9. B	12. C	15. B

TEST 5

1. B	4. A	7. C	10. E	13. B
2. C	5. C	8. A	11. C	14. C
3. B	6. C	9. C	12. A	15. C

LEVEL C

TEST 1

1. B	4. D	7. B	10. E	13. D
2. D	5. B	8. B	11. D	14. C
3. B	6. A	9. E	12. D	15. D

TEST 2

1. D	4. C	7. B	10. C	13. B
2. B	5. B	8. B	11. B	14. C
3. D	6. B	9. B	12. B	15. D

TEST 3

1. B	4. B	7. D	10. B	13. D
2. D	5. C	8. E	11. E	14. E
3. C	6. A	9. D	12. A	15. B

TEST 4

1. B	4. A	7. C	10. B	13. B
2. D	5. B	8. D	11. A	14. C
3. B	6. A	9. C	12. D	15. B

TEST 5

1. B	4. B	7. D	10. B	13. B
2. D	5. C	8. D	11. E	14. C
3. D	6. E	9. B	12. D	15. C

LEVEL D

TEST 1

1. C	4. D	7. E	10. B	13. C
2. C	5. C	8. D	11. A	14. D
3. E	6. B	9. A	12. B	15. C

TEST 2

1. C	4. B	7. B	10. C	13. C
2. D	5. D	8. B	11. E	14. B
3. E	6. D	9. D	12. B	15. E

TEST 3

1. C	4. B	7. E	10. B	13. C
2. A	5. B	8. B	11. C	14. B
3. E	6. B	9. A	12. C	15. E

TEST 4

1. E	4. B	7. B	10. D	13. D
2. D	5. C	8. B	11. A	14. E
3. C	6. E	9. C	12. B	15. C

TEST 5

1. D	4. C	7. C	10. D	13. A
2. C	5. C	8. D	11. D	14. B
3. A	6. B	9. B	12. D	15. E

Explanatory Answers

LEVEL A

TEST 1

1. **(D)** *Although* means "regardless of the fact that." Hence the missing noun must be *contrary* to the key word *smile,* that is, *frown.*

2. **(E)** What *kind* of handling of food would make them decide to forego Martha's cooking? (D) would be meaningless in this context, and (A) would be wrong because such handling would have the opposite effect. Martha's being "unworldly" (B) or "not unworldly" (C) would become a consideration *if* a more specific, more narrow adjective (E) were not available.

3. **(B)** The word *stigma* indicates that the job puts the jobholder in a disgraceful or unenviable position, so that it is *unattractive* (B) or *uninviting* (E). But *even* means "in spite of," so that the salary must be quite unlike the job. This eliminates (E) and makes (B), with its exact opposite adjectives, the best choice.

4. **(C)** The sentence structure, balancing "one" against "another," suggests contrast, difference. Contrast is not provided by (E), meaning right or privilege, since the first man already has the meat as *his* prerogative; nor by (A), which is another category of food or nourishment; nor by (B), since meat *is* the flesh of mammals; nor by (D), which is only a play on words. But (C) is a contrast, providing not nourishment but harm.

5. **(E)** What *kind* of management (handling) would make Joseph an object of jokes and ridicule, a fool (laughingstock)? (A) would earn him respect, and (B), disapproval. (D) would make the industry laugh *with* him, not *at* him. (C), meaning effusively sentimental, would not elicit ridicule so much as (E), meaning inept.

6. **(B)** To shift district lines in order to divide a bloc of voters, thus preventing them from exerting all their strength in one district, is, by definition, to *gerrymander.* This is done slyly, not by confrontation, ruling out (A). It does *cheat* the bloc of its *majority* in its own area (D), but *majority* would not sound idiomatic here. It does not *shift* the bloc in its entirety but rather cuts it up, ruling out (C), which would also be unidiomatic. Of the two choices using the correct word, *gerrymander,* (E) would be relevant (*out of hand* meaning at once, immediately, improperly) but (B) completes the meaning more effectively.

7. **(B)** What condition would a man be in after 90 days of solitary confinement? Unlikely are (C), since that's the state he *was* in and is now freed from; (E), meaning strength of mind; and (D), rightness in intellectual judgment. He could be in a state of exhaustion, torpor, or lethargy, which is what (A) means, but it's most likely that he is in a state of *decrepitude* (B), that is, of weakness, infirmity.

8. **(C)** There is nothing to suggest he has been omitted from the will (A) or will fight it in the courts (D). He seems to have got his money in one lump sum, not in installments like a pension (B). Although he may be described as a *winner* (E), that is not the legal term used for an heir, but *beneficiary* is.

9. **(C)** *Picayune* is the perfect adjective, meaning petty, mean, small-minded.

10. **(D)** High fever can produce a state of mental confusion. (A) and (B) are too mild, and (C) too severe. (E), meaning exceedingly arrogant or confident, sounds unlikely. But *delirious* is the proper word for someone in the state described.

11. **(E)** The context implies you would be taking unfair advantage of another, and so, in a moral sense, would lower, or *abase* yourself. There is no indication that you would scold or censure yourself, as (A) would mean, or that it would stimulate (C) or weaken (D) you. (B) would be meaningless repetition.

12. **(B)** This is an instance in which you might first try out the second word in each pair. The main idea is that the storm *refused to slacken:* you must find, for the second blank, a close synonym for *slacken.* Of two offered, *mitigate* (D), meaning alleviate, sounds too affected, but *abate,* meaning "diminish, subside," sounds idiomatic. (A) is contrary to what "We waited … for"; (E) would suggest "to travel," which would have a different meaning; and (C) would imply "to weakly refuse to change itself into a more acceptable form," which is remote from the context.

13. **(E)** Which of the five words offered has much to do with deciding between love and the throne? Only (E), meaning "to give up a high position." (A), meaning to lie, would be the opposite of deciding; (C) wouldn't tell us how or what he would alter, or change; (D) wouldn't say which one he would nullify or abolish, which is what *abrogate* would involve; and (B), meaning to cleanse or purify, seems pointless in this context.

14. **(D)** Choices (A), (B), and (E) can all be ruled out because they do not link idiomatically with *in:* a fence would not have sold, testified, or masterminded *in* a robbery. (C) does so link (*participated in*) but is still wrong because, we are told, he had *not* witnessed the crime. (D) does so link *and* makes good sense: a fence, ready to receive and sell stolen goods, can be seen as having *aided* and *abetted* (that is, encouraged, incited) *in* a robbery.

15. **(D)** "Extenuating circumstances" are those that make an offense less serious by providing partial excuses. Coupled with "the defendant's youth," such circumstances make it unlikely that the judge would have recommended (E) or (A) or wanted the defendant to stand trial again, as he would have had to after (C). The partial excuses already constituted (B). The judge clearly recommended *leniency,* implying mercy, restraint, forgiveness.

TEST 2

1. **(C)** Any person so fanatical and so uncompromising is, by definition, a *zealot.* (A) would make fewer sales if he didn't know when to give up on a customer. Neither (E), a minor official who certifies documents and takes oaths, nor (D), a person of unorthodox views, need necessarily be fanatical. (B) is ruled out because the blank requires a noun, not an adjective.

2. **(B)** The very word *strangers* and the fact that they should be "offering candy" to young people they do not know strongly suggests that the children not be (C), (D), or (E), but rather cautious, watchful, that is, *wary.* (A) is a trap for students who have heard the expression "wary of strangers" but are unable to spell or recapture the exact sound.

3. **(E)** The position taken is that people do things in response either to outer force or to inner will. (B), involving judgment, is close, but (E), meaning the power to will, choose, decide, is better in context.

4. **(B)** The phrase "respect for age" calls for strong positive regard or reverence for elder statesmen: they were *venerated.* (C) and (D) are negative, disrespectful; (A) is too mild and (E) too matter-of-fact, lacking in feeling.

5. **(C)** The length of the sermon indicates its effect on the congregation: boredom and resultant passivity. Hence the metaphor of the sermon as a *soporific,* a sleep-inducing drug, which would cure *insomnia,* or chronic wakefulness. The other choices repeat the pattern of medicine for a condition but do not account for the emphasis on the 45-minute presentation.

6. **(D)** The last phrase makes it clear that his attitude was obvious, that is, *manifest.* He did not keep it a secret (B), and there is no indication that it was *affected* (A) or that it was either (C) or (E).

7. **(C)** The result of her condition identifies it as *agoraphobia,* or fear of open spaces. (A) would be the opposite: fear of closed places. (E), or hatred of foreigners, can be suffered indoors or out. (D), a state of conflicting emotions, like love and hate for the same person, and (B), a blood deficiency, do not necessarily keep the sufferer indoors.

8. **(C)** Presumably their appetite has already been *whetted* (B), that is, stimulated; (A) is simply not idiomatic; (D) is meaningless in this context; (E), in the sense of facing or acknowledging, would serve if (C), meaning to indulge, were not better.

9. **(C)** The missing word must be a synonym for *badgering,* or harrying with persistent chiding or entreaty, pestering. (B) is too strong, (A) the opposite, (E) irrelevant in this context, (D) wrong because the speaker *wants* the child to do it on his own volition.

10. **(B)** Choice (C) can be ruled out because there is no indication that the speaker is computerized. He is, however, working in a formal relationship to a superior. His own feelings would be inappropriate—(A), (D), (E). *Authorized* would be the factual word for describing what he is and is not allowed to say.

11. **(D)** A magazine that publishes refined fiction might be considered a *bastion* (fortress) of literary good taste.

12. **(C)** A rudderless boat is certainly not in a *favored* (E) position. (C) is the most inclusive and accurate description: the ship is not suitable for occupancy; it is defenseless, subject to the erratic motion of the winds— ideas that are completed with the words *untenable* and *vagaries.*

13. **(A)** If the branches are moving, so are the shadows they cast. Hence (B) and (E), implying "staying in one place," are wrong. The shadows are not *clandestine* or secret (D), and it would be odd to call them *swarthy* (C). *Transient* (A), passing, is the best choice.

14. **(E)** *Into* gives you a clue. (D) is wrong because that would mean substituting one for the other; (A), because it would mean that the base metal is moved into gold. (C) is metaphoric, and (B) is completely inappropriate. (E), *transmute,* is the perfect word, meaning "to change from one form, nature, or substance into another."

15. **(A)** Choice (E) seems improbable; and (B), (C), and (D) make no sense. (A) only implies that the article was published and the birthday celebrated on the same day.

TEST 3

1. **(C)** The phrases "out of control" and "dropped the reins" make *careened* the best word: it means moved rapidly and in an uncontrolled manner; lurched; swerved. (E) would be appropriate only if the chariot had collided with something and rebounded. (A), (B), and (D) are less specific, less fitting.

2. **(E)** The sentence indicates that the speaker is warning someone not to stray from the main subject, that is, not to *digress* from the *crux,* or heart, of the matter. (A) would connote straying from the truth; (B), involuntary difficulty in speaking; (C) and (D) would both involve postponement but are ruled out mainly because "stick to the promptness/urgency" are not idiomatic.

3. **(A)** (B), (D), and (E) seem farfetched, (C) too mild, and (A) just right: *disconsolate* means beyond consolation, hopelessly sad.

4. **(E)** If it was an "unpopular war," there was little chance of (C) or (D). On the other hand, since recruits were needed, it is unlikely they would be *shot* (A), especially since they could be *conscripted.* All the recruits, whether volunteers or draftees, would have to be (B).

5. **(C)** If the fumes are poisoning the air, they are surely *noxious,* or harmful.

6. **(C)** The blank requires a verb that is used with *to.* Only (C) and (D) are so used. Since (D) is impossible, it's (C) by process of elimination: the state of the house gave testimony, *attested to* the fact, that it had been robbed.

7. **(C)** "Although" alerts you to expect a reversal of results: they will be different for "blows" and "gunshots." *Vulnerable* means susceptible to injury, not sufficiently protected; *invulnerable* means not susceptible, well protected. *Impervious* means incapable of being penetrated or affected. (A) does not fit into the syntax (we don't say "reachable *to*" or "proof *to*"). In (B), *vulnerable* makes sense, but *not susceptible* would contradict that. (D) would be wrong in both parts, (E) in its first part.

8. **(B)** The "belied" tells you that her words contradicted the beauty and elegance of her appearance. The only choice that offers the opposite of beauty and elegance is *uncouth,* meaning crude, rude, ungraceful.

9. **(D)** Apparently it's the quality, not the content, of the expressions he uses that makes them "insufferable," that is, unbearable. This rules out (E). Such succinct proverbs are not repetitive or wordy, as *redundant* (C) would mean, and they are not *cryptic* (B), that is, they do not contain hidden meanings. However, they are so overused,

so overfamiliar, that they no longer command our interest: they have become *trite.* (A) is a trap for the student unfamiliar with the correct spelling and sound of *trite.*

10. **(C)** The phrase "not permissive" rules out *liberal* (B) and *unrestrictive* (E). (A) would be a redundancy. Regulations may be both permissive and *uniform* (D). (C), meaning severe, makes sense in context.

11. **(D)** (A), meaning incapable of being measured or weighed precisely, would be wrong because it *is* possible to count population; (B) and (E), because they would gainsay the need for a Spanish-speaking employee; (C), because no neighborhood large enough to have a clinic would be completely any ethnic group. Most likely it would be (D), meaning mainly.

12. **(B)** Such a sky is neither a *belier,* that is, denier, of the possibility of a storm (C), nor is it a *proof,* or a guarantee, of a storm (D). It may be (A), but most likely it's a forerunner, or *precursor* (B), of a storm. (E) is a trap for hasty readers who free-associate from sky to stars.

13. **(A)** Judging from the title of the act alone, citizens can enjoy (A), but with no right to correct or rectify information on file, as (C) would mean. (E) would be a contradiction of the title, and (B) and (D) would be meaningless in this context.

14. **(A)** "Possible meanings" is your main clue. Any statement with more than one meaning is, by definition, *ambiguous,* (A). (B), meaning flippantly humorous; (C), meaning incorrect; (D), meaning coinciding; and (E) would not necessarily involve different meanings.

15. **(B)** A performance that was *auspicious,* or promising (A), or one that was *luscious,* sweet and pleasant (C), would hardly make him out a fool. A performance that was *interlocutory,* that is, involving a conversation (D), or one that was *internecine,* or mutually destructive (E), would not on those grounds alone be foolish. But *ludicrous* (B) means laughable, foolish, causing scornful laughter.

TEST 4

1. **(C)** Notice, it is the wrongdoer himself who is required to do something to the property. Thus (A) is ruled out because he cannot *confiscate* or seize his own property; (D) because to evaluate or *assess* his own property would hardly be a penalty; (E) because if he got the proceeds of the sale it would not be much of a punishment. To *destroy* the property (B) would deprive the state of its compensation. But to give the property up, that is, to *forfeit* it (C), would be a real penalty.

2. **(C)** A key link is *from:* the word supplied must make this connection idiomatically. *Distracted* is the only past participle (used as an adjective) here that is used with *from;* it means, literally, "drawn away, having the attention diverted."

3. **(B)** The Person Speaking, in criticizing the Person Spoken About, is not likely to explain PSA's failure to finish the job by saying that PSA is free from guilt, *inculpable* (E); or that PSA is poor, *indigent* (A), which would seem rather to be an incentive to work. Calling PSA uninteresting or unstimulating, in short, *insipid* (D), would also seem to be irrelevant. PS might cite PSA's being lenient or *indulgent* (C) as a reason if PSA is a boss easy on the employees doing the job, but this doesn't seem to be the case. The only remaining, and much more likely, choice is that PSA, be he boss or laborer, is lazy, *indolent.*

4. **(E)** There is no evidence for (A) or (D); it was but no longer is (B). That it was (C) can be included in a larger classification: it was a *hoax,* an act intended to trick people, either as a practical joke or as a serious fraud, in this case apparently the former.

5. **(C)** (A) denotes a physical imprint or psychological effect; (B), a sacrificial destruction or renunciation; (D), a warning; (E), the state or cause of disgrace. (C) is relevant: an *embargo* is a suspension or prohibition of trade. *Traps:* Memories of *impressment* of seamen might tempt some students to pick (A); the fact that an alert can be *declared* might influence some to pick (D); so you should declare a prohibition or an embargo on words that fit neither the context nor the syntax!

6. **(D)** *Slaughtering* (E) and *eating* (B) the oxen would never get the load home; *resting* (A) or *feeding* (C) them would delay their arrival; so the rationalization is complete for *goading* (D) them, that is, prodding them with a stick to make them move faster.

7. **(B)** (A) is wrong because he did not affirm, corroborate, or *attest* to the facts; (C), because tone of voice would not be the crucial factor in his defense; (D), because he was not conducting a liturgical prayer with responses by others; (E), because he did not bind or cement anything. Rather he had offered a *fabrication,* a totally false account of where he was at the time of the crime.

8. **(C)** (A) is wrong here because *fettle* is a noun that means condition or shape; it is usually used in a phrase like "in fine fettle" and is incorrectly offered here as an adjective. (B) would be okay only if he had claimed something wrong with his sanity. "Perfectly" *hectic* (D) and "perfectly" *decrepit* (E) are both nonsense. So (C) is right, both by process of elimination and by the test of meaning in context: *hale* means whole, free from defect, and *hearty* means vigorous, robust.

9. **(D)** Both words in the pair must be able to link with *about.* Only (D) meets this requirement. Beyond that, only (D) requires the "Although …" construction. All the others would make more sense with *and;* for example, (A): "She had doubts about the weather *and* she had no confidence, etc."

10. **(C)** (A) would be self-contradictory, since *foreclosure* involves barring, hindering, thwarting, or settling beforehand and usually refers to mortgage matters. (B) is not a consideration in this kind of work. (D) and (E) would be wrong because the police might conceivably accept such a report for *control* or *guidance,* even though they would not take the responsibility for *investigating* it.

11. **(B)** To be (A) they would have to eat everything; to be (C), meat. Since they eat only herbs, they are (B). Not all of these animals are *ruminants* (D), that is, cud-chewers, or *pachyderms* (E), that is, thick-skinned beasts.

12. **(D)** There is no indication of (A), (B), or (C). The bell does identify the scene as a boxing *ring* (E), but what about "in the thick of"? It has to be "in the thick of" the fight, the heated contest, that is, the *fray.*

13. **(E)** The verb you select has to be one that would fit syntactically with "from blocking." This eliminates (B) and (C). (A), too, does not work in context. (D) does not fit at all and is ridiculous in this context, for it means "deprived of the right to practice a profession," like preaching the gospel. Only (E) involves prohibition by legal action.

14. **(C)** True, the information is someplace on the *envelope* (D), but the envelope is the only thing listed that's NOT "on the letter." (A) indicates the letter's destination, not its origin, and (B) shows denomination and national origin. (E) is too general. Only the *postmark* gives date and local origin.

15. **(B)** Because the photos are placed in some specified order, (A) is wrong, since it means a state of disorder. (C) is meaningless, and (D), meaning danger, is ridiculous. As for (E), objects are not "placed in" collaboration. Two photos can only be "placed in" *juxtaposition,* that is, put side by side.

TEST 5

1. **(C)** Only (C), meaning "expressions of sympathy for another person's grief or pain," would be relevant. The others are irrelevant because (A) denotes flattery; (B), recognition of good fortune or outstanding achievement; (D), series of links or chains; (E), twistings out of shape.

2. **(C)** The "but" signals the opposite, and only *corpulent* is opposite, meaning fat. (D) and (E) are traps for people with a vague memory of (C), or vague knowledge that (D) and (E) have to do with the body. (A) means skillful and (B), negligent.

3. **(E)** A rude, impolite person is *boorish.* You might also call him (B) if you believe that such behavior is commonplace and trite, or (C) if you are biased against country folk and believe that they are all (E). Indeed,

such a bias is already built into the language: (A), meaning refined, elegant, suave, is obviously closely related to *urban*. (D) has nothing to do with manners: a *liberal* person—one open-minded, tolerant, generous—could be either urbane or boorish.

4. **(C)** They show their *interest* (A) by going to the polls, their lack of interest, or *apathy,* by staying away. (B), meaning excessive interest on loans, is an examiner's idea of a pun. In the context of elections, (E) would be the act of signing up as a voter. (D) is the faculty of making happy discoveries by accident, something possible only if one shows interest everywhere.

5. **(C)** How did the person take the exams? Certainly not with *indifference* (D), nor *aplomb* (A), nor *confidence* (B), since lack of preparation tends to undermine any of these forms of self-support. Not with *skepticism* (E) either, because the doubting that the skeptic does is a way of challenging beliefs, not one's own worth. This leaves the student taking exams with alarm, apprehension, maybe even some trembling—in short, with *trepidation.*

6. **(A)** Even if you had no image of colonists by the fireside, you could figure this one out by a process of elimination. You rule out (E) because there's not a blizzard in every thunderstorm. (D) and (B) make no sense, and (C) does not correlate with "winter." But you assume, given the technology of the time and the presence of virgin forests from coast to coast, that (A) was the prevalent condition—for those who had hearths.

7. **(C)** Tension in the air is likely to be *dispelled* (driven away) by a joke. None of the other choices makes any sense.

8. **(C)** The *facade* is the front. (D) is a trap for students unsure of the spelling of facade. (B) is unlikely to be found in the front of a building, and (E) is a domed structure surmounting the roof. To be safe, the occupants should have been in the rear of (A).

9. **(C)** If a witness is still to testify against him, then the case is still in the trial stage, and he has not yet been *convicted* (A) or proved *innocent* (E). Thus he cannot yet be described as (B) or (D), or even as a thief, but only as an *alleged* thief, that is, as one so accused but not so proved.

10. **(B)** We cannot say for sure whether she will act horselike, or *equine* (C), or whether she will be sluggish, dull, and cowlike, that is, *bovine* (D). But we do know she will be *ill-tempered* (E) and difficult to manage, that is to say, *intractable* (A), which is anything but submissive, or *docile.*

11. **(C)** If its eruption was unexpected, then they must have thought it was inactive, *dormant.* (A) is not a term used for inanimate matter, and (E) not for volcanoes. If it had been *disruptive* (D)—that is, causing disorder and confusion—they would not have been surprised by its activity. (B) refers to a three-syllable foot in poetry.

12. **(B)** Doctors agree that smoking is harmful, or *deleterious.* (C) is certainly inaccurate, and (D) is incorrect usage. Smoking is not *irrelevant* (E) to health: it certainly does have its effects. And it's not smoking that should be *disengaging* (A); it's the smoker who should extricate him- or herself from the habit.

13. **(B)** Since no voice can suspect anything, and this particular voice would never be so quiet as to arouse suspicion, it's unlikely to be called (C). Since a voice can't be seen, it's not (D). Since the word *copious,* meaning abundant, is not used to denote vocal power, this voice is not (E). Since it is capable of being heard, it is, by definition, *audible,* and, in this case, probably not (A) even when it whispers.

14. **(C)** You can rule out (A) because parents don't *chide,* or scold, their child for being diligently active, or *industrious;* (B), because parents are unlikely to regard a child as *superfluous,* or extra; (D), because parents don't punish a child who is self-reliant, or *independent;* and (E), because parents don't praise a child for being uncompromising, or *intransigent.* But parents do scold a child for being lazy, or *indolent.*

15. **(B)** A euphemism is an inoffensive term used instead of the offensive truth. In this case *portly* (B), which means confortably stout, is used in place of the blunt *fat.*

LEVEL B

TEST 1

1. **(C)** Certain kinds of reports do require (E), but not this kind. You do not "obtain" a *bystander* (A). No *charter* (D) is required, because such reports are demanded not only by law but by common sense. *Formulation* (B) of what? *Information* forms the starting point for any understanding or explanation.

2. **(C)** (E) is farfetched and unidiomatic. (D), no longer used as a transitive verb, must be rejected also as suggesting only favorable changes when unfavorable ones are also possible. (B) suggests that the change is harsh and brought about by physical assault, another unjustified conclusion. This brings you to an old bugaboo: the difference in the verbs *affect* (A) and *effect* (C). (A) means "to have an influence on"; (C), "to bring about, produce as a result," as in *A change in environment is very likely to effect a change in one's work habits.*

3. **(C)** (A), (B), and (E) can be ruled out because they are self-contradictory. People guilty of "typical diplomatic maneuvering" are not likely to avoid *diplomatic* language or the bureaucratic jargon known as *gobbledygook* or *cryptic* (secret) language. (B) is also wrong in using *gobbledygook* as an adjective. (D) is half-right: it's *plain* language that diplomats try to avoid, but they don't use a *summary* to do it. (C) is perfect: they used every *circumlocution*—literally, "roundabout expression"—to avoid *concise* expression.

4. **(D)** The reason for asking questions of a witness is to *elicit* (draw out) the truth. To accomplish this aim, the questions must often be *probing* (thorough).

5. **(C)** (A), (D), and (E) are wrong because if Santa Ana's forces had *declined* or been *isolated* or *absent,* they would not have won. The *felicitation* (B) or congratulation of his forces must have happened after his victory and could not have influenced the outcome. So both by elimination and by logic, (C) is correct. What makes the Alamo battle historic is that a small force held out for so long against an army overwhelmingly superior in numbers: that is, a *preponderant* army.

6. **(A)** *Turbid,* a synonym for *cloudy,* is defined as "having particles stirred up or suspended." To be described as *precipitous* (B), it would have to be extremely steep.

7. **(B)** No knowledge of flamenco dancing is necessary to ascertain, by a process of elimination, that (B) is the only word here describing an aesthetic position. When arms are *akimbo,* elbows are bowed outward. (E), meaning crooked, oblique, would be a vague substitute for (B). The dancer could not be "ready to perform" if his arms were already (C). (D) can describe an argument, but not a physical position. (A) seems to be a trap, a pun on *flame*(nco).

8. **(C)** The celebrity would not sue because his character had been *whitewashed* (E). He would sue because he believes his character has been blackened, that is, *defamed.* We do not speak of a character being *demoted* (A) or *implicated* (D) or *deplored* (B).

9. **(A)** Note the quotation marks. Without them, the word could have a different meaning. By definition, a "joiner" is one given to joining clubs, organizations, causes. She or he is not (E) but rather (A), that is, prone to move with or to form a group, to socialize with one's kind. This does not in itself guarantee that one will be (B) or (C). We put "joiner" in quotes because it's informal English, close to slang, and to distinguish it from joiner without quotes, in formal English. *That* joiner is a cabinet maker. (D) is a subtle trap.

10. **(D)** Here the right word is easy, and three of the wrong ones hard. (B) means stingy, (C) indicates a shape like the earth (a spheroid flattened at the poles), and *lilliputian* (E) means tiny, like the inhabitants of Lilliput in *Gulliver's Travels.* (A) means exceeding boundaries and would not be used to describe a person. *Obese* means extremely fat.

11. **(B)** To "want no more" is, by definition, to be *satiated* (B). (E) would mean you have flattered or cajoled your palate. (D) would be difficult to do well: the palate is the roof of the mouth. (C) even more so: have *imbibed* would mean have *drunk*—your palate? (A) is an unlikely result of eating such a soft food.

12. **(B)** (C), (D), and (E) would not "protect the respondents' privacy." The preposition *to* in (A) would not link properly with *questionnaires,* to which (since they are not people) nothing could be "referred" anyhow. Only (B) will link properly and "protect … privacy."

13. **(B)** A word made up of the initial letters of words in a phrase (like SAT for Scholastic Assessment Test) is called an *acronym.* (A) is a word that can have two or more meanings but only one pronunciation: for example, "pool of water"; "let's play pool." (C) is a word that differs in pronunciation when it differs in meaning: "row a boat"; "hurt in a row." (D) is a word's opposite: *cold* is an antonym for *hot.* (E) is an assumed name: Samuel Clemens' *pseudonym* was Mark Twain.

14. **(A)** Flood waters from a deluge are likely to endanger, or *imperil,* a town. None of the other choices makes any sense in this context.

15. **(B)** The test sentence provides a good definition of the verb to *procrastinate.* (E) means to announce or declare officially, as a decree or a policy; (D), to denounce or condemn; (C), to introduce or precede; (A), to divide proportionately, for example, half a year's allowance for six months.

TEST 2

1. **(C)** The climate is allegedly not conducive to good health, or not *salubrious.* (B) means very changeable, which is precisely what New York's climate often is. Climates can be healthful, but only living things can be *healthy* (D). (A) is too specific and narrow. *Pathogenic* (E) means disease-causing, but it is not a word you would use to describe a climate.

2. **(A)** *Defiles* (B), meaning makes filthy, and *harasses* (E), disturbs, bothers, pesters, are not laughing matters. *Buffoons* (D) are clowns; the word is never used as a verb. (C) *Irks* refers to mildly annoying behavior. *Derides* means "treats with contemptuous mirth," definitely laughing *at.*

3. **(B)** To grant concessions to enemies in order to maintain peace is *appeasement.* It is a special kind of *defeat* (A). (C), meaning urgent requests, and (D), a trick to avoid confrontation, are not the same as "giving in." (E), which refers to open, legal agreements between sovereign states, cannot be made with terrorists, who operate secretly and illegally.

4. **(B)** Even if the wooden beast did have *fetlocks* (E), projections on the lower legs, that was not what deceived the Trojans. Nor was it the horse's *prolixity* (D), or excessive use of language, since even live horses abstain. The whole incident did become a tragedy (A), but that was the result, not the cause, of the deception. Nor was it a *strategy* (C), because that is the overall science of military planning. Rather, it was one small part of strategy, a single maneuver or tactic, a *stratagem.*

5. **(C)** She is only pretending to be *nonchalant* (unconcerned), so the answer must be a word opposite in meaning. The only choice that fits is *worry.*

6. **(D)** The word *but* indicates that the words in the two blanks must be opposite in meaning. The best choice is (D): a *luxury* is by definition not an *essential.*

7. **(A)** The words chosen must add up to a wicked injustice. By definition, an *iniquity* is a *grossly* immoral act, a crime against morality. *Perjury* is the crime of giving false testimony, automatically ruled out here because an injustice cannot be *mendacious* (untruthful), only a person can (C). A *bias* is a preference that keeps one from being impartial, ruled out because injustice itself cannot be described as *slanted* (E). A *lobotomy,* (B) and (D), is a controversial brain operation; it may be evil, *pernicious* (D), but hardly senseless or silly, *inane* (B). You would not choose (D), however, because lobotomy does not *mean* injustice.

8. **(D)** The navy scoured the area for an entire month; the search was therefore necessarily *painstaking* (extremely thorough).

9. **(B)** *Assumption* (E) would be redundant. By definition, a *hypothesis* is a proposition stated as the basis for argument or experiment. Testing (A), (C), and (D) by stripping the subject of its modifying phrases, you find you can say "a hypothesis or an assumption was that …" but not "a *labyrinth,* an *outlay,* or an *itinerary* was that.…"

10. **(A)** The only adjective listed that is specifically related to facial expression is (A), which suggests being disdainful, raising the eyebrows, looking down the nose.

11. **(C)** Any wheel—first or 201st—would be (A), (B), and (E). In the usual four-wheel vehicle, only a fifth would be extra, unnecessary, that is, *superfluous*. (D), a trap, has to do not with *axle* but with *axilla,* the armpit.

12. **(C)** The only irreversible change would be one that abolished the legislature. A *parliamentary* (A) government is still a legislative democracy, and merely *contrasting* it with our democracy could not lead to irreversible change. (B) and (E), which would create awkward sentences, could still be legislated in and legislated out. Many democracies, including ours, have had at times three or more major parties (D). Only a *dictatorship* would destroy the mechanism for its own removal.

13. **(B)** *Onerous* (C), or "burdensome," would never describe a look. All dogs look *canine* (D), that is, doglike. They certainly do not look catlike or *feline* (A). Dogs are not subject to legal distinctions between misdemeanors, or petty crimes, and felonies, or major crimes (E). But the poodle probably does look *bellicose* (B), that is, warlike, in defense of his territory.

14. **(E)** The correct answer will be the opposite of *disregarded* or *ridiculed.* The only possible choice is *appreciated.*

15. **(B)** Both (C) and (D) are wrong because they both involve increase, and it is not possible to increase school attendance beyond the legal requirement, only to decrease it. (E) would require *for* instead of *in,* and would suggest the unlikelihood that he was moved to attend only during that week. (A) would suggest that the only time he attended consecutively would be that week. *Hiatus,* meaning gap, hence absence, makes sense all around.

TEST 3

1. **(E)** Soldiers who rent themselves to foreign armies are called *mercenaries.*

2. **(A)** "Countless" calls for *myriad,* an indefinite number that surpasses (C). (D) and (E) are syntactically incorrect. (B) is a wood nymph, here beguiling careless readers with an *-ad* ending like that in myriad.

3. **(B)** This task is never *passé* (E), or out of date, if you don't have the proper machinery. Apparently the peeler does *not* find peeling pertinent, suitable, or *relevant* (D). Hard work is rarely *infectious* (C), that is, catching. The peeler would not find both tasks *preferable* (A). But he surely could find undressing spuds burdensome, oppressive, *onerous.*

4. **(C)** *Entreated* (A) for mercy is not idiomatic, and *applauded* (B) does not fit with prostration. (D) would involve laying a formal curse on the listener, and (E) means belittled. (C) has the appropriate tone: They humbly asked, *begged....*

5. **(E)** *Contumacious* (D) would be redundant; it means obstinately rebellious. (B) is wrong because it means concealed; (C) means evident although unexpressed, which does not fit. (A) is an inappropriate descriptor. *Manifest,* clearly and openly revealed, sounds more as if he *wanted* his rebelliousness to be perceived.

6. **(D)** The answer is indicated by the phrase "quality is preferred to quantity." *Caliber* is a synonym for quality, and that is how the system is to be *judged.*

7. **(C)** You should pass right over (E); it denotes the use of more words than are necessary; over (A) because it denotes exaggerated patriotism; (B), servile flattery; and (D), anarchism. (C) is just right: *nepotism* is favoring relatives for appointment to high office.

8. **(B)** The word *but* indicates a change in meaning. Speech is not free when it is under *restriction.* Nevertheless, even when free speech is allowed, people seldom feel *blessed* by their liberty.

9. **(E)** From "although" you infer the engine is "just in case" the wind becomes less dependable, and the ship needs an additional source of power—not so much a complete *substitute* (B) as an auxiliary, a *subsidiary.* Sails don't need (A). (D) and (C) are irrelevant.

10. **(A)** *Resentment* (E) would be irrational. If (D) were true, why would the speaker have prepared so well? There would be no reason for belligerence or alarm, as (B) or (C) would signify. *Aplomb* (A) is the poise that comes from self-confidence.

11. **(E)** The speech was difficult to understand, that is, *abstruse*. (B) would be the opposite: clear and compact; (A), drawn out; (C), vile, filthy; (D), cautious.

12. **(C)** All life is (B) and (D), that is, limited. (E) is impossible; a subatomic particle is micro-, not *macroscopic*. (A) is meaningless in this context, but (C) is perfect: it means *short-lived*.

13. **(E)** At the *millenium* the world will be filled with peace and good will; even income taxes will disappear. A *milestone* (D) does not arrive; it is reached and passed. (C) does not arrive either; it is a grinding stone which, speaking metaphorically, can be a burden one carries "around the neck." (A) is a future period prophesied in the New Testament.

14. **(B)** Something that cures all the troubles of humanity would be by definition a *panacea* (cure-all).

15. **(D)** You cannot avoid, or *eschew* (B), a day, especially one already past. You might blot it out or *obliterate* (C) it "from your memory," but then you'd have to add those words. There's no sense in (E). You might well, in your disappointment, *regard* (A) the day with misgivings, but if you are disappointed, you'll remember it regretfully, that is, *rue* it (D).

TEST 4

1. **(E)** *Mathematical* (C) is nonsense. Failing to speak well of others has nothing to do with being very talkative, that is, *loquacious* (A); or being evasive, dishonest, or *oblique* (B); or being understood only by those with secret knowledge, that is, *arcane* (D). But such failure could indicate that one is dull, or *obtuse* (E), about social life.

2. **(B)** The second clause indicates the kind of elegance and the degree he attained in it: elegance in dress, that is, *sartorial* grace, and he is a good representative of it, the *epitome* of it. Other choices are ruled out because they do not relate well to the second clause: (A) deals with elegance in walking: (C), with sensuous pleasures; (D), with food; and (E), with a broad and general category that might work if *root* were not an odd word choice and (B) were not listed.

3. **(E)** What kind of rivalry could there be? (A) would be between brothers; (B), sisters; (C), parents; (D), mothers; and (E), between children having parents in common: *sibling* rivalry.

4. **(C)** *Interfered* (B) would be a natural first choice for meaning, but it does not fit the syntax: it would have to be "interfered *with*." (E) is wrong because such accusations hardly constitute *acknowledgment,* and (A), because they hardly supply *correction.* (D) is too strong for the facts we have. But *disconcerted* is suitable; it means upset, irked, ruffled.

5. **(C)** The English word is made up of two classical Greek forms: *astron,* star, and *nautes,* sailor.

6. **(B)** *Burn .. cauterize* (A) is ruled out because to *cauterize* is to burn tissue with a hot or cold instrument; (C), because to *husband* and to *economize* mean the same thing, to conserve; (D), because in this context these verbs too are synonyms; (E), because *alter* is awkward and unspecific in this context. But (B) makes sense, since *dissipate* means squander, waste, expend intemperately.

7. **(C)** *Lots* are defined as "objects used to make a choice by chance," that is, *randomly.* (A), (B), and (D) would each describe only one aspect of the process; limiting it as in (E) would defeat its purpose.

8. **(C)** You need know no history or biography at all to figure out this type of question: the text yields its meaning to the careful reader. "Eminence" is the word used in the first clause to describe Richelieu. The only adjective offered in the second clause that corresponds to *eminent* is *prominent.*

9. **(B)** A *conspirator* (A) has not necessarily broken a law; nor has a *transient,* or hobo. A *bystander* (D) may have witnessed a crime, but has not taken part. A *paragon* (E), or ideal, is surely not a criminal. (B) refers to someone who has simply crossed the boundary between legal and illegal activity.

10. **(E)** (B) is out because there's no hint *colleagues* are present; (D), because it's not a goodbye; (C), because they are not yet friends, and they might even include some foreign students. (A) would make no sense at all. (E) fits the occasion: they *greet* each other for the first time and he wishes to *salute* them.

11. **(E)** Since *have* can be either an independent verb taking an object or an auxiliary to a main verb (like *arrived*), (A) seems possible syntactically. But the second clause seems to be defining the missing word, which would then best be a noun in the object position: *forbearance,* meaning patience, lenience, restraint, meets these needs. (C), in this context, would mean ill humor, testiness.

12. **(C)** If the first clause is to explain the second, frequency (A), sound (B), and humidity (D) would all be irrelevant. Only increasing nearness (C) would reduce visibility. Lack of resistance (E) is to be expected.

13. **(B)** If the opening phrase is to help explain the rest of the sentence, a word meaning tireless would do the job best: *indefatigable* (B) is perfect. If she were (A), she would not make 15 yards; yet being (C) would not be enough. (D) and (E) are unlikely, unidiomatic words in this context.

14. **(D)** *Impromptu* is defined as given on the spur of the moment.

15. **(B)** The beneficial effects described indicate that the sun and exercise had a healthful, or *salutary,* effect. The dark circles under her eyes disappeared, or were *obliterated.*

TEST 5

1. **(B)** "Although" alerts you to look for the opposite of *aloof,* which means cool, distant, uninvolved. The only opposite listed is *gracious,* which means warm, courteous, sympathetic. (A) means somewhat unwilling; (C), evil, baneful; (D), seemingly truthful; (E), haughty.

2. **(C)** The "but" tells you that the two activities are being put into different categories. The word *crime* suggests that the second is more serious than the first. (A) is much too understated, as is (B): speeding is not a social blunder or false step, which is what *faux pas* means. (E) is greatly overstated, since neither murder generally (*homicide*) nor murder of a brother (*fratricide*) is indicated. By definition, a felony is more serious than a misdemeanor, so (D) has them wrong and (C) puts them in the right order.

3. **(B)** You have to put "skill" into an appropriate category. This is easy, since *craft* is a synonym for skill and implies dexterity with the hands. The entire range of his skills and crafts would be his *repertory,* in the singular.

4. **(A)** Remarks that are not worth taking seriously are likely to be *insipid* (dull or pointless).

5. **(C)** Familiarity with the countryside allowed them to *elude* (escape the notice of) their pursuers.

6. **(C)** Ruling out (D) because no one can elect the law, you have four choices for the second word that all indicate shady activity for a lawyer: to *abrogate* (nullify), *bend, evade,* or *obfuscate* (confuse, becloud) the law. The first word must then suit this shady activity. The only such choice is *unscrupulous.*

7. **(C)** Since the banker thrives on people who put money away for him to lend out at a profit, he will look at you with disapproval, that is, *askance.* Probably he looks at you sidewise, obliquely, not *directly* (D). He is unlikely to *respect* your decision (A). He might look at you *only* (B) if he felt romantic, not indicated here. *Subvertly* (E) is not a word, and the nearest possibility, *subversively,* is inappropriate.

8. **(A)** What the readers want is information causing shock or horror, that is, *lurid* information.

9. **(C)** "Worshipping her every move" did not of itself make him her kindest, most *beneficent* (A) admirer, nor did it necessarily prove that he was more worldly and *sophisticated* (D), more elegant, polite, *urbane* (E), or more unconsciously stupid, or *fatuous* (B), than her other admirers. It qualified him only to be called her most devoted, warm, most *ardent* admirer.

10. **(E)** Once you eliminate the only totally irrelevant choice—(D), meaning to spread through—you have four words all expressing some degree of opposition. But only *dissuade,* meaning to discourage by persuasion, fits gracefully into the syntax. To use (A), (B), or (C), you would have to recast the sentence.

11. **(C)** Only one of the five choices relates to money: *impecunious* means lacking money, penniless. The others are irrelevant.

12. **(A)** If people couldn't finish their meals, there was too much food, or a *surfeit*.

13. **(B)** Only state *subsidies,* or financial aid would enable the Arts Center to provide low-cost programs.

14. **(C)** *Successor* (E) would make some sense if we knew the general had retired. He can't order his (D) to do it; we don't know his relation to (A) or (B)—are they above or below him?—but we do know that his (C), his assistant, is the logical one for him to tap.

15. **(C)** By definition, a malingerer is someone who pretends to be ill, hurt, or otherwise unavailable in order to avoid his obligations. So (C) is the only choice. (D) is a trap: it could be used in a related statement, such as, "You can depend on him to *lack* a sense of duty."

LEVEL C

TEST 1

1. **(B)** The very word *pen*ding suggests her appointment is put into sus*pen*sion, that is, temporarily set aside, in *abeyance. Purgatory* (A) can imply indefinite suspension, such as virtuous but unbaptized people suffer after death, according to some theologians. (C) is a trap for students who sense that a word sounding like this is right. (D) and (E) you ruled out as soon as you made sure of the context.

2. **(D)** The evidence is not of a *feast* (E) or a *prom* (C) or a *contest* (A), but of a massive slaughter, that is, *carnage.*

3. **(B)** Since the school is small and prestigious, its requirements are likely to be strict, or *stringent.*

4. **(D)** *Plastic* (E) means capable of being shaped or formed. But (D) is more specific: *malleable* means capable of being shaped by hammering. (A) is the exact opposite, meaning susceptible to breakage under pressure. (B) means hard and inflexible as a diamond. In the presence of more specific words, (C) is too general; it also works badly in the sentence.

5. **(B)** An *aspersion*—slander, defamation—is always "cast." Only (B) works in this context.

6. **(A)** "His dictionaries" (lexicons, or wordbooks) and "abounded" suggest the books were not compiled for private use but published and indicate that Webster was a writer of wordbooks, that is, a *lexicographer.* He was also (E), but this was not the basis for his fame. (B) is a mapmaker; (C), a specialist in laser photography; and (D), an expert in the use of the dictograph.

7. **(B)** You need a word that denotes something contrary to business. The only such word here is *palaver,* meaning to chatter aimlessly. (A), meaning to assemble; (C), to pool mental resources for quick suggestions; and (D), to associate with, can all be used to describe facets of business. (E) is nonsensical in context.

8. **(B)** The second clause suggests that the missing word refers to deliberate and evil misuse and misinterpretation, that is, *perversion.* (A) means change, modification, with no evil intention necessarily implied; (C), a turning upside down; (D), an attack that involves penetration of enemy territory; (E), a scattering, distribution.

9. **(E)** In a civil war, conflicts are *internecine;* they take place between members of a given group or society.

10. **(E)** What he is missing is theory and formal instruction, without which his experience, no matter how extensive, remains empirical. (B) and (D) would suggest knowledge that includes theory, and (A), advanced knowledge known only to a few. (C) would indicate incomplete knowledge even on the empirical level.

11. **(D)** No special knowledge of economics is needed to see that his income will provide feasts when it goes up, famine when it goes down. Such irregularity is called *fluctuation.* (A) would mean always more famine; (B), a steady growth and more feasts. If *taxes* (C) were a factor, they too would have to fluctuate to produce these results. (E) is the process of liquidating a debt by installment payments or writing off expenditures by prorating them over a period of time.

12. **(D)** The listing of both *hung* and *hanged* suggests that proper usage will figure in the answer: pictures are hung, people are hanged. Hence (A) and (C) are ruled out. (B) is completely nonsensical. Surely he *reviewed* his order (E) but he has no power to *canonize,* that is, declare a person a saint. (D) makes sense all the way: he does have the right to review, change, or reverse his own command, that is, *countermand* it, and to grant a traitor a soldier's death by firing squad instead of civilian death on the gallows.

13. **(D)** The scientific names for plants and animals are *flora* and *fauna,* respectively.

14. **(C)** To bring them into her faith, she would have to do more than *educate* (A), *civilize* (B), and *protect* (D) them, she would have to *proselytize,* or convert them to her religious beliefs. There is nothing to suggest she would want to render them incapable of reproducing, as (E) suggests.

15. **(D)** Here "failed to touch him" means failed to affect his emotions. *Oppressive* (A) cannot be said of a stone. *Impassive* (D) gives us the whole story. It means not only devoid of feeling but also motionless, still. The other three words you rule out because you would never use them to describe a stone; (E), meaning timid; (C), pure, unblemished; (B), hesitant to speak out.

TEST 2

1. **(D)** The second clause suggests that the missing word has to do with returning to jail. (A) is syntactically incorrect; there might be *fewer criminals. Recidivism,* meaning a tendency to relapse into criminal habits, is the exact term called for. (E) is exaggerated patriotism.

2. **(B)** Of the five words offered, all meaning renewal in some sense, only (B) has a negative connotation: it means a revival of something undesirable or ill advised, like disease or civil war, after a dormant or inactive period. (A) and (C) denote a revival of intellectual activity, like the Harlem Renaissance or the Irish Literary Renaissance. (D) denotes a restoration to a former and better condition and (E), any renewal of life or consciousness.

3. **(D)** You can answer this by a process of elimination: (A) is a person who indulges in sexual promiscuity; (B), a retiree getting a pension; (C), a peeping Tom; (E), someone who derives pleasure from inflicting pain on others. *Reprobate* denotes a morally unprincipled person.

4. **(C)** The only word here related to wet eyes is *lachrymose,* meaning "tearful." (E) is cane sugar; (B) is related to fat; (D) means afflicted with coma; (A), warlike.

5. **(B)** Which word catches the essence of the second clause? Not (E), meaning spoken with pompous authority; nor (D), meaning set forth; nor (C), meaning producing abundant works or results; nor (A), meaning limited; but *prolix,* meaning wordy, verbose.

6. **(B)** Neither side has suffered a complete failure (C), nor an overwhelming defeat (D), nor a sudden collapse (E); yet neither side has won. If opposing forces are deadlocked, it's a *stalemate.* A battle cannot become a *truce* (A).

7. **(B)** The missing word must include prediction, secrecy, mystery. Three of the five choices have nothing at all to do with fortune-telling: *bovine* (E) means cowlike; *asinine* (D), unconsciously foolish; *aquiline* (C), like an eagle. *Illicit* (A) means secretive with a connotation of illegality, but *sibylline* means mysterious and prophetic.

8. **(B)** *Disbandment* (E) can be ruled out at once: you cannot direct a program that no longer exists. (A) would be the program's actual functioning, as distinct from (B), the point at which it was conceived; (C), its high point or climax; (D), its completion. Presumably she has seen the program from (B) through (A), and (C) and (D) have not yet occurred.

9. **(B)** The only trait that we hear about ("forever arguing") fits the only word offered that means quarrelsome: *contentious.* Such a person might also be *restless* (D), incapable of resting, or even *restive* (C), restless and resistant to control; but we have evidence only for (B).

10. **(C)** The word *not* indicates a shift in a meaning between the two parts of the sentence: if peace can be maintained only by the brave, the desire for peace cannot be equated with *cowardice*.

11. **(B)** Secret meetings for romantic purposes are called *trysts*.

12. **(B)** If he is corruptible, open to bribery, then he is *venal*. He might also have to be (E), that is, pretending to be moral when he isn't, and to the people making the bribes he may be (A), that is, compliant, submissive, maybe even (C), slavish. In the miscarriages of justice attendant upon his venality, he probably engages in *vilifying* (D) those who haven't paid him. But (B) is the central meaning of the missing word.

13. **(B)** *Promiscuous .. orgy* (A) seems unlikely because it is not impossible to extricate oneself from that situation. (C) is ruled out because *counterfeit* is not used as a noun in this way; (D), because it's not idiomatic: we don't talk about being caught in a prison; (E), because *anathema* is a denunciation or excommunication, and this is not an idiomatic use of the word. (B) makes sense: getting involved with cheap, shoddy, *sleazy* politicians can get you trapped in a bog, or *quagmire,* from which, by definition, it's impossible to escape.

14. **(C)** The missing word must fit the explanation given in the second clause. This rules out (E) and (A), since Algebra I cannot be taken instead of Algebra II or simultaneously. (D) is irrelevant, meaning a job that pays well with little work. (B) is correct in the sense that I occurs before II, but (C) is stronger because it makes I a requirement as well.

15. **(D)** The easiest word to fit in means "a least bit" and is normally used in the negative: "not a *whit* wiser." (E) would be suitable if we were talking about reaching the end: *omega* is the last letter of the Greek alphabet. (B), a unit of distance in astronomy, and (C) are not even metaphorically used to measure intelligence. (A) might do, suggesting that wisdom can be weighed, but in the presence of (D) it is inferior.

TEST 3

1. **(B)** If both parties can live with the solution, it can be considered *tenable*.

2. **(D)** *Postprandial* means after a meal, especially a dinner. (A) would shift the meaning. Other choices are irrelevant: (B) is a grammatical term; (C) has a variety of meanings in travel, military life, and communications; (E) is a term for the buttocks.

3. **(C)** There is nothing to suggest that he uses this experience as either (D) or (E), or that he has withdrawn from the world for these studies, which is what *eremite* (B) would imply, or that he bases his opinions on varied sources, which is what *eclectic* (A) would imply. However, he is without doubt an *authority* on this particular subject.

4. **(B)** The word you choose should link their esteem with his statesmanship. That rules out (D), in chronic bad health; (A), having to do with sexual intercourse; and (C), easily forgiven. There is no hint of a farewell, which is what (E) is about. But (B) fits because he is revered, *venerated*.

5. **(C)** There is no way of measuring a *threat* (A), a *fantasy* (E), or a *circumstance* (B). We would not say that a *graph* (D) has been reduced. But *incidence* makes sense, denoting extent or frequency.

6. **(A)** To escape pursuit, the film star would seek *refuge* (shelter) in her palatial home.

7. **(D)** *Thank .. trouble* (B) can be ruled out: it seems unlikely that anyone would thank a teacher for this; we do like to be thanked for our trouble in doing something, but "my trouble to do so" is not idiomatic. (C) is ruled out because it also sounds unlikely that a teacher would be fired for this or declare it a pleasure; (E), because it is not idiomatic: it might be "a matter of honor *to do so,*" but not "*my* honor." (A) and (D), both referring to a right, seem close. But *privilege* would connote some benefit or advantage to the teacher, while *prerogative* means simply an exclusive right.

8. **(E)** The first clause implies that his lying is beyond his control; it's a compulsion, a matter of mental illness: he is *psychopathic*. (C) would be redundant; *prevaricating* means lying.

9. **(D)** The second clause explains what the missing word means. Only (D) suffices: *hegira* means "a flight from danger." (A) and (B) connote some pleasant excitement. (C) refers to a dispersion, a scattering of people.

10. **(B)** The word *but* signifies a change in meaning between the two parts of the sentence. Snakebites may sometimes cause death, but they are not *inevitably,* or necessarily, fatal.

11. **(E)** *Blade* (C) would do if the palm were grass, but a palm leaf is called a *frond.*

12. **(A)** You need an adjective that tells the kind of job. (B), meaning concise but comprehensive, would be incongruous here. (E) would mean pretentious, boastfully showy. (C) is potentially untrue: his day can include traffic management and delivering babies as well as guarding payrolls, and the frequency of the last kind of activity denies (D). (A), meaning chief, main, or first, is correct by both logic and process of elimination.

13. **(D)** If quick recognition fails you, then a simple elimination of unlikely first words would leave you the most likely one. A rocking motion is not likely to make one feel *oily, bionic,* or *callow.* It might make one feel *languid* (listless), but that would not be followed by an attack of *panic.* The only possible choice is (D).

14. **(E)** Soup is best served in a deep, broad, covered dish called a *tureen.*

15. **(B)** A tower on a mosque is, by definition, a *minaret. Gibbets* (A) are gallows. A *jihad* (C) is a holy war. *Staffs* (D) may project upward, but not on a building. A weapon that combines an axelike blade with a pointed spear is a *halberd* (E).

TEST 4

1. **(B)** By definition, a *staccato* rhythm is a "choppy beat."

2. **(D)** The second clause indicated she reacted with swiftness, a synonym for *celerity.* That means she did not hold back, did not display any *reserve* (C). (A) and (B)—the latter meaning vitality, liveliness—would not be alarming; and she would hardly say yes to a proposal with sharpness, or *acerbity* (E).

3. **(B)** It sounds not only dull but insipid, weak, insubstantial—*jejune.* There is nothing about (A), meaning concerned with current events; (C), meaning concerned with past events; (D), meaning intellectual and spiritual to the exclusion of the sensuous and physical; or (E), meaning self-admiring, that would necessarily make a novel dull.

4. **(A)** The sentence would make no sense if the judge were *determined* (D) or if he *vowed* (C) to stick to the truth, and certainly he would not use coaxing or flattery, which is what (E) would involve. On the other hand, he would make an earnest, solemn appeal, which is what (A) means. (B) is irrelevant in this context, meaning the act or result of a judge's hearing and settling a case.

5. **(B)** The bottled water was necessary because the well water was tainted with chemicals and no longer *potable* (safe to drink).

6. **(A)** Choice (B) is illogical. (D) is begging the question: how much weight does the envelope or container add? (E) would mean that anything, of any weight *except* 70 pounds, could be mailed. (A) and (C) express the idea of setting a realistic limit, but (C) is awkward and unidiomatic.

7. **(C)** The crucial words are "government" and "company." A large grant of money given to a private enterprise by a government, usually in support of a project regarded as in the public interest, is a *subsidy.* (B) is irrelevant because it's a brief summary of a larger composition; (D), because *memoranda* are used for internal, not external, communication. (E) is fixed compensation, paid at regular intervals to an industrial employee for work done. (A) is money given for some special service, usually to a finder who is unknown at the time the *reward* is posted.

8. **(D)** Answer (C) is ruled out because such proof would require service in the job, not just previous experience; (E), because this word, reserved for laws, doctrines, policies, means "announced to the public," usually by a government. (A) and (B) would be unidiomatic and meaningless in this context. (D) is the only choice that makes sense.

9. **(C)** As breeding places for disease and crime, slums have an extremely negative effect on their inhabitants and on society. The only answer choice with a negative meaning is *undermine.*

10. **(B)** The word *but* alerts you to a change to an opposite condition; another key word, estuary, means that wide part of a river where it blends with the sea. There the sweet water would become salty, briny, that is, *brackish.* There it would no longer be drinkable, or *potable* (E). There is no indication that (A), (C), or (D) would be true.

11. **(A)** The second clause describes the kind of societies that by definition would be democratic. (E) is the next nearest, as it refers to the lower classes. (C) means agricultural; (B) and (D) refer to governments that have a single ruler with absolute power.

12. **(D)** If you did not know that *minatory* means menacing, threatening, you could arrive at the right answer by eliminating (A) and (B) because there is no indication of anything sexual in the communication, (C) because there is no mention of laser photography, (E) because it is redundant and not so specific as (D): it is already clear, since he is "charged with" something, that it is *proscribed,* that is, forbidden, whereas (D) assumes that and gives the charge a name.

13. **(B)** In order to pick his teacher's brain, the pupil must have the right to approach it, and the means of doing so; that is, by definition, he must have *access* to it. (A), (C), (D), and (E) do not fit the idiom of the first clause.

14. **(C)** A person who has drawn up his will in legal fashion is a *testator.* The *deceased* (E) testator would no longer have the chance. Being a *witness* (A), that is, a *testifier* (D), or even an embezzler, swindler, or *peculator* (B), would have no bearing on a person's right to testate.

15. **(B)** The only word listed that has to do with snoring is *stertorous,* meaning sounding like a snore. One trap here is (A), which means relating to the sternum—*all* breathing might be described this way. Another trap is (C) since it is related to sleep, meaning sleep-inducing. (E) may sound like snoring, but it refers to the student who ranks second in his graduation class and so qualifies to deliver the salutatory, the speech of welcome. (D) is far off, being not an adjective but a verb meaning to channel some unacceptable form of expression into some acceptable form of expression.

TEST 5

1. **(B)** Even if you never heard of Buck Rogers, you get the idea that he was the original, the model for all the space cadets who followed. This makes him more than just a *pioneer* (D), it makes him a *prototype.*

2. **(D)** If her novels were so widely read, her admirers must have been *legion* (numerous).

3. **(D)** The word *but* indicates that the two clauses have opposite meanings. The other crew members panicked, but she remained very calm, or *imperturbable.*

4. **(B)** You get the main idea from the phrase "explicit love scenes," even if you miss the sexual implication of the title (*The Art of Love,* a work by Ovid). You get another clue from the parallel structure: "the authorities thought it too ----; [the authorities thought] its more explicit love scenes, ----." (A) and (C) are ruled out then because they might *want* those scenes *deleted* or *eliminated,* but they can't *think* them so; (D), because there's nothing scandalous about being pastoral or rustic; (E), because *depicted* is a meaningless word here. But (B) works because *erotic* ties in with "explicit love scenes," and the authorities can think of it as *taboo.*

5. **(C)** The second clause gives you the clue to the two missing words in the first clause. The first word must correspond with "how to" (implying instruction), the second word with "fire and brimstone" (implying strong language that makes readers fear hellfire). (A) gives these, but in the wrong order; (B) makes both of them instructional. (D) and (E) don't come near our requirement. But (C) does: *didactic* = how to, and *inspirational* = fire and brimstone.

6. **(E)** You need no knowledge of the play, only the ability to decipher the text. If the person she dismissed had prevented Juliet from being alone with her lover, then that person might have been a chaperone. The person dismissed is unlikely to be a shipworker (A). A 14-year-old would rarely have *students* (B), and a *confidante* (C) would not stand in the way of love. (D) would have been another lover—highly unlikely. (E) refers to a servant who acts as a chaperone.

7. **(D)** This can be a fast decision if you see that *termagant* is the only word that applies exclusively to a woman: it means a scolding, quarrelsome woman, a shrew. (A), hater of women, is most likely to refer to a man. (B) is also ruled out because she is not described as morally unprincipled, which is what *sinner* implies; (C), because she is not a male villain, a *knave*. Even if she does talk like one, she isn't really (E), an affectionate word for sailor (short for *tarpaulin*).

8. **(D)** You can rule out (C) because *corespondent* relates to adultery, not money. *Domicile* (E) is a word for home, or legal residence. (D) is defined as someone who stands in special relation of trust, confidence, or responsibility, one who holds something in trust for you, a *trustee*.

9. **(B)** His net worth could not be weighed or assessed, and so by definition it was *imponderable*. True as the other choices may be, none so exactly states the situation as (B).

10. **(B)** Your main clues are the words *freedom* and *revenge,* suggesting that he has just been released from captivity and intends to retaliate against those who put him into *incarceration*. (C) and (A) would be contradictions of the second clause, meaning, respectively, a feeling of remorse for one's sins and an act performed to show contrition.

11. **(E)** "On the other hand" implies a contrast, in this case between workers and some opposing group. Only (E) provides the appropriate relationship.

12. **(D)** People who think the province they live in is all the world are *provincial,* that is, narrow in their interests and curiosity. The word is used here ironically, because it is the word city people use to describe country people out in the provinces beyond the metropolis. (A), meaning internationally sophisticated, is belied by the second clause in the sentence. (B), meaning cautious, and (C), meaning prepared for the future, are traps, words close enough to (D) to distract the hasty test-taker.

13. **(B)** The word to describe "voice" must be related to "loudness" as the second missing word is related to "honest heart." Of the five words describing voices, only *sonorous*—meaning full in sound—is paired with a word related to "honest heart," that is, *candor*. A *silky* voice (D) would surely be smooth, but it is paired with *shenanigans,* which are hardly in demand.

14. **(C)** Choice (E) would be a pointless repetition of *unconsciously* in the main cause, while (A) and (B) would contradict the word. (D) makes no sense in context. Either by a process of elimination or through insight, you choose (C), meaning through another person's experience, through a substitute who takes the risks for us.

15. **(C)** The main clue is *hostile*. While hostility can be expressed physically, it is unlikely that he would feel (A), more likely that he would sense an attitude. A hostile crowd would not have *sympathy* (B). The only word describing a negative attitude is *animus* (C), a synonym for hatred. (D) is debris; (E), an evil spirit who rapes women in their sleep.

LEVEL D

TEST 1

1. **(C)** It couldn't be (E) because *role* would need an "of" to link with "Bubbles"—"role of Bubbles." (A) would make sense if "Bubbles" were a title of respect. (C) is much more appropriate, for a *sobriquet* is an affectionate, humorous nickname. (B) is a coquettish maiden in an operetta. (D), a block of fuel, and (B) both have slight similarities in spelling and sound to (C).

2. **(C)** Which of the five choices for the first blank seems like a common, "usual" reason? *Festive* (E) seems appropriate until you realize that *aesthetic* (C) is even more so, since an aesthetic arrangement can both strike the desired mood (festive or funereal) and be beautiful. *Practical* follows through with the expected opposite meaning. *Lugubrious,* meaning "sad," hardly seems suitable, especially when paired with *elation* (D), which

is not idiomatic in this structure anyhow. (B) sounds possible, but not likely on a regular basis. Used to describe a marriage between a member of royalty and a commoner, *morganatic* (A) is way off.

3. **(E)** If you were "unable to read" it, you wouldn't know how "flawless" the *grammar* (A), *spelling* (B), or *rhetoric* (C) was, or even if it had *meter* (D). But you could judge the penmanship, handwriting, or *calligraphy* (E).

4. **(D)** From context and the use of the word *threw,* you can plainly pick choice (D), meaning scornfully, mockingly, cynically.

5. **(C)** If you didn't know that (C) is by definition a hearty eater, you could arrive at it by eliminating (A), because an *aesthete* wouldn't do anything so piggish; (B), because a *spartan* lives a life of restraint and austerity; (D), because *gourds* are not people but hollowed-out shells of certain fruits; and (E), because being a specialist in nutrition says nothing about one's eating habits.

6. **(B)** The only word here related to "tattered beggars" is *ragamuffins.* There is nothing about their being beggars in rags that would necessarily mean that they are criminals or *felons* (C), villains or *miscreants* (D), or base cowards, *poltroons* (E). (A) is the reliable trap for the hasty reader.

7. **(E)** If the governor had not changed her mind, she would have been, by definition, *adamant,* or hard as a diamond. You hesitate over (A) and (B)—but committed or uncommitted to what?—and eliminate (D) because there's no hint she was aggravated or *exacerbated,* and (C) because she must have remained as *governor* if she granted the pardon.

8. **(D)** Since "augmentation" means increase—that is, they were now losing even more money—the directors must have expressed negative feelings to the manager. And there's only one negative word in the choices listed: *reprobation,* meaning disapproval. The deficit would hardly call forth flattery, or *adulation* (A), praise, or *commendation* (B), approval, or *approbation* (C), congratulation or *felicitation* (E).

9. **(A)** You do not need to know what is meant by "a Philadelphia lawyer"; you need only pick up the clue in the words "he could never be pinned down." In other words, he was tricky, shifty, slippery; he had *lubricity.* There are no signs that he was an accomplice in anything, which (B) would imply; engaged in double-dealing, or *duplicity* (C); certainly none that he had clarity, that is, *lucidity* (D), or boldness, *temerity* (E). A "Philadelphia lawyer," by the way, is one expert in discovering and manipulating subtle legalisms. He is slippery, elusive, lubricious.

10. **(B)** The word missing in the first clause must relate meaningfully to the second clause. (B), meaning stubborn or persistent, is the only choice that makes sense.

11. **(A)** The guilty one seems likely to escape scot-free, so his smile is very likely to be *sardonic* (mocking).

12. **(B)** If there are fountains at every corner, they may be considered *ubiquitous* (existing everywhere).

13. **(C)** One cannot "grant" *federation* (A). On the other hand, *autonomy* means self-government, and a kingly "I" could grant it. He could also grant (D), rule by one person, but that would not allow "them" to "govern themselves." (E), meaning control of one country by another, seems to be what the "I" is considering giving up. (B) would do if (C) were not a more specific word for freedom and self-government.

14. **(D)** Either you spot *hiatus* immediately because you know it means a gap, an interruption, or you reason it out by eliminating (A) because such a long illness could not be called a *vacation;* (B), because it would hardly create an excess, a *surplus* of schooling; (E), because this word suits "illness" more than it does education. (C) would do if (D) were not far more specific.

15. **(C)** The main clues are "beneath," "civilization," and "feral," the last meaning characteristic of a wild, savage beast. (C) springs into place at once then because *veneer* is a thin finishing or surface layer, and *beast* matches "feral." The four pairs containing Freudian terms are all traps because the *psyche* (A) contains much more than just the *feral*—it includes humans' civilized mental powers; (B), the *superego,* or conscience, is the opposite of feral; (D) and (E), the *subconscious* and the *id* both include much that is not feral but creative.

TEST 2

1. **(C)** To experience it *directly* (A) you would have to be present then; *infinitely* (E) is equally impossible because no human experience can be endless; *reminiscently* (B) would require your being there in actuality before you could think back on it; *subliminally* (D) would be only a partial experience even of the reading, which includes a lot of conscious as well as subconscious impressions. So the right word is *vicariously,* that is, through imaginative participation in the experiences of others.

2. **(D)** Since they do not indicate distance, (C) and (E) have no meaning in this context. (B) would be impossible with stationary buildings. (A) would not be close enough. (D) would mean that our houses actually touched.

3. **(E)** The words "rich," "even though," and "uneducated" suggest the two men are being contrasted in terms of their relative wealth and education. (A) plausibly completes the neighbor's description, but creates repetition in the orphan's. (B) creates a contradiction in the neighbor, impossibly making him both poor (*indigent*) and rich at the same time. (C) creates redundancy in both descriptions, since rich and *opulent* are synonyms, and so are *unschooled* and uneducated. (D) does likewise—*affluent* means rich, and *untutored* means uneducated. (E) creates the full contrast intended: one is rich and *educated,* the other *poor* and uneducated.

4. **(B)** The sentence describes three stages in the growth of a disagreement. The missing word then might be halfway between "friendly argument" and "blows." That rules out (A), which denotes a disastrous collapse or defeat; (C), meaning legal action, which should not lead to blows; and (D), a brawl, which would already have involved blows. (E), meaning a heated argument, would do except that, used in this sense, *rhubarb* is slang, and this sentence is formal English. (B), which also means a heated quarrel, is formal enough to fit.

5. **(D)** Since Satan is not a saint, the "he" is not really a doctor. The only word here that describes a person who does not have the medical skills he pretends to have is *quack,* a particular kind of impostor. (A), a synonym for Satan, would add nothing to the description, while (B) and (C), denoting different ranks of angels, would contradict the second clause. (E), a wise man, also contradicts the meaning of the second clause.

6. **(D)** Choice (E) can be ruled out because *spartan* means austere, rigorous. (A), (B), and (C) are all pleasant to recollect, but there is a better word that includes all their meanings and more. (D) means calm, golden, prosperous, carefree.

7. **(B)** If Einstein claimed no greatness in mathematics, then physics must have been his field of eminence. So (A) is out, since it means an object of dread and concern. (E) is out because it means a disastrous defeat. (C) and (D) are pastimes, not one's most serious activity. That leaves *forte,* meaning area of expertise.

8. **(B)** The correct word must describe the situation between them if they had em*bittered* each other. Hardly marriage, *matrimony* (A), or statements under oath, *testimony* (D). (C) is ruled out because *alimony* cannot be shared. It could possibly be legal action, *litigation* (E). But (B) is definite: it means bitterness, animosity.

9. **(D)** You need the word closest in meaning to "in balance" probably in a psychological, not a literal, sense. That rules out (E), meaning out of proportion; (C), spotless, unpolluted; and (A) or (B), balanced (but in a physical, material sense). (D) means unshakably calm, undisturbed—the closest of the five.

10. **(C)** You infer that "they" are trying to convert "my people" from one religion to another, in other words, by definition, to *proselytize* them. This does not always mean they have to punish them for their present beliefs (A) or change any of their religious activities into worldly ones—for example, change religious into civil marriage, that is, *secularize* marriage (E). "They" can't *baptize* (D) "my people" until "they" have converted them. "They" may *orient* (B) "my people," but this is not what "they" are "attempting" to do.

11. **(E)** The word "only" indicates that "art" was the lesser of his two pursuits, about which nothing is said except that "he could paint." In politics, on the other hand, he achieved superiority in skill and strength ("prowess"), indicating it was his main activity, his vocation. Art, then, was his hobby, his *avocation,* an activity engaged in aside from his regular profession.

12. **(B)** The word chosen must name a suitable response to his nobility and generosity, and it must fit into the syntactical frame "had … for." Only *adulation* (warm praise) indicates a positive response, and only adulation uses "for." The last three choices all denote negative responses: (C) means great distress; (D), dread or alarm; (E), sudden amazement or frustration. (A), meaning an act of moderating in force or intensity, is irrelevant here.

13. **(C)** No matter how far away (A), (B), (D), and (E) may be, they are all outdistanced by (C), which means, by definition, "a place exactly on the opposite side of the globe."

14. **(B)** The stress on honest dealing tells us that dishonesty is what is being denied. Only (B), meaning deception or trickery, fits. (C) would be men who trick and deceive, not the act itself. (D), meaning joy, liveliness, and (E), a bruise, are irrelevant. While related to card-playing, (A) would create a nonsensical statement.

15. **(E)** Choices (B) and (C) can be ruled out because they denote formal agreements, whereas the party is suffering from disagreement. This produces not a gap (A) but a division, a *schism* into two contradictory parts or opinions. (D) would denote having two or more meanings.

TEST 3

1. **(C)** You need know nothing about the famous Dreyfus case to find the correct answer in the context itself. The sentence could just as well read "Smith was ---- when Rodriguez.…" By definition, if a man is proved innocent, he is declared blameless, *exonerated*. Being proved innocent does not lead to being formally charged, or *indicted* (A) but to just the opposite: being cleared. Dreyfus (or Smith) would have to be cloned to be *proliferated* (B), meaning multiplied rapidly, and he certainly was not *exasperated* (D), that is, angered, irked, or annoyed. (E) means "fruitful" and is irrelevant.

2. **(A)** The main clue is "loose fat," which indicates that the person spoken to is flabby, or *flaccid*.

3. **(E)** The sentence structure requires two compatible words. Only (E) offers this: *altruism,* meaning concern for others, makes sense when linked with *selfless*. A person known for *communism* would not be dubbed *conservative* but radical (A); for *economy,* not *profligate* (wasteful, uneconomical) but prudent in management (B); for *virtue,* not *wanton* (immoral, lewd) but moral, chaste (C); for *conservatism,* not *leftist* but rightist (D).

4. **(B)** Choice (E) would serve as a word for "little faults," but (B) is better because *peccadillos* mean, literally, "small faults." (C) is a trap for readers who vaguely remember a word ending in *-adillos* used in this connection. (D) is too strong, meaning "practices considered deviant," and (A) is contradictory to what is needed.

5. **(B)** You need an adjective meaning the opposite of "long-winded." That rules out (A) and (E), both of which mean wordy, and (D), which means drawn-out. (C) is the nonsense choice, meaning abolished, nullified. (B) means concise, terse, brief, and to the point.

6. **(B)** The phrase "perfect balance" and the first example, "the social and the personal," indicate you must supply opposites for "objectivity" and for "emotion," in that order. Objectivity is that state of mind that views outer reality factually, without reference to personal feelings, in a way that all people could agree on. Opposite is the state of mind that views outer reality in terms of personal emotions and individual need: *subjectivity*. In this context, the opposite of emotion is *reason*. Hence (B) is correct.

7. **(E)** Context supplies the answer, in this case "gobbledygook," a modern word describing unclear, verbose language full of bureaucratic or technical jargon. The word was coined from the sound a turkey makes plus *gook,* meaning sticky, slimy stuff. So, while *gook* suggests you can *smell* (A), *taste* (B), *touch* (C), or, generally speaking, *sense* (D) it, the full word means, in effect, that you can't *understand* (E) it.

8. **(B)** You need not know that IRS stands for Internal Revenue Service; you need know only that someone says that X takes all his money and thus makes him a ----. (B) makes sense, since a *mendicant* is a penniless person, a beggar.

9. **(A)** Don't worry about who Fiedler was. Context tells you all you need know: he performed as a conductor with "brilliance." And that is the definition of *eclat*. (B), meaning style, flair, would do if (A) were not listed. (E) is a formal tribute or eulogy; (C), the best or most skilled people of a given group; and (D), a French pastry.

10. **(B)** A *monologue* (A) is a dramatic soliloquy, and only one person does the speaking; (B) is perfect, for it denotes a long, monotonous harangue, while (C) is much too general and weak. The others are farfetched: (E) means an intuition of some future event, (D), a commission promoting an officer to higher rank without higher pay.

11. **(C)** Grave robbers are properly called *ghouls* (from the Arabic). (B), as they used to be called, and (D), as they prefer to be called now, usually bury corpses rather than dig them up. There is nothing to indicate that these ghouls are (A) or (E).

12. **(C)** The best approach is to start with the word most closely related to "riddles." That's (C), a riddle in which a fanciful question is answered with a pun. For example, "What does a cat get when it crosses the desert?" "Sandy claws." There is no indication that the person being addressed is either antagonistic (A) or tolerant (B).

13. **(C)** Choice (E) can be ruled out at once: it's a room where meals are served; (D) too, with a bit more thought: it means cranky, irritable, troublemaking. (B), denoting a possession that cannot be transferred to another person (e.g., *inalienable* rights) does not fit well. (A) sounds right—it means defensible, logical—but the last four words describe something not amenable to logic. He is dug in, ready for a last-ditch battle.

14. **(B)** You can arrive at the answer by a process of elimination: (A) is ruled out because houses were destroyed too, and *defoliation* refers only to plant life; (C), because there is no evidence of moral corruption or *depravity,* only of a policy of leaving nothing for an enemy to thrive on; (D), because such destruction could not take place after death; (E), because *asceticism,* or self-denial, involves an act of will.

15. **(E)** It makes sense to assume that the missing word denotes something in contrast to "spirit." *Illusory* (A) is not a good contrast to spiritual; (E), meaning related to the body, is a sharper contrast. (D) is wrong because troubles of the spirit would have to be *personal*—it's his spirit. (B) and (C) are traps for the hasty reader who free-associates from "spirit" to clergy and laity.

TEST 4

1. **(E)** The word selected must include spiteful, irritable as part of its meaning. (A) is way off: it means repentant. (D), meaning emotionally upset from fear, pain, or worry, and (C), meaning frantic to the point of frenzy, do not connote the malice of spitefulness. (B) is too general: it means, simply, emotional. (E) is closest: *splenetic* means irritable, peevish, ill-tempered.

2. **(D)** The first missing word must be related to "thick, black smoke," the second missing word, to "evil-smelling and noxious." Only (D) offers such a pair. *Effluvium* means an outflow of vapor or fumes; *noisome* means offensive, disgusting, filthy.

3. **(C)** You need know nothing about a Stradivarius violin in order to answer this question. From context, the crucial fact about a Stradivarius seems to be its "tone." Of the five choices offered, the word most closely related to tone is *timbre*. When used in reference to a musical instrument or a voice, timbre refers to its distinctive tone. (B) is ruled out because nothing has a unique *pitch;* pitch is simply an indication of how high or low a sound is in the register of sounds. Many instruments and many voices can duplicate any given pitch (including that of a Stradivarius). (A), (D), and (E) are components of a string instrument; but none of them can produce the instrument's characteristic tone by itself.

4. **(B)** Ask yourself: Which of the five choices pertains to travel and can be "carefully planned"? (A) and (E) both need to be well organized, but a *pogrom* is a massacre of a minority group, and *diet* is a regulated selection of foods. An *adjournment* (C) is undertaken by a group, not a single person: it involves a suspension of that group's proceedings until a later time. True, a candidate makes appearances, but they are not "carefully

planned" to be ghostly, as the word *apparition* (D) would imply. (B) is the appropriate word, denoting a route or a proposed route for a journey.

5. **(C)** Eliminate (A) because there is nothing about *stalactites* (deposits of minerals pointing downward from a cave ceiling) that would in themselves terrify children; (B), because we describe as *ferocious* (savage, fierce) something alive or at least moving, like a lion or a storm; (D) and (E), because neither *coldness* nor *location* would themselves so affect children. (C) makes sense: *tenebrous* means dark and gloomy, explaining both the terror and the need for children to get close to whatever light is available.

6. **(E)** Whatever it is that "abated" (diminished, lessened), it is characterized by "bitter" feelings. This rules out (A), not normally connected with bitterness; (B), which is good-natured teasing or joshing; (C), which is the art and science of debate; and (D), which is indifference. (E) denotes acrimony, animosity, sharpness—in short, bitterness itself.

7. **(B)** The sentence as it stands is a fair definition of *procrastinate,* which means to put off doing (something) until the morrow. To *premeditate* (C) is to plan or arrange (a future deed or happening) beforehand. To *proscribe* (D) is to denounce or forbid (something or someone). To *prorate* (A) is to divide (something) proportionately; to charge someone $\frac{7}{30}$ of the month's rent for a week's occupancy, or to pay him $\frac{1}{12}$ of a year's pay for one month's work, would be to prorate rent or wage, in any case dividing future obligations proportionately. To *prevaricate* (E) is to fail to tell the whole truth.

8. **(B)** Any romance that is filled with unbridled passions is surely *torrid* (scorching).

9. **(C)** The choices offered would pose different threats to her financial security. Such an overall, practically absolute statement about security requires a verb that covers all possibilities. (A), (B), (D), and (E) are thus ruled out because each represents a limited and specific threat: (A) would mean to gain possession by proving prior right; (B), by taking legal action; (D), by persuading and pleading; (E), by violating her trust. But (C) covers all these and more: it means to usurp, obtain by pulling violently with twisting motions; extract by guile, extortion, or persistent effort.

10. **(D)** The force drawing the ship landward must have been a gentle one, because it just "touched" the sails and moved the ship "slowly." These requirements rule out a *storm* (A) and *gales* (E), which act more forcefully; *sirocco* (C), which is a Mediterranean wind; and *nimbuses* (B), which are rain clouds. But *zephyrs* are gentle breezes, usually from the west.

11. **(A)** You rule out (E) because a *codger* is a man. (C), denoting an ill-mannered person, would do if (A) were not offered. A *virago* is a noisy, domineering woman, a scold; the word is a synonym for "shrew."

12. **(B)** He will never become alcoholic if he just *buys* (A), *accumulates* (D), or stores liquor in a hiding place, which is what both (C) and (E) would mean. He must drink it, too, which means he *imbibes* it.

13. **(D)** (A) and (B) are tempting because either would complete a common phrase, but neither would make sense joined with the rest of the sentence. (E) sounds unlikely unless he were a masochist, and (C) is rather extreme for such a temporary discomfort, and both (E) and (C) sound unidiomatic. But (D) does make sense and does complete another common phrase meaning "in a sullen, angry, indignant mood or humor."

14. **(E)** (C) and (D) are unlikely: this was hardly the time for the soldiers to undertake such a long process as sharpening or polishing their spears. (A) and (B) seem extreme. They waved, flourished, or *brandished* their spears in a menacing manner that could be seen by the enemy troops and had the described effect.

15. **(C)** "Smaller" suggests that these "islands" are being compared with larger islands. Certainly they would not be called "smaller islands" if they were being compared with a *commonwealth* (A) or a *peninsula* (E); and what they are being compared with is "populated," so it can't be a body of water (B, D). It makes sense that the larger islands would be the more populated ones, the smaller islands unpopulated or "unspoiled." Such a chain or series of islands is called an *archipelago.*

TEST 5

1. **(D)** You rule out (E) because it means without humor; (C), because it means arousing pity; (B), because it means vague; (A), because it means disheartened. (D) is perfect: it means agreeably exciting.

2. **(C)** From the characteristics of the two examples you must decide: Which type of figure of speech do they belong to? Being "wretched" is the same as being "miserable." A "prototype" is the same as an "original" type. "Miserably" and "original" add nothing to the words they seemingly modify. His writing, then, is replete with redundancies, needless use of the same sense in different words—that is, *tautologies*. You could arrive at the answer by a process of elimination. The two quoted phrases are not *apologies* (B) in any sense of the word; they are not exaggerations (A); neither are they certain figures of speech (D and E).

3. **(A)** The President can't be *neutral* (C), because the word means "uncommitted to either side." His success may be dependent, or *contingent* (D), on Congress's help, but *he* can't be contingent. (B) and (E) are exactly the opposite of the situation described: the President is ill-*equipped*, not *potent* enough to achieve his goals, which leaves you with (A): *impotent*.

4. **(C)** The context makes it clear that some (unnamed) action by the Senate is required before a treaty becomes valid, legal, binding. Which choice denotes a definite result, a conclusion of a process of treaty-making? (D) would mean that the process had been indefinitely suspended. (A) and (B) describe inconclusive stages of the process. Not even (E) can be said to put the treaty "into effect," because the voting could go either way, for approval or rejection. You are left with (C), the result of a favorable vote.

5. **(C)** Your main clue is the phrase "the grace time," meaning that the city won temporary immunity from the penalties that could have been exacted for missing its deadline, or the "due date" of payment. Such a temporary suspension is called a *moratorium*. The city would not have wanted to get a *lien* (A) or *foreclosure* (B), which would have brought on the penalties in full. (E) would have been an impossible dream for the city, an impossible nightmare for the bondholders. (D) is a place where bodies are cremated.

6. **(B)** A *potpourri* is a combination of various incongruous elements, like a Louis XIV escritoire and a stereo system.

7. **(C)** If you don't spot *puerile* at once as the best word—it means boyish, juvenile, immature—you will arrive at it by a process of elimination. The word "strictly" makes other choices incompatible with "like a child." Strictly *senile* (E) behavior—that is, feebly aged? Strictly *febrile* (D) behavior—consistently feverish? Strictly *kittenish* (A) behavior referring to a man? Strictly *playful* (B) behavior—does this sound idiomatic? To cover all aspects of childlike behavior you need the broad, general word *puerile*.

8. **(D)** *Perversity* is behavior that can be described as obstinate persistence in an error. (A) sounds likely in meaning, but it's not idiomatic. (B) would be impossible—she couldn't do this out of hardship, which is what *adversity* means; it's a choice intended to trap the student who has a vague idea of the sound of the right word. (C) would be considered a plausible explanation—some bravery is needed to maintain such a foolish course— if the broader psychological term were not offered. (E) would be a contradiction: a *pragmatist* would be one who would especially look for the meaning of a course of action in its results.

9. **(B)** To make up for a quarrel, a person would send flowers as a *conciliatory* gesture (one intended to regain good will).

10. **(D)** (B) is irrelevant: it means scolded abusively. (C) would have bad connotations, meaning his confidence was blown up excessively. (A), meaning pleasantly excited, sounds too slight and temporary to describe such a profound reaction as new "confidence." (E) would be absurd, meaning "paid [him] back." So the test results must have inspired, permeated, that is, *imbued* him with self-assurance.

11. **(D)** Rule out (A) right off: it would mean the circumstances are favorable. It couldn't be (C), meaning impulsive, sudden, or (E), accidental, unplanned, because this very sentence shows it is premeditated. (B) would be too strong: there would be nothing irregular, abnormal, or incorrect about asking; it would just be (the only remaining choice) unwise, inexpedient, that is, not good politics, *impolitic* (D), right now.

12. **(D)** Jogging is not an exercise to be called *light* (A); nor is it symbolic of the real thing, that is, *token* exercise (E), and certainly not false, counterfeit, or *spurious* (B). At the other extreme, it's not dangerous, not *hazardous* (C). But since it does require great effort and exertion, it can be called so *strenuous* as to require a doctor's okay.

13. **(A)** The call could not have been *asinine* (B)—foolish, or like an ass's call—if it yielded "valuable information." It wasn't *private* (C) if it pertained to public business. To have such an effect, it would obviously have to be open, frank, fair, truthful, that is, *candid* (D)—so why would that be mentioned? In this context it seems unlikely that the call was *obscene* (E). But if a person communicating something in writing or in speech "refused to give his name," the communication is called *anonymous*.

14. **(B)** If the newspaper leaves ethical judgments to the reader, it is making no attempt to reflect on *morality*. It is doing no more than recording *events*.

15. **(E)** A person who could control everything would by definition be *omnipotent*.

Critical Reading

WHAT IS CRITICAL READING?

Critical reading questions test your ability to understand what you read. You may be asked to read a single passage in the area of humanities, social science, natural science, or nonfictional or fictional narrative, or you may be asked to read two passages about a single topic or based on a common theme. In all cases, the passage or passages contain or imply the information you need to answer the questions that follow. You will be called on to interpret an author's turn of phrase, to define words in context, and to analyze and evaluate the author's work.

How to Answer Critical Reading Questions

Critical reading passages vary in difficulty. You may want to follow one strategy for easy passages, and another for difficult ones.

When you encounter a reading passage that is easy for you to follow, read it all the way through before you consult the questions. As you read, underscore the major ideas. Then, when you read the questions, you will find it easy to identify the author's assumptions and main points.

On the other hand, when you decide to work on a passage that is *not* easy to follow, read all the questions about the passage first, *before* you read the passage itself. In this way, you will know what to look for as you read.

Types of Critical Reading Questions

There are four types of SAT critical reading questions.

1. *Vocabulary-in-context questions* ask about the meaning of a particular word within the selection.

2. *Interpretation questions* ask the reader to interpret a word or phrase as it relates to the ideas in the selection.

3. *Evaluation questions* ask the reader to identify the main point of a selection or the key assumptions of the author.

4. *Synthesis/analysis questions* ask about the logical structure of the selection.

To illustrate the different question types, let's look at the following critical reading "double" passage.

Below are two excerpts from essays on the rule of King Richard III of England. Richard III was the brother of Edward IV. When Edward died, the throne was left to his twelve-year-old son, Edward V. Richard intercepted the boy on the road to London. After convincing the boy's mother to release Edward IV's other son to join Edward in Richard's care, Richard hid the boys away in the Tower of London. They were never seen again. Richard arranged to disinherit the boys and had himself crowned in 1483. In 1485 Richard was defeated and killed in the Battle of Bosworth Field by Henry Tudor, who became Henry VII.

Passage 1

Richard III was without any doubt whatsoever the most evil man ever to have worn the crown of England. Attached to his name are so many crimes, and crimes that are so heinous and unnatural, that it
(5) is scarcely credible that such a monster could exist. He not only committed murder on a number of occasions, but many of those he murdered he had either sworn to protect or should have been expected to defend with his last ounce of strength if he had
(10) anything approaching human feeling.

First on the list of his crimes was the death of his sovereign, Henry VI. Granted that Henry had been deposed by Richard's brother, and hence could not easily claim Richard's loyalty. But Henry was a
(15) broken man, and for most of his life had been essentially a cipher, doing whatever those around him wished. He was almost an imbecile, and certainly was not a threat to the new regime. Furthermore, he was safely locked away in the Tower.
(20) There was no need to have him killed, especially since the forces that had come together to "liberate" Henry had been decisively beaten in the Battle of Barnet. Yet Richard, all of 19 at the time, supervised his death. There are no records that the new mon-
(25) arch, Edward IV, had either consulted with his Council or given Richard an order concerning such a grave matter. Thus, one of Richard's first acts as Constable of England, whose chief responsibility was the preservation of law and order, was regicide.
(30) The next major crime in Richard's career was the death of his other brother, the Duke of Clarence. The records of the time claim that Richard pleaded for his brother's life. However, as we shall see, Richard's words were typically at antipodes to his plans. Also,
(35) the method of Clarence's death—being drowned headfirst in a barrel of wine—was so unusual that all contemporary witnesses noted the bizarreness of it.

But it was the actions that Richard took in the interval between his brother's death in April 1483,
(40) and his own coronation on July 6 of the same year that have earned him his just reputation of being a monster. During that interval he had his mother proclaimed an adulteress and his brother, who had heaped honors and power upon Richard's head,
(45) declared to be illegitimate. Later he claimed that his brother was also a bigamist (though he never could decide which of three other women were allegedly married to his brother before Edward married the mother of his children). He coerced the young king
(50) to join him on the trip to London while dismissing the boy's closest friends and advisers. He threatened his nephew's mother with violence while she was in sanctuary in a monastery if she did not hand over her other son to him. (In threatening her, he
(55) incidentally gave his solemn word that no harm would come to either child.) He had his late brother's closest adviser summarily beheaded.

Richard then callously had his nephews murdered and buried secretly in the Tower, without
(60) even the slightest remorse or twinge of conscience. The two boys were only 12 and 10 at the time. Richard spent the 25 months of his reign looking fearfully for traitors under every bed and killing off those who had helped him to power.

Passage 2

(65) There are two major dangers in the study of history. One is that the historian might well forget that no matter how well he might come to know the person he is studying, there is an untraversable gulf between his own time and the time in which his

(70) subject lived. The second danger is that, no matter how tempting it may be, he is not free to claim a godlike knowledge of all that transpired in connection with any particular event.

(75) Richard III is an unusual case because we all "know" what he was like. The greatest playwright of the English language has given us a portrait of him so vivid that it is hard to imagine that Richard had been dead more than a century before the Bard wrote the play. And what kind of person was this (80) Richard? Shakespeare has him speak to us at the very beginning of the play: I, that am curtail'd of this fair proportion, Cheated of feature by dissembling nature, Deform'd, unfinish'd, sent before my time … And that so lamely and unfashionable That (85) dogs bark at me, as I halt by them;… I am determined to prove a villain,… Plots I have laid, inductions dangerous,…

Shakespeare has painted a man twisted in both body and soul, and his artistry has made us accept (90) this creature for the man. Because we already see Richard this way, we are prepared to interpret all the events around him in such a way as to justify our opinion of him. Rejecting the sincerity of Richard's pleading for his brother Clarence is an example of (95) this tendency. But this is merely deepening prejudice, not expanding our understanding.

Richard's first "crime" was his alleged supervision of the death of Henry VI. First of all, there is no proof that Henry was actually murdered. One of the (100) main reasons that his death has been viewed as suspicious is that it occurred at a relatively convenient time for Edward IV. But even if it were murder, the gravity of it would be such that not even King Edward would wish to be held respon- (105) sible for it. So it would come as no surprise that there would be no "smoking gun" in Edward's handwriting. With a crime so grave that the king would not want to be associated with it, it seems unlikely that Richard would take it upon himself.

(110) Much has been made of his treatment of his brother's widow and her children. What is not pointed out is that Edward's widow, Elizabeth Woodville, had spent her time on the throne plotting to replace all of her husband's family in power with (115) her own family. She pursued this policy to the point of forcing some nobles to marry her sisters and cousins. Elizabeth could not be expected to treat her brother-in-law with any mercy at this stage. All the treachery that Richard indeed did was not so much (120) a measure of his character as of the entrenched position of Elizabeth. This leads us to the final point of this essay. By leaving out the background, we see Richard striking out in a hideous fashion. Once we add in the actions of his opponents, his actions, (125) while not noble, were not monstrous. As we add in the tone of the times, as presented in such works as *The Prince,* by Machiavelli, Richard becomes almost understandable, if not lovable.

Now let's look at each individual critical reading question type.

Vocabulary-in-context questions

Here is an example of a typical vocabulary-in-context question:

The word *heinous* in line 4 means

(A) awful

(B) secretive

(C) bloody

(D) deceitful

(E) dishonest

To answer a vocabulary-in-context question, look at the surrounding sentences as well as the sentence that contains the word. To distinguish between choices (A) and (C) requires you to note that the word is being used to amplify the evil of the murder. Since it is not apparent from the passage that Richard hacked anyone to pieces, *bloody* can be disqualified. If you picked *secretive,* you mistook the methods that the author ascribes to Richard with the fundamental element that the author claims makes him a monster. Only (A) is correct.

Note that in this type of question, often the answers will include more than one synonym for the word in question. In the example, *deceitful* might be an appropriate synonym for *heinous* in some circumstances, but in line 4 it is not.

Interpretation questions

Here is an example of a typical interpretation question:

> Why does the author of Passage 1 call Richard a monster (line 5)?
>
> (A) Because Richard murdered people
>
> (B) Because Richard was deformed, as pointed out in the Shakespeare quote
>
> (C) Because Richard was ambitious
>
> (D) Because Richard allowed no point of honor or family feeling to hold him back
>
> (E) Because Richard supported Henry VI against his own brother

If you chose (B), you either read into the passage more than was there or attempted to fuse two passages.

To answer an interpretation question, first eliminate any choices that are blatantly untrue. In the example, Choice (E) is factually incorrect. Next, look for evidence elsewhere in the passage to help you make a choice. Choice (A) looks appealing, but keep in mind that the author remarks that it was more than the number of people that Richard murdered that made him evil. Choice (C) is close, but nowhere in the passage does the author make any statement against ambition as such.

Don't be afraid of an answer that paraphrases the passage. It is very likely to be correct. In the example, the correct answer is (D). The sentiment expressed in the choice is clearly in line with what the author is writing, despite the fact that the wording is slightly different. This forces you to respond to the content, rather than the form, of the material.

Evaluation questions

Here is an example of a typical evaluation question:

> Which of the following remarks is closest to the views of the author of Passage 1 on the way to judge a person?
>
> (A) Birds of a feather flock together.
>
> (B) Deeds, not words, define the man.
>
> (C) Shoot first and ask questions later.
>
> (D) A man must be judged in the context of his times.
>
> (E) Where there's smoke, there's fire.

To answer evaluation questions, try to summarize the author's point of view or main idea. Summarizing Passage 1, you could say that the author makes the case that Richard III is a monster because of the crimes he committed and because of the way he committed them. The author has clearly collected evidence before reaching this conclusion, which means that (C) is not appropriate. Choice (D) is more appropriate to the author of Passage 2, because that author tries to rehabilitate Richard by pointing out that he was not totally free to act as he wished. Choices (A) and (E) are not supported by the passage. Only (B) is an accurate reflection of the author's point of view, based on the passage.

Synthesis/analysis questions

Here is an example of a typical synthesis/analysis question:

> The author of Passage 2 uses the quote from Shakespeare in order to
>
> (A) give an accurate description of Richard III
>
> (B) give a contemporary portrait of Richard III
>
> (C) present the traditional picture of Richard III
>
> (D) refute the claims of the author of Passage 1
>
> (E) show that the author of Passage 1 was essentially correct, though mistaken in some details

To answer a synthesis/analysis question, hunt for clues within the passage that allow you to eliminate choices. The overall point of the author of Passage 2 is that the image of Richard III is far more tarnished than it should be. Thus, any answer that implies that the author really agrees with the position of the author of Passage 1 is wrong. That rules out choices (A) and (E). Choice (B) can be discarded based on a clue given within the passage. The passage states that "Richard had been dead more than a century when the Bard wrote the play. . . ." Clearly, Shakespeare and Richard III were not contemporaries.

Always read the surrounding context carefully. In the example, the quote from Shakespeare does have Richard say damning things about himself, so the quote itself appears to support the view of the author of Passage 1. Therefore, choice (D) is unlikely—you know that the author's purpose is to refute the claims of Passage 1, but this quote does not support that purpose. It *does* support the idea that we are prejudiced against Richard because of the way he has been portrayed in popular culture. A quote from Shakespeare makes the point that in literature Richard has already been convicted of being a monster. (C) is the correct answer.

PRE-TEST QUIZ

This quiz contains both a relatively simple and a relatively complicated passage. Attack each passage according to the suggested guidelines in the "Question Analysis." Circle the letter that appears before your answer.

In the consistent development of our previous efforts toward the saving and safeguarding of our national life, I have continued to recognize three related steps. The first is relief, because the primary
(5) concern of any government dominated by the humane ideals of democracy is the simple principle that in a land of resources no one should be permitted to starve. Relief was and continues to be our first consideration. It calls for large expenditures and
(10) will continue in modified form to do so for a long time to come. We may as well recognize that fact. Relief comes from the paralysis that arose as the after-effect of that unfortunate decade characterized by a mad chase for unearned riches, and an
(15) unwillingness of leaders in almost every walk of life to look beyond their own schemes and speculations.

In our administration of relief we followed two principles: first, that direct giving should, wherever possible, be supplemented by provision for useful
(20) and remunerative work and, second, that where families in their existing surroundings will in all human probability never find an opportunity for full self-maintenance, happiness and enjoyment, we shall try to give them a new chance in new
(25) surroundings.

The second step was recovery, and it is sufficient for me to ask each and every one of you to compare the situation in agriculture and in industry today with what it was fifteen months ago.
(30)   At the same time, we have recognized the necessity of reform and reconstruction—reform because much of our trouble today and in the past few years has been due to lack of understanding of the elementary principles of justice and fairness by those in
(35) whom leadership in business and finance was placed, reconstruction because the new conditions in our economy as well as old but neglected conditions had to be corrected.

1. The main purpose of the three steps mentioned in this passage is to
   (A) increase exports
   (B) decrease imports
   (C) raise farm subsidies
   (D) increase the national surplus
   (E) none of these

2. The top priority envisioned in this passage is
   (A) justice
   (B) economy
   (C) efficiency
   (D) honesty
   (E) relief

3. According to this passage, the need for reform is caused by those charged with responsibility for such enterprises as
   (A) plumbing and heating
   (B) food and restaurant supplies
   (C) real estate
   (D) banks and stock markets
   (E) farms and filling stations

4. "That unfortunate decade characterized by a mad chase for unearned riches" probably refers to
   (A) the last decade in the last century
   (B) the third decade in the twentieth century
   (C) the last decade in this century
   (D) the second decade in this century
   (E) the first decade in this century

5. According to this passage, two of the economic facets which had been hardest hit were
   (A) shipping and mining
   (B) sports and the media
   (C) radio and television only
   (D) agriculture and industry
   (E) medicine and real estate

We are poor, enslaved, unhappy; speak to us of bet-
ter material conditions, of liberty, of happiness. Tell
us if we are doomed to suffer forever, or if we too
may enjoy in our turn. Preach Duty to our masters,
(5) *to the classes above us which treat us like machines,*
and monopolize the blessings which belong to all.
To us speak of rights; speak of the means of vindi-
cating them; speak of our strength. Wait till we have
a recognized existence; then you shall speak to us
(10) *of duties and of sacrifice.*

This is what many of our workingmen say, and
follow teachers and associations which respond to
their desires. They forget one thing only, and that
is, that the doctrine which they invoke has been
(15) preached for the past fifty years without producing
the slightest material improvement in the condition
of the working people.

For the past fifty years whatever has been done
for the cause of progress and of good against abso-
(20) lute governments and hereditary aristocracies has
been done in the name of the Rights of Man; in the
name of liberty as the means, and of well-being as
the object of existence. All the acts of the French
Revolution and of the revolutions which followed
(25) and imitated it were consequences of a Declaration
of the Rights of Man. All the works of the philosophers who prepared it were based upon a theory of
liberty, and upon the need of making known to every
individual his own rights. All the revolutionary
(30) schools preached that man is born for happiness,
that he has the right to seek it by all the means in
his power, that no one has the right to impede him in
this search, and that he has the right of overthrowing
all the obstacles which he may encounter on his
(35) path. And the obstacles were overthrown; liberty
was conquered! It endured for years in many countries; in some it still endures. Has the condition of
the people improved? Have the millions who live
by the daily labor of their hands gained the least
(40) fraction of the well-being hoped for and promised
to them?

And nevertheless, in these past fifty years, the
sources of social wealth and the sum of material
blessings have steadily increased. Production has
(45) doubled. Commerce, amid continual crises, inevitable in the utter absence of organization, has acquired a greater force of activity and a wider sphere
for its operations. Communication has almost

everywhere been made secure and rapid, and the
(50) price of commodities has fallen in consequence of
the diminished cost of transport. And, on the other
hand, the idea of rights inherent in human nature is
today generally accepted; accepted in word and,
hypocritically, even by those who seek to evade it
(55) in deed. Why, then, has the condition of the people
not improved? Why is the consumption of products, instead of being divided equally among all
the members of the social body in Europe, concentrated in the hands of a small number of men
(60) forming a new aristocracy? Why has the new impulse given to industry and commerce produced,
not the well-being of the many, but the luxury of the
few?

The answer is clear to those who will look a little
(65) closely into things. Men are creatures of education,
and act only according to the principle of education
given to them.

6. The author of this passage is speaking out against

   (A) ideals and duties
   (B) self-interest and the preoccupation with
       individual rights
   (C) revolution
   (D) education
   (E) the aristocracy

7. One can infer that this passage was written
   during the

   (A) late 18th century
   (B) mid-19th century
   (C) mid-17th century
   (D) early Renaissance
   (E) Napoleonic Era

8. According to the author of this passage, the
   Declaration of the Rights of Man had success in

   (A) improving the conditions of workers
   (B) the 19th century
   (C) the 18th century
   (D) making the upper class more sympathetic
       to the needs of the laboring class.
   (E) none of the above

9. According to this passage, when man had achieved the right to seek happiness and to overthrow all obstacles in his path to happiness,

    (A) poverty was conquered

    (B) a utopia was achieved

    (C) liberty was conquered

    (D) the aristocracy was liquidated

    (E) liberty, equality, and fraternity reigned

10. According to this passage, decreases in the cost of merchandise resulted from

    (A) decreases in costs of movement of goods

    (B) increases in the amount of available slave labor

    (C) equal division of consumption of material goods

    (D) more laborers becoming merchants

    (E) better rapport between capital and labor

Explanatory Answers

1. **(E)** The main purpose of the three steps is stated in the opening sentence: the saving and safeguarding of our national life.

2. **(E)** The first paragraph states: "The first is relief, because the primary concern of any government dominated by the humane ideals of democracy is the simple principle that in a land of resources no one should be permitted to starve." Then it reiterates: "Relief was and continues to be our first consideration."

3. **(D)** The last paragraph begins: "At the same time, we have recognized the necessity of reform and reconstruction—reform because much of our trouble today and in the past few years has been due to lack of understanding of the elementary principles of justice and fairness by those in whom leadership in business and finance was placed…."

4. **(B)** It is common knowledge that the first and only administration in the United States to mount a coordinated program of relief, recovery, reform, and reconstruction in response to a purely *economic* condition was that of Franklin D. Roosevelt (1932–45). The decade immediately preceding Roosevelt's first term (1920–30), the third decade of the twentieth century, was characterized by the "mad chase for unearned riches" that culminated in the stock market crash of 1929.

5. **(D)** The third paragraph says, "The second step was recovery, and it is sufficient for me to ask each and every one of you to compare the situation in agriculture and in industry today with what it was fifteen months ago."

6. **(B)** This question should be considered a "title" question; it deals with the over-all theme of the passage. The first paragraph shows the workers' demands for change ("To us speak of rights….") and for "the blessings which belong to all." The second paragraph shows that the revolutions made in the name of labor "were consequences of a Declaration of the Rights of Man," but suggests that the gain of "rights" was accompanied by a loss of liberty. The third paragraph says that the fifty years following the Declaration of the Rights of Man resulted in a perpetuation of the suppression of the common worker because the ruling class considered it *their* right and privilege to preserve their share of the wealth that was produced. Throughout the passage the author makes it clear that he feels that self-interest and the preoccupation with individual rights on the part of workmen have precluded any improvement in their lot.

7. **(B)** The second and third paragraphs speak of "the past fifty years," which, one can infer from the context, began following the French revolution and the first Declaration of the Rights of Man. Since the French revolution began in 1789, we can calculate that this passage was written about the mid-nineteenth century.

8. **(E)** The implication in the next to last paragraph is that because the Declaration of the Rights of Man allowed all men to protect their rights and self-interests from all and by any means, the privileged classes used their available resources to preserve the status quo.

9. **(C)** According to the second paragraph, "All the revolutionary schools preached that man is born for happiness, that he has the right to seek it by all the means in his power, that no one has the right to impede him in this search, and that he has the right of overthrowing all the obstacles which he may encounter on his path. And the obstacles were overthrown; liberty was conquered!"

10. **(A)** Speaking of an improvement in commerce, the third paragraph says, "Communication has almost everywhere been made secure and rapid, and the price of commodities has fallen in consequence of the diminished cost of transport."

LEVEL A CRITICAL READING

Each passage below is followed by a series of questions that require you to analyze, interpret, or evaluate the written work. Answer these questions on the basis of what each passage states or implies. Circle the letter that appears before your answer.

Test 1   (Answers on Page 186)

Katherine Prescott Wormeley was born in England and moved with her family to the United States in the late 1840s. When the Civil War broke out, she joined the United States Sanitary Commission, a private organization designed to supplement the United States Army's medical division. She was in a place called Harrison's Landing when Abraham Lincoln came to meet General McClellan and discuss the fight for control of Richmond.

For the last two hours I have been watching President Lincoln and General McClellan as they sat together in earnest conversation on the deck of a steamer close to us. I am thankful, I am *happy*, that
(5) the President has come—has sprung across that dreadful intervening Washington, and come to see and hear and judge for his own wise and noble self.

While we were at dinner someone said, chancing to look through a window: "Why, there's the Presi-
(10) dent!" and he proved to be just arriving on the *Ariel*, at the end of the wharf close to which we are anchored. I stationed myself at once to watch for the coming of McClellan. The President stood on deck with a glass, with which, after a time, he inspected
(15) our boat, waving his handkerchief to us. My eyes and soul were in the direction of general headquarters, over where the great balloon was slowly descending. Presently a line of horsemen came over the brow of the hill through the trees, and first
(20) emerged a firm-set figure on a brown horse, and after him the staff and bodyguard. As soon as the General reached the head of the wharf he sprang from his horse, and in an instant every man was afoot and motionless. McClellan walked quickly
(25) along the thousand-foot pier, a major general beside him, and six officers following. He was the shortest man, of course, by which I distinguished him as the little group stepped onto the pier. When he reached the *Ariel* he ran quickly up to the afterdeck, where

(30) the President met him and grasped his hand. I could not distinguish the play of his features, though my eyes still ache with the effort to do so. He is stouter than I expected.... He wore the ordinary blue coat and shoulder straps; the coat, fastened only at the
(35) throat, and blowing back as he walked, gave to sight a gray flannel shirt and a—suspender!

They sat down together, apparently with a map between them, to which McClellan pointed from time to time with the end of his cigar. We watched
(40) the earnest conversation which went on, and which lasted until 6 P.M.; then they rose and walked side by side ashore—the President in a shiny black coat and stovepipe hat, a whole head and shoulders taller, as it seemed to me, than the General. Mr. Lincoln
(45) mounted a led horse of the General's, and together they rode off, the staff following, the dragoons presenting arms and then wheeling round to follow, their sabres gleaming in the sunlight. And so they have passed over the brow of the hill, and I have
(50) come to tell you about it. The cannon are firing salutes—a sound of strange peacefulness to us, after the angry, irregular boomings and the sharp scream of the shells to which we are accustomed....

1. What does the author mean by "that dreadful intervening Washington" (lines 5–6)?

   (A) Politics are always interfering with the war.

   (B) Lincoln's office stands in the way of his leadership.

   (C) Lincoln has crossed Washington to come to Harrison's Landing.

   (D) The fame of a previous President keeps Lincoln in the shadows.

   (E) Washington is mediating between North and South.

2. How does the author feel toward Lincoln?

   (A) She trusts his judgment.

   (B) She suspects his motives.

   (C) She regrets his arrival.

   (D) She finds him undistinguished.

   (E) She has no opinion.

3. The word "glass" is used in line 14 to refer to

   (A) a goblet

   (B) a mirror

   (C) a window

   (D) a telescope

   (E) bifocals

4. The "great balloon slowly descending" (lines 17–18) is apparently

   (A) the sun setting

   (B) remnants of a firestorm over the Potomac

   (C) the moon over the river

   (D) a mirage

   (E) McClellan's transport arriving

5. Why do the author's eyes ache?

   (A) She has been sobbing for hours.

   (B) She struggled to see Lincoln's expression.

   (C) The wind has blown smoke from the battle.

   (D) She is writing in darkness.

   (E) There was glare over the water.

6. The phrase "by which I distinguished him" (lines 26–27) might be rewritten

   (A) "which made him seem elegant"

   (B) "in that way I understood his speech"

   (C) "it was easy to see"

   (D) "I was more refined than he"

   (E) "which is how I picked him out"

7. A synonym for "dragoons" (line 46) might be

   (A) wagons

   (B) troops

   (C) horses

   (D) haulers

   (E) demons

8. Why does Wormeley refer to the cannon salutes as peaceful?

   (A) They are far quieter than the scream of shells.

   (B) A truce has been declared.

   (C) She is contrasting them to the cannonfire of war.

   (D) both A and B

   (E) both C and D

Test 2 (Answers on Page 186)

Thomas Bulfinch (1796–1867) translated and popularized myths of the ancient Greeks, Romans, and other cultures. Here he describes the legends surrounding Orion, the hunter for whom a constellation is named.

Orion was the son of Neptune. He was a handsome giant and a mighty hunter. His father gave him the power of wading through the depths of the sea, or, as others say, of walking on its surface.

(5)   Orion loved Merope, the daughter of Œnopion, king of Chios, and sought her in marriage. He cleared the island of wild beasts, and brought the spoils of the chase as presents to his beloved; but as Œnopion constantly deferred his consent, Orion (10) attempted to gain possession of the maiden by violence. Her father, incensed at this conduct, having made Orion drunk, deprived him of his sight and cast him out on the seashore. The blinded hero followed the sound of a Cyclops' hammer till he (15) reached Lemnos, and came to the forge of Vulcan, who, taking pity on him, gave him Kedalion, one of his men, to be his guide to the abode of the sun.

Placing Kedalion on his shoulders, Orion proceeded to the east, and there meeting the sun-god, was
(20)   restored to sight by his beam.

After this he dwelt as a hunter with Diana, with whom he was a favourite, and it is even said she was about to marry him. Her brother was highly displeased and often chid her, but to no purpose. One
(25)   day, observing Orion wading through the sea with his head just above the water, Apollo pointed it out to his sister and maintained that she could not hit that black thing on the sea. The archer-goddess discharged a shaft with fatal aim. The waves rolled the
(30)   dead body of Orion to the land, and bewailing her fatal error with many tears, Diana placed him among the stars, where he appears as a giant, with a girdle, sword, lion's skin, and club. Sirius, his dog, follows him, and the Pleiads fly before him.

(35)   The Pleiads were daughters of Atlas, and nymphs of Diana's train. One day Orion saw them and became enamoured and pursued them. In their distress they prayed to the gods to change their form, and Jupiter in pity turned them into pigeons, and
(40)   then made them a constellation in the sky. Though their number was seven, only six stars are visible, for Electra, one of them, it is said left her place that she might not behold the ruin of Troy, for that city was founded by her son Dardanus. The sight had
(45)   such an effect on her sisters that they have looked pale ever since.

1. When Bulfinch says "as others say" in line 4, he probably is referring to
    (A) the meaning of "wade" in other languages
    (B) Orion's powers as described by the gods themselves
    (C) other translations or interpretations of the myth
    (D) a Christian explanation of the myth
    (E) the fact that Orion could perform both feats

2. The word "spoils" (line 8) means
    (A) leftovers
    (B) stains
    (C) joys
    (D) damage
    (E) booty

3. The word "chid" (line 24) means
    (A) remarked
    (B) lost
    (C) embraced
    (D) irked
    (E) scolded

4. The "black thing on the sea" (line 28) is
    (A) a seal
    (B) a boat containing Diana's beloved
    (C) Orion's head
    (D) Diana's reflection
    (E) impossible to determine from the information given

5. The word "discharged" (line 28) is used to mean
    (A) performed
    (B) shot
    (C) executed
    (D) emptied
    (E) dismissed

6. The word "train" (line 36) is used to mean
    (A) locomotive
    (B) gown
    (C) veil
    (D) series
    (E) entourage

7. Unlike the first three paragraphs, the last
    (A) deals with a constellation other than Orion
    (B) explains Orion's death
    (C) connects myth to the world of nature
    (D) both A and B
    (E) both B and C

8. The purpose of this myth seems to be to
    (A) teach a lesson about responsibility
    (B) review the powers of the Greek gods
    (C) explain certain astronomical phenomena
    (D) both A and B
    (E) both C and D

Test 3   (Answers on Page 186)

Sigmund Freud lived most of his life in Vienna, Austria. He trained in medicine and established The International Psychoanalytic Association in 1910. This excerpt is from a translation of a 1923 work, The Ego and the Id.

There are certain people who behave in a quite peculiar fashion during the work of analysis. When one speaks hopefully to them or expresses satisfaction with the progress of the treatment, they show
(5) signs of discontent and their condition invariably becomes worse. One begins by regarding this as defiance and as an attempt to prove their superiority to the physician, but later one comes to take a deeper and juster view. One becomes convinced, not only
(10) that such people cannot endure any praise or appreciation, but that they react inversely to the progress of the treatment. Every partial solution that ought to result, and in other people does result, in an improvement or a temporary suspension of symptoms
(15) produces in them for the time being an exacerbation of their illness; they get worse during the treatment instead of getting better. They exhibit what is known as a 'negative therapeutic reaction.'
   There is no doubt that there is something in these
(20) people that sets itself against their recovery, and its approach is dreaded as though it were a danger. We are accustomed to say that the need for illness has got the upper hand in them over the desire for recovery. If we analyse this resistance in the usual
(25) way—then, even after allowance has been made for an attitude of defiance towards the physician and for fixation to the various forms of gain from illness, the greater part of it is still left over; and this reveals itself as the most powerful of all obstacles to recov-
(30) ery, more powerful than the familiar ones of narcissistic inaccessibility, a negative attitude towards the physician and clinging to the gain from illness.
   In the end we come to see that we are dealing with what may be called a 'moral' factor, a sense of
(35) guilt, which is finding satisfaction in the illness and refuses to give up the punishment of suffering. We shall be right in regarding this disheartening explanation as final. But as far as the patient is concerned this sense of guilt is dumb; it does not tell
(40) him he is guilty; he does not feel guilty, he feels ill. This sense of guilt expresses itself only as a resistance to recovery which it is extremely difficult to overcome. It is also particularly difficult to convince the patient that this motive lies behind his
(45) continuing to be ill; he holds fast to the more obvious explanation that treatment by analysis is not the right remedy for his case.

1. How does Freud feel about the syndrome he describes?
    (A) He feels it is curious.
    (B) He feels it is routine.
    (C) He feels it is unmanageable.
    (D) He feels it is predictable.
    (E) He feels it is ridiculous.

2. The word "defiance" (line 7) is used to mean
    (A) boldness
    (B) respect
    (C) scorn
    (D) recalcitrance
    (E) contempt

3. The word "juster" (line 9) means
    (A) more honest
    (B) more lawful
    (C) fairer
    (D) clearer
    (E) more precise

4. By "reacting inversely" (line 11), Freud means that these patients
    (A) act contrary to a physician's expectations
    (B) get worse when they should get better
    (C) get better when they should get worse
    (D) both A and B
    (E) both B and C

5. The word "exacerbation" (line 15) means
    (A) intensification
    (B) discharge
    (C) enforcement
    (D) hatred
    (E) inference

6. The "approaching danger" Freud refers to in line 21 is

(A) the need to feel sick

(B) negative attitudes

(C) despair

(D) recovery from illness

(E) a sense of guilt

7. Freud's study of this syndrome leads him to think that

(A) most patients respond badly to praise

(B) patients' guilt may keep them from getting well

(C) patients need to trust their physicians

(D) both A and B

(E) both B and C

8. The word "dumb" (line 39) is used to mean

(A) slow

(B) dull

(C) dense

(D) stupid

(E) silent

9. Does Freud feel that analysis is not right for the patients he describes?

(A) Yes, he feels they are in love with their illness.

(B) Yes, he feels that they are too ill to recover.

(C) Yes, he senses that they need another remedy.

(D) No, but the patients often feel that way.

(E) No, but analysis may harm such patients.

10. A good title for this passage might be

(A) "Doctors and Patients"

(B) "Guilt and Suffering"

(C) "An Inverse Reaction to Progress"

(D) "The Need for Analysis"

(E) "Narcissism"

Test 4   (Answers on Page 186)

Edwin Markham was primarily a poet. He was associated with the "muckraking movement" of the early twentieth century. Muckrakers were a loosely allied set of novelists, essayists, and magazine editors whose goal was the raising of society's consciousness and the exposure of social ills. This excerpt is from a 1906 essay Markham wrote for the muckraking magazine Cosmopolitan.

In the North…, for every one thousand workers over sixteen years of age there are eighty-three workers under sixteen…; while in the South, for every one thousand workers in the mills over sixteen years of
(5)   age there are three hundred and fifty-three under sixteen. Some of these are eight and nine years old, and some are only five and six. For a day or a night at a stretch these little children do some one monotonous thing—abusing their eyes in watching the
(10)   rushing threads; dwarfing their muscles in an eternity of petty movements; befouling their lungs by breathing flecks of flying cotton; bestowing ceaseless, anxious attention for hours, where science says that "a twenty-minute strain is long enough for a
(15)   growing mind." And these are not the children of recent immigrants, hardened by the effete conditions of foreign servitude. Nor are they Negro children who have shifted their shackles from field to mill. They are white children of old and pure colo-
(20)   nial stock. Think of it! Here is a people that has outlived the bondage of England, that has seen the rise and fall of slavery—a people that must now fling their children into the clutches of capital, into the maw of the blind machine…

(25)   Fifty thousand children, mostly girls, are in the textile mills of the South. Six times as many children are working now as were working twenty years ago. Unless the conscience of the nation can be awakened, it will not be long before one hundred
(30)   thousand children will be hobbling in hopeless lockstep to these Bastilles of labor….

Think of the deadly drudgery in these cotton mills. Children rise at half-past four, commanded by the ogre scream of the factory whistle; they hurry, ill (35) fed, unkempt, unwashed, half dressed, to the walls which shut out the day and which confine them amid the din and dust and merciless maze of the machines. Here, penned in little narrow lanes, they look and leap and reach and tie among acres and (40) acres of looms. Always the snow of lint in their faces, always the thunder of the machines in their ears. A scant half hour at noon breaks the twelve-hour vigil, for it is nightfall when the long hours end and the children may return to the barracks they call (45) "home," often too tried to wait for the cheerless meal which the mother, also working in the factory, must cook, after her factory day is over. Frequently at noon and at night they fall asleep with the food unswallowed in the mouth. Frequently they snatch (50) only a bite and curl up undressed on the bed, to gather strength for the same dull round tomorrow, and tomorrow, and tomorrow.

1. The words "abusing," "dwarfing," and "befouling" (lines 9–11) are used by Markham to show

    (A) the health hazards for children of life in the mills

    (B) the quality of the workers in the mills

    (C) how little respect for life millworkers have

    (D) how adults fare no better than children

    (E) the varying jobs available for children

2. Markham quotes "science" (line 14) to support his point that

    (A) young muscles are built by hard labor

    (B) mill work is dangerous

    (C) children should not work long hours

    (D) both A and B

    (E) both B and C

3. The word "effete" (line 16) means

    (A) decent

    (B) flourishing

    (C) childless

    (D) barren

    (E) unwholesome

4. By "shifted their shackles from field to mill" (lines 18–19), Markham means

    (A) taken their slaves from country to city

    (B) changed from field slaves to slaves of the mills

    (C) moved their money indoors

    (D) slipped the bonds of slavery to work in the mills

    (E) left a life of servitude for a better life

5. By the "maw of the blind machine" (line 24), Markham compares mill labor to

    (A) a senseless device

    (B) a matriarchal society

    (C) a cruel, unfeeling mother

    (D) a Cyclops-like ogre

    (E) a tool that blinds workers

6. What does Markham mean by "Bastilles of labor" (line 31)?

    (A) America needs a revolution.

    (B) The mills are prisons.

    (C) Children work for freedom.

    (D) Work is the drug of the masses.

    (E) We are no better than Europeans.

7. Paragraph 3 continues Markham's metaphor of

    (A) prisons

    (B) monsters

    (C) flight

    (D) both A and B

    (E) both B and C

8. The word "penned" (line 38) is used to compare the children to

    (A) writers

    (B) animals

    (C) wrestlers

    (D) pigs

    (E) ranchhands

9. The word "barracks" (line 44) is used to refer to the fact that the children's home is

   (A) in a camp

   (B) manned by armed guards

   (C) dreary and uniform

   (D) militarily clean

   (E) old and run-down

10. Markham repeats the word "tomorrow" (line 52) to

    (A) remind us that the future is here

    (B) imply endless repetitiveness

    (C) suggest that it is not too late to change

    (D) arouse us to the fact that these children will grow up

    (E) contrast the past with the present

Test 5   (Answers on Page 186)

Ralph Waldo Emerson is one of America's best-known essayists. In 1837 he was called on to give the Phi Beta Kappa address to Harvard students and their guests. He spoke on "The American Scholar."

It is remarkable, the character of the pleasure we derive from the best books. They impress us with the conviction that one nature wrote and the same reads. We read the verses of one of the great English poets,
(5) of Chaucer, of Marvell, of Dryden, with the most modern joy,—with a pleasure, I mean, which is in great part caused by the abstraction of all *time* from their verses. There is some awe mixed with the joy of our surprise, when this poet, who lived in some
(10) past world, two or three hundred years ago, says that which lies close to my own soul, that which I also had well-nigh thought and said. But for the evidence thence afforded to the philosophical doctrine of the identity of all minds, we should suppose some
(15) preestablished harmony, some foresight of souls that were to be, and some preparation of stores for their future wants, like the fact observed in insects, who lay up food before death for the young grub they shall never see.
(20)   I would not be hurried by any love of system, by any exaggeration of instincts, to underrate the Book. We all know, that as the human body can be nourished on any food, though it were boiled grass and the broth of shoes, so the human mind can be fed by
(25) any knowledge. And great and heroic men have existed who had almost no other information than by the printed page. I would only say that it needs a strong head to bear that diet. One must be an inventor to read well. As the proverb says, "He that
(30) would bring home the wealth of the Indies, must carry out the wealth of the Indies." There is then creative reading as well as creative writing. When

the mind is braced by labor and invention, the page of whatever book we read becomes luminous with
(35) manifold allusion. Every sentence is doubly significant, and the sense of our author is as broad as the world. We then see, what is always true, that as the seer's hour of vision is short and rare among heavy days and months, so is its record, perchance, the
(40) least part of his volume. The discerning will read, in his Plato or Shakespeare, only that least part,—only the authentic utterances of the oracle;—all the rest he rejects, were it never so many times Plato's and Shakespeare's.
(45)   Of course there is a portion of reading quite indispensable to a wise man. History and exact science he must learn by laborious reading. Colleges, in like manner, have their indispensable office,—to teach elements. But they can only highly
(50) serve us when they aim not to drill, but to create; when they gather from far every ray of various genius to their hospitable halls, and by the concentrated fires, set the hearts of their youth on flame.

1. By "one nature wrote and the same reads" (line 3), Emerson means that

   (A) the author is rereading his own work

   (B) nature writing is read by the same people

   (C) author and reader live in the same era

   (D) author and reader are in accord

   (E) the reader does not remember his own writing

2. The word "abstraction" (line 7) is used to mean

   (A) conception

   (B) notion

   (C) preoccupation

   (D) elimination

   (E) inattention

3. Emerson uses the image of insects (line 17) to parallel his discussion of

    (A) past writers storing knowledge for future readers

    (B) authors working in grubby surroundings

    (C) soulless parents toiling blindly for unknowing children

    (D) the act of creating art

    (E) the food chain

4. A good title for paragraph 2 might be

    (A) "Creative Writing"

    (B) "Creative Reading"

    (C) "Rating Books"

    (D) "The Wealth of the Indies"

    (E) "Visions of the Past"

5. The proverb Emerson cites (lines 29–31) is used to support his theory that

    (A) one must apply knowledge to extract knowledge

    (B) the rich need more education than the poor

    (C) all the wealth in the world will not make a man a genius

    (D) the wealth of the present is found in the past

    (E) only a writer can be a good reader

6. The word "braced" (line 33) is used to mean

    (A) upset

    (B) beamed

    (C) paired

    (D) clamped

    (E) bolstered

7. By "manifold allusion" (line 35), Emerson means

    (A) diverse references

    (B) numerous mentions

    (C) mechanical fantasies

    (D) multiple delusions

    (E) many-sided remarks

8. The word "oracle" (line 42) means

    (A) wonder

    (B) seer

    (C) composer

    (D) naturalist

    (E) reader

9. The word "office" (line 48) is used to mean

    (A) site

    (B) employment

    (C) department

    (D) duty

    (E) study

10. Emerson calls for an educational system that

    (A) includes works of the masters

    (B) teaches students to write brilliantly

    (C) inspires creativity in scholars

    (D) both A and B

    (E) both B and C

LEVEL B CRITICAL READING

Each passage below is followed by a series of questions that require you to analyze, interpret, or evaluate the written work. Answer these questions on the basis of what each passage states or implies. Circle the letter that appears before your answer.

Test 1   (Answers on Page 186)

Jean Toomer was one of the most interesting writers of the Harlem Renaissance of the 1920s. He wrote experimental plays, poetry, and the novel Cane, from which this excerpt is taken.

For a long while she was nothing more to me than one of those skirted beings whom boys at a certain age disdain to play with. Just how I came to love her, timidly, and with secret blushes, I do not know. But
(5) that I did was brought home to me one night, the first night that Ned wore his long pants. Us fellers were seated on the curb before an apartment house where she had gone in. The young trees had not outgrown their boxes then. V Street was lined with them.
(10) When our legs grew cramped and stiff from the cold of the stone, we'd stand around a box and whittle it. I like to think now that there was a hidden purpose in the way we hacked them with our knives. I like to feel that something deep in me responded to the
(15) trees, the young trees that whinnied like colts impatient to be let free… On the particular night I have in mind, we were waiting for the top-floor to go out. We wanted to see Avey leave the flat. This night she stayed longer than usual and gave us a chance to
(20) complete our plans of how we were going to stone and beat that feller on the top floor out of town. Ned especially had it in for him. He was about to throw a brick up at the window when at last the room went dark. Some minutes passed. Then Avey, as uncon-
(25) cerned as if she had been paying an old-maid aunt a visit, came out…. I just stood there like the others, and something like a fuse burned up inside of me. She never noticed us, but swung along lazy and easy as anything…. Some one said she'd marry that feller
(30) on the top floor. Ned called that a lie because Avey was going to marry nobody but him. We had our doubts about that, but we did agree that she'd soon leave school and marry some one. The gang broke up, and I went home, picturing myself as married.

(35)   Nothing I did seemed able to change Avey's indifference to me. I played basketball, and when I'd make a long clean shot she'd clap with the others, louder than they, I thought. I'd meet her on the street, and there'd be no difference in the way
(40) she said hello. She never took the trouble to call me by my name…. It was on a summer excursion down to Riverview that she first seemed to take me into account. The day had been spent riding merry-go-rounds, scenic-railways, and shoot-the-chutes.
(45) We had been in swimming, and we had danced. I was a crack swimmer then. She didn't know how. I held her up and showed her how to kick her legs and draw her arms. Of course she didn't learn in one day, but she thanked me for bothering with her. I was also
(50) somewhat of a dancer. And I had already noticed that love can start on a dance floor. We danced. But though I held her tightly in my arms, she was way away. That college feller who lived on the top floor was somewhere making money for the next year. I
(55) imagined that she was thinking, wishing for him. Ned was along. He treated her until his money gave out. She went with another feller. Ned got sore. One by one the boys' money gave out. She left them. And they got sore. Every one of them but me got sore….

1. The word "disdain" (line 3) means

    (A) dislike
    (B) contend
    (C) regard
    (D) offend
    (E) unnerve

2. "The first night that Ned wore his long pants" (lines 5–6) is used to reveal

    (A) that the events took place long ago
    (B) that the boys involved were fairly young
    (C) that Ned was younger than the narrator
    (D) both A and B
    (E) both B and C

3. The word "whittle" (line 11) means

   (A) cut

   (B) signal

   (C) knock

   (D) dull

   (E) play

4. Toomer's narrator compares himself to a tree in terms of his

   (A) sturdiness

   (B) youth

   (C) desire to break free

   (D) both A and B

   (E) both B and C

5. The word "flat" (line 18) is used to refer to a

   (A) remark

   (B) soda

   (C) joke

   (D) lodging

   (E) tire

6. By "take me into account" (line 42), the narrator means

   (A) "employ me"

   (B) "forgive me"

   (C) "notice me"

   (D) "interest me"

   (E) "chastise me"

7. The word "sore" (line 59) is used to mean

   (A) pained

   (B) angry

   (C) tender

   (D) bruised

   (E) wounded

8. The passage tells a tale of

   (A) wounded pride

   (B) envy and regret

   (C) unrequited love

   (D) sorrow and guilt

   (E) unfounded fears

Test 2   (Answers on Page 186)

Best known as the author of Robinson Crusoe, *Daniel Defoe was a prolific writer. His* Journal of the Plague Year, *published in 1722, is the convincing "journal" of a man identified only as "H.F." It tells of a real plague that decimated the Continent the year Defoe was five.*

It was now the beginning of August, and the plague grew very violent and terrible in the place where I lived, and Dr. Heath coming to visit me, and finding that I ventured so often out in the streets, earnestly

(5) persuaded me to lock myself up, and my family, and not to suffer any of us to go out of doors; to keep all our windows fast, shutters and curtains close, and never to open them; but first, to make a very strong smoke in the room where the window or door was to

(10) be opened, with rosin and pitch, brimstone or gunpowder, and the like; and we did this for some time; but as I had not laid in a store of provision for such a retreat, it was impossible that we could keep within doors entirely. However, I attempted, though

(15) it was so very late, to do something towards it; and first, as I had convenience both for brewing and baking, I went and bought two sacks of meal, and for several weeks, having an oven, we baked all our own bread; also I bought malt, and brewed as much

(20) beer as all the casks I had would hold, and which seemed enough to serve my house for five or six weeks; also I laid in a quantity of salt butter and Cheshire cheese; but I had no flesh meat, and the plague raged so violently among the butchers and

(25) slaughterhouses on the other side of our street, where they are known to dwell in great numbers, that it was not advisable so much as to go over the street among them.

And here I must observe again that this necessity

(30) of going out of our houses to buy provisions was in a great measure the ruin of the whole City, for the people caught the distemper on these occasions one of another, and even the provisions themselves were often tainted; at least I have great reason to

(35) believe so; and therefore I cannot say with satisfaction what I know is repeated with great assurance,

that the market people and such as brought provisions to town were never infected. I am certain the butchers of Whitechapel, where the greatest part of
(40) the flesh meat was killed, were dreadfully visited, and that at last to such a degree that few of their shops were kept open, and those that remained of them killed their meat at Mile End and that way, and brought it to market upon horses.

(45)   However, the poor people could not lay up provisions, and there was a necessity that they must go to market to buy, and others to send servants or their children; and as this was a necessity which renewed itself daily, it brought abundance of unsound people
(50) to the markets, and a great many that went thither sound brought death home with them.

      It is true people used all possible precaution; when anyone bought a joint of meat in the market they would not take it off the butcher's hand, but
(55) took it off the hooks themselves. On the other hand, the butcher would not touch the money, but have it put into a pot full of vinegar, which he kept for that purpose. The buyer carried always small money to make up any odd sum, that they might take no
(60) change. They carried bottles of scents and perfumes in their hands, and all the means that could be used were used, but then the poor could not do even these things; and they went at all hazards.

1. When the doctor says "not to suffer any of us to go out of doors" (line 6), he means

    (A) going outdoors will cause suffering

    (B) the narrator should not allow his family to go out

    (C) they should go outdoors to avoid the suffering inside

    (D) going outdoors will prevent suffering

    (E) the narrator should not prevent his family from going out

2. The word "fast" (line 7) is used to mean

    (A) fleet

    (B) steadfast

    (C) swift

    (D) fastened

    (E) permanent

3. By "laid in a store of provision" (line 12), the narrator refers to

    (A) putting up a supply of food

    (B) telling a story of salvation

    (C) preserving the past

    (D) lying in a bed of flour sacks

    (E) sleeping in his place of business

4. The word "retreat" (line 13) is used to mean

    (A) departure

    (B) evacuation

    (C) flight

    (D) escape

    (E) refuge

5. The "distemper" (line 32) refers to

    (A) the plague

    (B) bad feelings

    (C) anger

    (D) fear

    (E) a disease common to dogs

6. How does the narrator feel about the meat available in the city?

    (A) Only flesh meat is available.

    (B) It comes from within the city.

    (C) It is inedible.

    (D) It seems it is never infected.

    (E) It is tainted.

7. The word "sound" (line 51) is used to mean

    (A) severe

    (B) solid

    (C) clamorous

    (D) drifting

    (E) healthy

8. The last paragraph mainly discusses

    (A) the inability of the poor to protect themselves

    (B) the effects of the plague on business

    (C) symptoms of the plague

    (D) safeguards against getting the plague

    (E) doctors' advice and warnings

9. In general, the narrator believes that the plague was worsened by people's need to

(A) socialize

(B) self-medicate

(C) shop

(D) travel abroad

(E) fight

10. The narrator implies that the people worst hit were

(A) city-dwellers

(B) doctors

(C) children

(D) servants

(E) the poor

Test 3   (Answers on Page 187)

Sarah Orne Jewett was born in Maine in 1849. At the age of twenty, she published her first story, and she went on to write stories and novels about the Mainers she knew. This excerpt is from "The Hiltons' Holiday," first published in 1896.

An hour later the best wagon was ready, and the great expedition set forth. The little dog sat apart, and barked as if it fell entirely upon him to voice the general excitement. Both seats were in the wagon,
(5) but the empty place testified to Mrs. Hilton's un-yielding disposition. She had wondered why one broad seat would not do, but John Hilton meekly suggested that the wagon looked better with both. The little girls sat on the back seat dressed alike in
(10) their Sunday hats of straw with blue ribbons, and their little plaid shawls pinned neatly about their small shoulders. They wore gray thread gloves, and sat very straight. Susan Ellen was half a head the taller, but otherwise, from behind, they looked much
(15) alike. As for their father, he was in his Sunday best—a plain black coat, and a winter hat of felt, which was heavy and rusty-looking for that warm early summer day. He had it in mind to buy a new straw hat at Topham, so that this with the turnip seed
(20) and the hoe made three important reasons for going.

"Remember an' lay off your shawls when you get there, an' carry them over your arms," said the mother, clucking like an excited hen to her chick-ens. "They'll do to keep the dust off your new
(25) dresses goin' an' comin'. An' when you eat your dinners don't get spots on you, an' don't point at folks as you ride by, an' stare, or they'll know you come from the country. An' John, you call into Cousin Ad'line Marlow's an' see how they all be,
(30) an' tell her I expect her over certain to stop awhile before hayin'. It always eases her phthisic to git up here on the highland, an' I've got a new notion about doin' over her best-room carpet sense I see her

that'll save rippin' one breadth. An' don't come
(35) home all wore out; an', John, don't you go an' buy me no kick-shaws to fetch home. I ain't a child, an' you ain't got no money to waste. I expect you'll go, like's not, an' buy you some kind of a foolish boy's hat; do look an' see if it's reasonable good straw, an'
(40) won't splinter all off round the edge. An' you mind, John"—

"Yes, yes, hold on!" cried John impatiently; then he cast a last affectionate, reassuring look at her face, flushed with the hurry and responsibility of
(45) starting them off in proper shape. "I wish you was goin' too," he said, smiling. "I do so!" Then the old horse started, and they went out at the bars, and began the careful long descent of the hill. The young dog, tethered to the lilac bush, was frantic with
(50) piteous appeals; the little girls piped their eager goodbys again and again, and their father turned many times to look back and wave his hand. As for their mother, she stood alone and watched them out of sight.

(55) There was one place far out on the high-road where she could catch a last glimpse of the wagon, and she waited what seemed a very long time until it appeared and then was lost to sight again behind a low hill. "They're nothin' but a pack o' child'n
(60) together," she said aloud; and then felt lonelier than she expected. She even stooped and patted the unresigned little dog as she passed him, going into the house.

1. The words "great expedition" are used by the author

(A) literally

(B) ironically

(C) snidely

(D) cruelly

(E) matter-of-factly

2. The word "voice" (line 3) is used to mean

    (A) sing

    (B) vote

    (C) desire

    (D) call

    (E) express

3. The author's description of John's apparel

    (A) reveals his relative poverty

    (B) shows his stylishness

    (C) explains his behavior

    (D) contrasts his appearance with his character

    (E) is mean-spirited

4. The mother is compared to a hen in terms of her

    (A) brooding nature

    (B) coloration

    (C) eating habits

    (D) lazy good temper

    (E) concern over her children

5. The mother is worried that her children might

    (A) misbehave in their cousin's home

    (B) eat more than they should

    (C) be taken for hicks

    (D) both A and B

    (E) both B and C

6. The word "kick-shaws" (line 36) apparently refers to

    (A) money

    (B) something to eat

    (C) a kind of hat

    (D) odds and ends

    (E) parasols

7. The author's feeling toward her characters can be summed up as

    (A) unyielding

    (B) affectionate

    (C) uncaring

    (D) troubled

    (E) mystified

8. The tone of the final paragraph emphasizes

    (A) gratitude

    (B) remorse

    (C) dreariness

    (D) impulsiveness

    (E) isolation

Test 4   (Answers on Page 187)

Patrice Lumumba (1925–1961) was president of the Congolese National Movement and the first Prime Minister of the Congo after it achieved independence from Belgium. Amidst the unrest that followed independence, he was deposed and assassinated. This speech was given in 1959 to an audience in Brussels, Belgium.

We have capable men who are just waiting for a chance to get to work. I visited Guinea recently: there are eleven ministers in the government, and seven state secretaries who have ministerial status. (5) Only three of these eighteen ministers have studied at a university; the others have finished high school, held jobs, and acquired a certain amount of experience, and the government of Guinea has brought in French technicians to help it in the field of law, (10) economics, agronomy, and every other area of activity. So I think it is possible today to set up a Congolese government.

We have chosen January 1961 as our deadline. We thus have two years in which to prepare ourselves, (15) and we are convinced that two years from now we will be in a position to take over the responsibilities of running our country, with the Belgians working side by side with us to help us and

guide our footsteps. If Belgium understands us, if
(20) Belgium takes this fervent desire—the desire of the
Congolese people—into consideration, she will be
entitled to our friendship. The people will see for
themselves that when the proper moment came and
we decided we were capable of self-rule, the Bel-
(25) gians did not stand in our way. On the contrary: they
will have helped and guided us. The question of
future relations between Belgium and the Congo
will resolve itself automatically. There will be no
difficulty whatsoever. We are the ones to say: look,
(30) we still need Belgium in this field of endeavor, we
still need European technicians. But if the Belgian
people, the Belgian government, refuse to take our
demands into consideration, what will happen as a
result? The government perpetuates bitterness and
(35) fosters a climate of continual discontent, and whatever the Belgians may say, whatever their wishes in
the matter may be, we are going to gain our independence, come what may. In the end the Congolese
people are liable to say: "Belgium has always been
(40) opposed to our emancipation. We've had enough of
that now; we're going our own separate way...."
And that is precisely the problem. Everyone—the
financiers, the colonialists—keeps asking for guarantees. But such guarantees depend entirely on
(45) them, because winning our independence does not
mean that we are going to seize property belonging
to Belgians; we are not thieves, we respect other
people's property. It is a matter of a gentleman's
agreement with the status of an international right;
(50) when any citizen finds himself in another country,
his property and his person must be protected. This
is the problem as we see it.

So today we want our country to be independent.
We want to run our country now so that we may
(55) draw up agreements between an independent Congo
and an independent Belgium on an equal footing,
and thus foster friendship between these two peoples.
I am very happy to meet young Belgians here who
share our ideas, progressive young Belgians who
(60) agree with us, who will help press for Congolese
independence tomorrow and are joining forces with
us. This is encouraging. It proves that they are
dissatisfied, that they disapprove of the attitude of
certain Belgians in the Congo today. I do not want
(65) to make any sort of sweeping general statement:
there are Belgians in the Congo—certain civil

servants, certain colonists, certain doctors, certain
missionaries—who have always treated Africans in
a dignified way. But they are no more than a minor-
(70) ity. Why are the majority opposed? Belgians in the
Congo believe that when the blacks get their independence tomorrow, they are going to seize everything Belgians own. This is still the usual reaction
among typical Europeans, even after the new policy,
(75) even after the declaration on January 13. They keep
saying, "These are the blacks who are going to take
our places tomorrow, and where will that put *us?*
Where will we go?"

1. Lumumba brings in the example of Guinea to
   demonstrate that
   (A) colonial power can hold a country
       together
   (B) those who would govern need a back-
       ground in law
   (C) liberation from the French is possible
   (D) ministers need not be educated
   (E) an independent African government can
       exist

2. The word "fervent" (line 20) means
   (A) impassioned
   (B) maniacal
   (C) hotheaded
   (D) dispassionate
   (E) torpid

3. How does Lumumba feel about friendship with
   Belgium?
   (A) It is unlikely to come about for many
       years.
   (B) It is possible if Belgium helps the Congo.
   (C) It is not possible if Belgium opposes the
       Congolese.
   (D) both A and B
   (E) both B and C

4. Paragraph 2 moves back and forth between

   (A) humor and bitterness

   (B) pleasantries and deference

   (C) warnings and recommendations

   (D) raillery and lightheartedness

   (E) profanity and charity

5. The words "gentleman's agreement" (line 49) refer to

   (A) a deal without benefit for either side

   (B) a bargain sealed in blood

   (C) a written contract

   (D) an unspoken understanding

   (E) an oath of allegiance

6. Paragraph 3 is primarily

   (A) about young Belgians

   (B) used to contrast with paragraph 2

   (C) a specious argument

   (D) an analysis of Belgian resistance

   (E) a summation of Lumumba's main points

7. The word "press" (line 60) is used to mean

   (A) publish

   (B) constrict

   (C) push

   (D) crush

   (E) iron

8. According to Lumumba, why are Belgians afraid?

   (A) They are racist.

   (B) They think a Congolese government will imprison them.

   (C) They think the Congolese will take what they have.

   (D) both A and B

   (E) both B and C

Test 5   (Answers on Page 187)

In 1865 the naturalist Louis Agassiz, accompanied by his wife and a party of scientists and volunteers, embarked on a journey to Brazil to record information about fish and other wildlife in the rivers of that nation. Aboard ship, Agassiz talked to his assistants about the proper study of nature. As usual, his discussion was recorded by his wife.

When less was known of animals and plants the discovery of new species was the great object. This has been carried too far, and is now almost the lowest kind of scientific work. The discovery of a
(5) new species as such does not change a feature in the science of natural history, any more than the discovery of a new asteroid changes the character of the problems to be investigated by astronomers. It is merely adding to the enumeration of objects.
(10)   We should look rather for the fundamental relations among animals; the number of species we may find is of importance only so far as they explain the distribution and limitation of different genera and families, their relations to each other and to the
(15) physical conditions under which they live. Out of such investigations there looms up a deeper question for scientific men, the solution of which is to be the most important result of their work in coming generations. The origin of life is the great question
(20) of the day. How did the organic world come to be as it is? It must be our aim to throw some light on this subject by our present journey. How did Brazil come to be inhabited by the animals and plants now living there? Who were its inhabitants in past times?
(25) What reason is there to believe that the present condition of things in this country is in any sense derived from the past? The first step in this investigation must be to ascertain the geographical distribution of the present animals and plants. Suppose
(30) we first examine the Rio San Francisco. The basin of this river is entirely isolated. Are its inhabitants, like its waters, completely distinct from those of other basins? Are its species peculiar to itself, and not repeated in any other river of the continent?
(35) Extraordinary as this result would seem, I nevertheless expect to find it so. The next water-basin we

shall have to examine will be that of the Amazons, which connects through the Rio Negro with the Orinoco. It has been frequently repeated that the
(40) same species of fish exist in the waters of the San Francisco and in those of Guiana and of the Amazons. At all events, our works on fishes constantly indicate Brazil and Guiana as the common home of many species; but this observation has never been
(45) made with sufficient accuracy to merit confidence. Fifty years ago the exact locality from which any animal came seemed an unimportant fact in its scientific history, for the bearing of this question on that of origin was not then perceived. To say that any
(50) specimen came from South America was quite enough; to specify that it came from Brazil, from the Amazons, the San Francisco, or the La Plata, seemed a marvellous accuracy in the observers. In the museum at Paris, for instance, there are many speci-
(55) mens entered as coming from New York or from Pará; but all that is absolutely known about them is that they were shipped from those sea-ports. Nobody knows exactly where they were collected. So there are specimens entered as coming from the Rio
(60) San Francisco, but it is by no means sure that they came exclusively from that water-basin. All this kind of investigation is far too loose for our present object. Our work must be done with much more precision; it must tell something positive of the
(65) geographical distribution of animals in Brazil.

Therefore, my young friends who come with me on this expedition, let us be careful that every specimen has a label, recording locality and date, so secured that it will reach Cambridge safely. It would
(70) be still better to attach two labels to each specimen, so that, if any mischance happens to one, our record may not be lost. We must try not to mix the fishes of different rivers, even though they flow into each other, but to keep our collections perfectly distinct.
(75) You will easily see the vast importance of thus ascertaining the limitation of species, and the bearing of the result on the great question of origin.

1. How does Agassiz feel about the discovery of new species?
   (A) It is taking place less and less.
   (B) All species have now been cataloged.
   (C) It cannot take the place of true science.
   (D) It is the great goal of science.
   (E) It is no longer particularly important.

2. Agassiz wants to focus upon
   (A) the enumeration of animals and plants
   (B) the interrelationships of species
   (C) a scientific study of man
   (D) both A and B
   (E) both B and C

3. The word "genera" (line 13) refers to
   (A) classifications
   (B) brain power
   (C) plants
   (D) habits
   (E) people

4. Agassiz sees his future work as answering the question
   (A) "Can we learn from history?"
   (B) "Is there a God?"
   (C) "How many species are there?"
   (D) "Where did man come from?"
   (E) "How did life originate?"

5. The word "distribution" (line 28) is used to mean
   (A) shipping
   (B) dispersion
   (C) donation
   (D) offering
   (E) quality

6. How might you paraphrase the sentence "Are its inhabitants … from those of other basins" (lines 31–32)?
   (A) Do the animals here resemble the water?
   (B) Do the inhabitants of this basin ever visit other basins?
   (C) Can we distinguish the animals of these waters from each other?
   (D) Since these waters differ from others, are the animals found here different as well?
   (E) Can we tell the difference between this basin and another?

7. The word "common" (line 43) is used to mean
   (A) familiar
   (B) collective
   (C) provincial
   (D) typical
   (E) unremarkable

8. Agassiz uses the phrase "a marvellous accuracy" (line 53) to
   (A) show how unlikely it was for observers to be so specific
   (B) give his opinion about the current generation of scientists
   (C) make a heartfelt plea for understanding
   (D) both A and B
   (E) both B and C

9. Agassiz urges his young colleagues to be
   (A) prudent
   (B) daring
   (C) meticulous
   (D) curious
   (E) adventurous

10. By "perfectly distinct" (line 74) Agassiz means that the collections should be
    (A) wholly dissimilar
    (B) flawlessly obvious
    (C) completely lucid
    (D) absolutely separate
    (E) quite clear

LEVEL C CRITICAL READING

Each pair of passages below is followed by a series of questions that require you to analyze, interpret, evaluate, compare, and contrast the written works. Answer these questions on the basis of what each passage states or implies. Circle the letter that appears before your answer.

Test 1   (Answers on Page 187)

The emancipation of African-Americans and the emancipation of women were two entwined issues of the mid-nineteenth century. These excerpts from an autobiographical letter by a former slave and from a speech by a leader in the fight for women's rights show that they shared a common foe.

Passage A—James L. Bradley, former slave (1835)

I will begin as far back as I can remember. I think I was between two and three years old when the soul-destroyers tore me from my mother's arms, somewhere in Africa, far back from the sea. They carried
(5) me a long distance to a ship; all the way I looked back, and cried. The ship was full of men and women loaded with chains; but I was so small, they let me run about on deck.

After many long days, they brought us into
(10) Charleston, South Carolina. A slaveholder bought me, and took me up into Pendleton County. I suppose that I staid with him about six months. He sold

me to a Mr. Bradley, by whose name I have ever since been called. This man was considered a won-
(15) derfully kind master; and it is true that I was treated better than most of the slaves I knew. I never suffered for food, and never was flogged with the whip; but oh, my soul! I was tormented with kicks and knocks more than I can tell. My master often
(20) knocked me down, when I was young. Once, when I was a boy, about nine years old, he struck me so hard that I fell down and lost my senses. I remained thus some time, and when I came to myself, he told me he thought he had killed me. At another time, he
(25) struck me with a currycomb, and sunk the knob into my head....

I used to work very hard. I was always obliged to be in the field by sunrise, and I labored till dark, stopping only at noon long enough to eat dinner.
(30) When I was about fifteen years old, I took what was called the cold plague, in consequence of being over-worked, and I was sick a long time. My master came to me one day, and hearing me groan with

pain, he said, "This fellow will never be of any more
(35) use to me—I would as soon knock him in the head, as if he were an opossum." … My master had kept me ignorant of everything he could. I was never told anything about God, or my own soul. Yet from the time I was fourteen years old, I used to think a great
(40) deal about freedom. It was my heart's desire; I could not keep it out of my mind. Many a sleepless night I have spent in tears, because I was a slave. I looked back on all I had suffered—and when I looked ahead, all was dark and hopeless bondage. My heart
(45) ached to feel within me the life of liberty.

Passage B—Elizabeth Cady Stanton, from "Address to the Legislature of New York on Women's Rights" (1854)

Look at the position of woman as mother. There is no human love so strong and steadfast as that of the mother for her child; yet behold how ruthless are your laws touching this most sacred relation. Nature
(50) has clearly made the mother the guardian of the child; but man, in his inordinate love of power, does continually set nature and nature's laws at open defiance. The father may apprentice his child, bind him out to a trade, without the mother's consent—
(55) yea, in direct opposition to her most earnest entreaties, prayers and tears.…

Again, as the condition of the child always follows that of the mother, and as by the sanction of your laws the father may beat the mother, so may he
(60) the child. What mother can not bear me witness to untold sufferings which cruel, vindictive fathers have visited upon their helpless children? Who ever saw a human being that would not abuse unlimited power? Base and ignoble must that man be who, let
(65) the provocation be what it may, would strike a woman; but he who would lacerate a trembling child is unworthy the name of man. A mother's love can be no protection to a child; she can not appeal to you to save it from a father's cruelty, for the laws
(70) take no cognizance of the mother's most grievous wrongs. Neither at home nor abroad can a mother protect her son. Look at the temptations that surround the paths of our youth at every step; look at the gambling and drinking saloons, the clubrooms, the
(75) dens of infamy and abomination that infest all our villages and cities—slowly but surely sapping the very foundations of all virtue and strength.

By your laws, all these abominable resorts are permitted. It is folly to talk of a mother moulding the
(80) character of her son, when all mankind, backed up by law and public sentiment, conspire to destroy her influence. But when women's moral power shall speak through the ballot-box, then shall her influence be seen and felt.…

1. By "soul-destroyers" (Passage A, line 3), Bradley apparently refers to
   (A) religious zealots
   (B) white women
   (C) slaves
   (D) Africans
   (E) slave traders

2. How does Bradley feel about his master, Mr. Bradley?
   (A) He was a wonderfully kind master.
   (B) He treated Bradley well.
   (C) He was not as kind as people thought.
   (D) He was no better than a slave.
   (E) He got along with him well.

3. Why did Bradley's "heart ache" (line 45)?
   (A) He was homesick.
   (B) He wanted a friend.
   (C) He was dreadfully ill.
   (D) He was treated badly.
   (E) He longed for freedom.

4. In Passage B, what does "steadfast" mean (line 47)?
   (A) Rapid
   (B) True
   (C) Habitual
   (D) Frequent
   (E) Vacillating

5. The word "sanction" (Passage B, line 58) means
   (A) permission
   (B) devoutness
   (C) lucidity
   (D) rank
   (E) eloquence

6. Stanton uses the word "infest" (line 75) to imply that

(A) our country is overrun with domineering men

(B) power is slowly changing hands

(C) drinking causes disease

(D) immorality is a kind of creeping plague

(E) the atmosphere of cities is festive

7. Bradley would probably agree with Stanton that

(A) a man who strikes a child is unworthy

(B) gambling and drinking sap one's strength

(C) moral power can speak through the ballot-box

(D) both A and B

(E) both B and C

8. Stanton's main point seems to be that

(A) laws pit mother against child

(B) sons will always follow their fathers' paths

(C) laws remove a mother's right to protect her child

(D) a mother's influence on her sons is unimportant

(E) few can argue with laws that protect children

9. A quotation from Passage B that might apply to Passage A is

(A) "Who ever saw a human being that would not abuse unlimited power?"

(B) "Neither at home nor abroad can a mother protect her son."

(C) "Look at the temptations that surround the paths of our youth at every step...."

(D) both A and B

(E) both B and C

10. As Bradley's master kept him ignorant of God, so

(A) might a father apprentice his child to a master

(B) does a mother remain ignorant of her child's welfare

(C) is a mother witness to sufferings of her child

(D) can parents keep their children home from school

(E) can a father keep his son ignorant of morality

Test 2   (Answers on Page 187)

All cultures teach an element of respect for the elderly and sick, and nearly all cultures present moralistic tales to stress this lesson. Here are two very different tales, one from the Indians of the Northeast and one from the Hispanic Southwest.

Passage A—"An Unwelcome Visitor," a legend of the Iroquois

When the frosts were unlocked from the hillsides there came into one of the villages of the red men a mild and quiet old man whom none of them had ever seen before. He stood beside the field where the
(5) young men played at their games, and when some of the fathers approached to bid him welcome to their village and wigwams they saw that his body was covered with sores, and they made excuses to turn aside that they might not meet him. When none went
(10) to him and called him brother, he turned to the village and walked slowly from door to door of the wigwams. The women saw him and as he approached their doors they covered their children's faces that they might not see his features, and
(15) wished in their hearts that he would not enter. When the little man read their thoughts, with saddened eyes and heavy steps he would turn away and seek another habitation, where he would again see that he was not welcome and turn his weary footsteps from
(20) the door. When he had visited all the wigwams in the village without finding a welcome in any, he went suddenly to the forest and they saw him no more....

Finally there remained but two more villages to visit and he feared that he should find none who

(25) would bid him enter their homes that they might minister to his wants. At last, however, as he approached a humble cabin his eyes brightened, for he read in the heart of the woman who saw him coming that she had taken pity on his forlorn condition and
(30) that her hospitality would overcome the dread his appearance caused. Said the woman: "Thou art welcome, my brother, for thou art a stranger."

Then said the strange man: ... "Listen, my sister: Thou of all thy race hast had in thy heart pity and
(35) love for a suffering and friendless creature that have led thee to give him shelter in thy house. Know then, my sister, that thy name shall henceforth be great. Many wonders shall be taught thee, and thy sons will be made chiefs and thy daughters princesses. I
(40) am Quarara, and bear messages from the Great Spirit." Then Quarara described to the woman a plant which she went forth into the forest and procured. She returned to the hut and prepared it as he bade her, and when it was administered to him he
(45) recovered from his sickness and the sores left him. Quarara remained at the woman's wigwam many moons and brought upon himself all manner of fevers, plagues and diseases, and for each one he described the medicine root or herb that would
(50) perform its cure.…

Then said the strange man, Quarara, to her: "Thou, Oh! sister, knowest now what the Great Spirit would have thee teach his children freely. Thou hast been patient and kind and thy heart is
(55) filled with gentleness. The sons that shall be born to thee shall be called Sagawahs, the healers, and thou and thy family shall be remembered throughout all generations."

Passage B—"The Boy and His Grandfather," a tale of the Hispanic Southwest

In the old days it was not unusual to find several
(60) generations living together in one home. Usually, everyone lived in peace and harmony, but this situation caused problems for one man whose household included, besides his wife and small son, his elderly father.
(65) It so happened that the daughter-in-law took a dislike to the old man. He was always in the way, she said, and she insisted he be removed to a small room apart from the house.

Because the old man was out of sight, he was
(70) often neglected. Sometimes he even went hungry.

They took poor care of him, and in winter the old man often suffered from the cold. One day the little grandson visited his grandfather.

"My little one," the grandfather said, "go and
(75) find a blanket and cover me. It is cold and I am freezing."

The small boy ran to the barn to look for a blanket, and there he found a rug.

"Father, please cut this rug in half," he asked his
(80) father.

"Why? What are you going to do with it?"

"I'm going to take it to my grandfather because he is cold."

"Well, take the entire rug," replied his father.

(85) "No," his son answered, "I cannot take it all. I want you to cut it in half so I can save the other half for you when you are as old as my grandfather. Then I will have it for you so you will not be cold."

His son's response was enough to make the man
(90) realize how poorly he had treated his own father. The man then brought his father back into his home and ordered that a warm room be prepared. From that time on he took care of his father's needs and visited him frequently every day.

1. What is it that keeps the villagers from greeting the old man in Passage A?

   (A) He is a stranger.

   (B) He is old.

   (C) He is covered with sores.

   (D) They are unfriendly.

   (E) They fear attack.

2. The word "minister" (Passage A, line 26) is used to mean

   (A) mind

   (B) tend

   (C) assemble

   (D) preach

   (E) negotiate

3. The word "great" (line 37) is used to mean

   (A) excellent

   (B) prodigious

   (C) weighty

   (D) exalted

   (E) spacious

4. The word "procured" (line 43) means

   (A) obtained

   (B) captured

   (C) dried

   (D) restored

   (E) healed

5. The words "many moons" (line 47) refer to

   (A) people's faces

   (B) the name of a place

   (C) a measure of size

   (D) a length of time

   (E) a strange natural occurrence

6. The last paragraph of Passage A could be called a(n)

   (A) repetition

   (B) fantasy

   (C) oath

   (D) summary

   (E) blessing

7. Quarara turns the woman and her children into

   (A) toads

   (B) chiefs

   (C) a new race

   (D) medicine men and women

   (E) ministers

8. By "several generations" (Passage B, lines 59-60), the author means

   (A) many years

   (B) separate lifetimes

   (C) children, parents, and grandparents

   (D) several breeding periods

   (E) more than one beginning

9. One difference between Passage A and Passage B is that

   (A) Passage A takes place in the past

   (B) people in Passage B ignore an old man

   (C) people in Passage A ignore an old man

   (D) Passage A deals with illness as well as age

   (E) Passage B has no moral

10. The woman in Passage A and the man in Passage B learn that

    (A) illness is not a crime

    (B) respecting one's elders can be beneficial

    (C) children may understand more than adults

    (D) both A and B

    (E) both B and C

LEVEL D CRITICAL READING

Each passage or pair of passages below is followed by a series of questions that require you to analyze, interpret, evaluate, compare, and contrast the written works. Answer these questions on the basis of what each passage states or implies. Circle the letter that appears before your answer.

Test 1   (Answers on Page 187)

In 1869, naturalist John Muir spent the summer in the Sierra Mountains. Muir, who would become the foremost conservationist in the country, had just moved to California, and this was the first of hundreds of trips he would take to the Sierra. He recorded his sights and impressions in a diary, from which this passage is excerpted.

Sugar pine cones are cylindrical, slightly tapered at the end and rounded at the base. Found one today nearly twenty-four inches long and six in diameter, the scales being open. Another specimen nineteen

(5) inches long; the average length of full-grown cones on trees favorably situated is nearly eighteen inches. On the lower edge of the belt at a height of about

twenty-five hundred feet above the sea they are smaller, say a foot to fifteen inches long, and at a
(10) height of seven thousand feet or more near the upper limits of its growth in the Yosemite region they are about the same size. This noble tree is an inexhaustible study and source of pleasure. I never weary of gazing at its grand tassel cones, its perfectly round
(15) bole one hundred feet or more without a limb, the fine purplish color of its bark, and its magnificent outsweeping, down-curving feathery arms forming a crown always bold and striking and exhilarating. In habit and general port it looks somewhat like a
(20) palm, but no palm that I have seen yet displays such majesty of form and behavior either when poised silent and thoughtful in sunshine, or wide-awake waving in storm winds with every needle quivering. When young it is very straight and regular in form
(25) like most other conifers; but at the age of fifty to one hundred years it begins to acquire individuality, so that no two are alike in their prime or old age. Every tree calls for special admiration. I have been making many sketches, and regret that I cannot draw every
(30) needle. It is said to reach a height of three hundred feet, though the tallest I have measured falls short of this stature sixty feet or more. The diameter of the largest near the ground is about ten feet, though I've heard of some twelve feet thick or even fifteen. The
(35) diameter is held to a great height, the taper being almost imperceptibly gradual. Its companion, the yellow pine, is almost as large. The long silvery foliage of the younger specimens forms magnificent cylindrical brushes on the top shoots and the
(40) ends of the upturned branches, and when the wind sways the needles all one way at a certain angle every tree becomes a tower of white quivering sun-fire. Well may this shining species be called the silver pine. The needles are sometimes more than a
(45) foot long, almost as long as those of the long-leaf pine of Florida.

1. The word "scales" (line 4) is used to mean
   (A) measures
   (B) weights
   (C) scrapings
   (D) husks
   (E) balances

2. By "favorably situated" (line 6), Muir probably means
   (A) in an approved site
   (B) positioned pleasantly
   (C) newly planted
   (D) far from the sea
   (E) having suitable sun and water

3. The word "bole" (line 15) means
   (A) trunk
   (B) top
   (C) tree
   (D) leaf
   (E) branch

4. By "general port" (line 19), Muir means
   (A) a place where ships dock
   (B) the manner in which one bears oneself
   (C) placement to the left
   (D) an opening for intake
   (E) a hole for firing weapons

5. In comparing the pine to a palm, Muir
   (A) finds the pine less majestic
   (B) finds the palm less majestic
   (C) assigns the pine human characteristics
   (D) both A and B
   (E) both B and C

6. In his description, Muir includes the pine's
   (A) height and thickness
   (B) coloration
   (C) planting time
   (D) both A and B
   (E) both B and C

7. Which of the following would be a good title for this passage?
   (A) "Sugar from the Pine"
   (B) "A Noble Tree"
   (C) "The Trees of the Sierra"
   (D) "Comparing Pines and Firs"
   (E) "The Yellow Pine"

8. Muir's attitude toward the pine might almost be called

    (A) deferential

    (B) daunted

    (C) imperious

    (D) contrite

    (E) charitable

In many cultures, the wealthy hired servants or kept slaves to take care of their children. These two narratives, one the true story of an ex-slave and one a work of fiction by a Nobel Prize-winning Indian writer, tell of children's occasional inexplicable cruelty toward the class that raised them.

Passage A—from the Narrative of James Curry, former slave (1840)

My mother was cook in the house for about twenty-two years. She cooked for from twenty-five to thirty-five, taking the family and the slaves to-gether. The slaves ate in the kitchen. After my
(5) mistress's death, my mother was the only woman kept in the house. She took care of my master's children, some of whom were then quite small, and brought them up. One of the most trying scenes I ever passed through, when I would have laid down
(10) my life to protect her if I had dared, was this: after she had raised my master's children, one of his daughters, a young girl, came into the kitchen one day, and for some trifle about the dinner, she struck my mother, who pushed her away, and she fell on
(15) the floor. Her father was not at home. When he came, which was while the slaves were eating in the kitchen, she told him about it. He came down, called my mother out, and, with a hickory rod, he beat her fifteen or twenty strokes, and then called his
(20) daughter and told her to take her satisfaction of her, and she did beat her until she was satisfied. Oh! it was dreadful, to see the girl whom my poor mother had taken care of from her childhood, thus beating her, and I must stand there, and did not dare to crook
(25) my finger in her defence.

Passage B—from "My Lord, the Baby" by Rabindranath Tagore (1916)

Raicharan was twelve years old when he came as a servant to his master's house. He belonged to the same caste as his master, and was given his master's
little son to nurse. As time went on the boy left
(30) Raicharan's arms to go to school. From school he went on to college, and after college he entered the judicial service. Always, until he married, Raicharan was his sole attendant.

But, when a mistress came into the house,
(35) Raicharan found two masters instead of one. All his former influence passed to the new mistress. This was compensated for by a fresh arrival. Anukul had a son born to him, and Raicharan by his unsparing attentions soon got a complete hold over the child.
(40) He used to toss him up in his arms, call to him in absurd baby language, put his face close to the baby's and draw it away again with a grin.

Presently the baby was able to crawl and cross the doorway. When Raicharan went to catch him, he
(45) would scream with mischievous laughter and make for safety. Raicharan was amazed at the profound skill and exact judgment the baby showed when pursued. He would say to his mistress with a look of awe and mystery: "Your son will be a judge some-
(50) day."

New wonders came in their turn. When the baby began to toddle, that was to Raicharan an epoch in human history. When he called his father Ba-ba and his mother Ma-ma and Raicharan Chan-na, then
(55) Raicharan's ecstasy knew no bounds. He went out to tell the news to all the world....

One afternoon the rain cleared. It was cloudy, but cool and bright. Raicharan's little despot did not want to stay in on such a fine afternoon. His lordship
(60) climbed into the go-cart. Raicharan, between the shafts, dragged him slowly along till he reached the rice-fields on the banks of the river. There was no one in the fields, and no boat on the stream. Across the water, on the farther side, the clouds were rifted
(65) in the west. The silent ceremonial of the setting sun was revealed in all its glowing splendor. In the midst of that stillness the child, all of a sudden, pointed with his finger in front of him and cried: "Chan-na! Pitty fow."
(70) Close by on a mud-flat stood a large *Kadamba* tree in full flower. My lord, the baby, looked at it with greedy eyes, and Raicharan knew his mean-ing.... But Raicharan had no wish that evening to go splashing knee-deep through the mud to reach
(75) the flowers. So he quickly pointed his finger in the opposite direction, calling out: "Oh, look, baby, look! Look at the bird." And with all sorts of curious

noises he pushed the go-cart rapidly away from the tree. But a child, destined to be a judge, cannot be
(80) put off so easily…. The little Master's mind was made up, and Raicharan was at his wits' end. "Very well, baby," he said at last, "you sit still in the cart, and I'll go and get you the pretty flower. Only mind you don't go near the water."
(85)   As he said this, he made his legs bare to the knee, and waded through the oozing mud toward the tree.

9. The numbers "twenty-five to thirty-five" (Passage A, lines 2–3) refer to
   (A) the age Curry's mother was when she was cook
   (B) the number of people Curry's mother cooked for
   (C) the years during which Curry's mother cooked
   (D) a system of measurement now obsolete
   (E) the number of consecutive hours Curry's mother worked without a break

10. The word "trying" (line 8) means
   (A) daring
   (B) troublesome
   (C) secure
   (D) binding
   (E) elementary

11. The word "trifle" (line 13) means
   (A) knickknack
   (B) jest
   (C) unimportant thing
   (D) trace
   (E) toy

12. By "take her satisfaction of her" (line 20), Curry means
   (A) please her
   (B) punish her until content
   (C) give her trinkets
   (D) show her the correct way
   (E) pacify her

13. The best description of Curry's feelings at this scene might be
   (A) apathy
   (B) helplessness
   (C) horror
   (D) both A and B
   (E) both B and C

14. In Passage B, the word "caste" (line 28) means
   (A) job
   (B) performance
   (C) company
   (D) post
   (E) class

15. The tone of paragraph 4, Passage B, is
   (A) ironic
   (B) dark
   (C) foreshadowing
   (D) both A and B
   (E) both B and C

16. The word "despot" (line 58) means
   (A) terminal
   (B) arsenal
   (C) repository
   (D) outrage
   (E) slave driver

17. In paragraph 5, it becomes clear that the author thinks the child is
   (A) tyrannical and spoiled
   (B) sweet and innocent
   (C) loud and witless
   (D) loving but foolish
   (E) amusingly gregarious

18. The word "mind" (line 83) is used to mean
   (A) consider
   (B) reason
   (C) take care
   (D) follow
   (E) sense

19. Like Passage A, Passage B tells of

    (A) a cook who becomes a child's nurse

    (B) a man living as a house servant

    (C) the early life of a slave

    (D) inhuman conditions under colonialism

    (E) a child's cruelty to a caretaker

20. Unlike the main character in Passage A, the one in Passage B

    (A) seems to enjoy his job

    (B) takes care of girls and boys

    (C) does not earn a salary

    (D) both A and B

    (E) both B and C

Test 2   (Answers on Page 188)

William Hazlitt (1778–1830) was an essayist and literary critic known for his studies of the romantic poets and Elizabethan playwrights. This passage is from an essay entitled "On Familiar Style," first published in 1821.

It is not easy to write a familiar style. Many people mistake a familiar for a vulgar style, and suppose that to write without affectation is to write at random. On the contrary, there is nothing that requires
(5) more precision, and, if I may so say, purity of expression, than the style I am speaking of. It utterly rejects not only all unmeaning pomp, but all low, cant phrases, and loose, unconnected, *slipshod* allusions. It is not to take the first word that offers, but
(10) the best word in common use; it is not to throw words together in any combinations we please, but to follow and avail ourselves of the true idiom of the language. To write a genuine familiar or truly English style, is to write as any one would speak in
(15) common conversation, who had a thorough command and choice of words, or who could discourse with ease, force, and perspicuity, setting aside all pedantic and oratorical flourishes. Or to give another illustration, to write naturally is the same thing
(20) in regard to common conversation, as to read naturally is in regard to common speech. It does not follow that it is an easy thing to give the true accent and inflection to the words you utter, because you do not attempt to rise above the level of ordinary life
(25) and colloquial speaking. You do not assume indeed the solemnity of the pulpit, or the tone of stage-declamation: neither are you at liberty to gabble on at a venture, without emphasis or discretion, or to resort to vulgar dialect or clownish pronunciation.
(30) You must steer a middle course. You are tied down to a given and appropriate articulation, which is determined by the habitual associations between sense and sound, and which you can only hit by

entering into the author's meaning, as you must find
(35) the proper words and style to express yourself by fixing your thoughts on the subject you have to write about. Any one may mouth out a passage with a theatrical cadence, or get upon stilts to tell his thoughts: but to write or speak with propriety and
(40) simplicity is a more difficult task. Thus it is easy to affect a pompous style, to use a word twice as big as the thing you wish to express: it is not so easy to pitch upon the very word that exactly fits it. Out of eight or ten words equally common, equally intelli-
(45) gible, with nearly equal pretensions, it is a matter of some nicety and discrimination to pick out the very one, the preferableness of which is scarcely perceptible, but decisive.

1. By "familiar" (line 1), Hazlitt means

    (A) public

    (B) accepted

    (C) informal

    (D) well-known

    (E) famous

2. By "purity of expression" (line 5), Hazlitt means

    (A) sweet face

    (B) religious speech

    (C) innocent statements

    (D) pious manner

    (E) clear wording

3. The word "cant" (line 8) means

    (A) tilted

    (B) inclined

    (C) sung

    (D) jargonistic

    (E) negative

4. Hazlitt compares writing a familiar style to

   (A) ascending a pulpit

   (B) wearing an old shoe

   (C) writing a letter

   (D) writing in a journal

   (E) speaking naturally

5. The word "perspicuity" (line 17) means

   (A) clarity

   (B) stuffiness

   (C) pedantry

   (D) insensitivity

   (E) sweat

6. The word "colloquial" (line 25) means

   (A) oratorical

   (B) pleasant

   (C) worldly

   (D) religious

   (E) everyday

7. Hazlitt believes that a writer must "steer a middle course" (line 30) between

   (A) familiar and unfamiliar

   (B) theatrics and bombast

   (C) clowning and sobriety

   (D) vulgarity and pomposity

   (E) discrimination and judgment

8. The general tone of this passage is

   (A) disdainful

   (B) reverent

   (C) scholarly

   (D) witty

   (E) pompous

9. How might you paraphrase Hazlitt's final sentence?

   (A) Common, everyday words may be pretentious, but it is nice to choose the correct one.

   (B) Common language is often discriminated against, but a writer should be decisive when choosing it.

   (C) It hardly matters which word you choose when all your choices have similar meanings and usages.

   (D) Judgment will help you decide whether to use a common word or one with more pretensions.

   (E) Choosing the word with the precise shade of meaning you desire is difficult but indispensable.

10. Hazlitt's main idea seems to be that

    (A) writing in a familiar style is harder than it looks

    (B) it is easier to write familiarly than vulgarly

    (C) the common touch should be used only with commoners

    (D) familiar language is only appropriate on certain occasions

    (E) an author must be consistent in style and tone

Throughout history, people have found themselves at the mercy of unyielding rulers to whom they have had to beg for mercy. The letters below were written perhaps 1800 years apart, yet each is a heartfelt plea to a man in a position of power.

Passage A—from Agrippina to her son, the emperor Nero, responding to charges of treason

Don't you know, my son, the affection all mothers naturally bear their children? Our love is unbounded, incessantly fed by that tenderness unknown to all but ourselves. Nothing should be more dear to us
(5)   than what we have bought with the risk of our lives; nothing more precious than what we have endured such grief and pain to procure. These are so acute and unbearable that if it were not for the vision of a successful birth, which makes us forget our agonies,
(10)   generation would soon cease.

Do you forget that nine full months I carried you in my womb and nourished you with my blood? How likely is it, then, that I would destroy the dear child who cost me so much anguish to bring into the
(15)   world? It may be that the just gods were angry at my excessive love of you, and used this way to punish me.

Unhappy Agrippina! You are suspected of a crime of which nobody could really think you
(20)   guilty.… What does the title of empress mean to me, if I am accused of a crime that even the basest of women would abhor? Unhappy are those who breathe the air of the court. The wisest of people are not secure from storms in that harbor. There even a calm
(25)   is dangerous. But why blame the court? Can that be the cause of my being suspected of parricide?…

Tell me, why should I plot against your life? To plunge myself into a worse fate? That's not likely. What hopes could induce me to build upon your
(30)   downfall? I know that the lust for empire often corrupts the laws of nature; that justice has no sword to punish those who offend in this way; and that ambition disregards wrong so long as it succeeds in its aim.… Nay, to what deity could I turn for
(35)   absolution after I had committed so black a deed?…

What difficulties have I not surmounted to crown your brow with laurels? But I insult your gratitude by reminding you of my services. My innocence ought not to defend itself but to rely wholly on your
(40)   justice.

Farewell

Passage B—from Elizabeth Barrett Browning to Napoleon III, pleading for mercy for a fellow artist

Sire,

I am only a woman and have no claim on your Majesty's attention except that of the weakest on the strongest. Probably my very name as the wife of an
(45)   English poet and as named itself a little among English poets, is unknown to your Majesty. I never approached my own sovereign with a petition, nor am skilled in the way of addressing kings. Yet having, through a studious and thoughtful life, grown
(50)   used to great men (among the Dead at least) I cannot feel entirely at a loss in speaking to the Emperor Napoleon.

And I beseech you to have patience with me while I supplicate you. It is not for myself nor for
(55)   mine.

I have been reading with wet eyes and a swelling heart (as many who love and some who hate your Majesty have lately done) a book called the 'Contemplations' of a man who has sinned deeply against
(60)   you in certain of his political writings, and who expiates rash phrases and unjustifiable statements in exile in Jersey. I have no personal knowledge of this man; I never saw his face; and certainly I do not come now to make his apology. It is indeed pre-
(65)   cisely because he cannot be excused, that, I think, he might worthily be forgiven. For this man, whatever else he is not, is a great poet of France, and the Emperor who is the guardian of her other glories should remember him and not leave him out.

(70)   Ah sire, what was written on "Napoleon le petit" does not touch your Majesty; but what touches you is, that no historian of the age should have to write hereafter, "While Napoleon the Third reigned Victor Hugo lived in exile." What touches you is, that
(75)   when your people count gratefully the men of commerce, arms and science secured by you to France, no voice shall murmur, "But where is our poet?" … What touches you is, that when your own beloved young prince shall come to read these poems (and
(80)   when you wish him a princely nature, you wish, sire, that such things should move him) he may exult to recall that his imperial father was great enough to overcome this great poet with magnanimity.…

I am driven by an irresistible impulse to your
(85)   Majesty's feet to ask this grace. It is a woman's

voice, Sire, which dares to utter what many yearn for in silence. I have believed in Napoleon the Third. Passionately loving the democracy, I have under-stood from the beginning that it was to be served *(90)* throughout Europe in you and by you. I have trusted you for doing greatly. I will trust you besides for pardoning nobly. You will be Napoleon in this also.

Elizabeth Barrett Browning

11. Agrippina's first two paragraphs (Passage A) appeal to Nero's

    (A) remembrance of his youth

    (B) power as a leader

    (C) love of women

    (D) belief in the gods

    (E) filial feelings

12. "Storms in that harbor" (line 24) is a metaphor referring to

    (A) tempests in teapots

    (B) political upheavals at court

    (C) adventurers in government

    (D) pirates at sea

    (E) Nero's early life as a sailor

13. When she says that "ambition disregards wrong" (line 33), Agrippina means that

    (A) it is right to grasp power

    (B) excessive ambition is wrong

    (C) ambitious people commit crimes

    (D) wickedness comes with rank

    (E) few kings are kind

14. Agrippina's final paragraph hints at her

    (A) desire for the crown

    (B) dislike of the present queen

    (C) gratitude toward Nero

    (D) trust in the gods

    (E) manipulation of Nero's career

15. When Browning claims to be "used to great men" (Passage B, line 50), she means that she

    (A) has studied heroic lives

    (B) knows a great many kings

    (C) has been ill-used by her sovereign

    (D) grew up in a famous house

    (E) has a famous husband

16. The word "supplicate" (line 54) means

    (A) astound

    (B) consume

    (C) petition

    (D) render

    (E) depose

17. Browning suggests the Emperor should forgive Hugo because

    (A) his crime is not great

    (B) she knows him personally

    (C) no one deserves exile

    (D) he is a great French poet

    (E) his deed is excusable

18. The word "touch" as it is used throughout paragraph 4, Passage B, means

    (A) caress

    (B) meet

    (C) affect

    (D) move

    (E) feel

19. Unlike Browning, Agrippina is pleading

    (A) for mercy

    (B) for her own life

    (C) for a greater cause

    (D) both A and B

    (E) both B and C

20. Unlike Agrippina, Browning

    (A) admits her own weakness

    (B) apologizes

    (C) denies the crime

    (D) both A and B

    (E) both B and C

Answer Key

For explanations see page 189.

LEVEL A

TEST 1

1. C	4. E	7. B
2. A	5. B	8. C
3. D	6. E	

TEST 2

1. C	4. C	7. A
2. E	5. B	8. C
3. E	6. E	

TEST 3

1. A	4. D	7. B	10. C
2. D	5. A	8. E	
3. C	6. D	9. D	

TEST 4

1. A	4. B	7. D	10. B
2. C	5. D	8. B	
3. E	6. B	9. C	

TEST 5

1. D	4. B	7. A	10. C
2. D	5. A	8. B	
3. A	6. E	9. D	

LEVEL B

TEST 1

1. A	4. E	7. B
2. D	5. D	8. C
3. A	6. C	

TEST 2

1. B	4. E	7. E	10. E
2. D	5. A	8. D	
3. A	6. E	9. C	

TEST 3

1. B	4. E	7. B
2. E	5. C	8. E
3. A	6. D	

TEST 4

1. E	4. C	7. C
2. A	5. D	8. C
3. E	6. E	

TEST 5

1. E	4. E	7. B	10. D
2. B	5. B	8. A	
3. A	6. D	9. C	

LEVEL   C

TEST 1

1. E	4. B	7. A	10. E
2. C	5. A	8. C	
3. E	6. D	9. D	

TEST 2

1. C	4. A	7. D	10. B
2. B	5. D	8. C	
3. D	6. E	9. D	

LEVEL   D

TEST 1

1. D	5. E	9. B	13. E	17. A
2. E	6. D	10. B	14. E	18. C
3. A	7. B	11. C	15. A	19. E
4. B	8. A	12. B	16. E	20. A

TEST 2

1. C		5. A		9. E		13. C		17. D
2. E		6. E		10. A		14. E		18. C
3. D		7. D		11. E		15. A		19. B
4. E		8. D		12. B		16. C		20. A

Explanatory Answers

LEVEL A

TEST 1

1. **(C)** This passage is quite literal. Lincoln has crossed Washington, which lay between his starting point and his destination.

2. **(A)** Lincoln has come to "judge for his own wise and noble self" (line 7), for which the author is thankful.

3. **(D)** Any of these choices could be a synonym for *glass,* but only one fits the context.

4. **(E)** Again, the line is quite literal. McClellan is arriving by hot-air balloon.

5. **(B)** The author specifically explains this in line 32.

6. **(E)** Plugging the choices into the context of the sentence will prove that only (E) is an exact translation.

7. **(B)** The context gives this away, even if you have never seen the word before.

8. **(C)** The last sentence of the excerpt contrasts these strangely peaceful cannon salutes to the terrible sounds "to which we are accustomed."

TEST 2

1. **(C)** Bulfinch assigns Orion two potential powers—wading through the depths and walking on the water. He appears to prefer the former, but acknowledges that some say the latter—presumably other translators.

2. **(E)** *Booty,* or *loot,* makes sense in context.

3. **(E)** *Chid* is an archaic word, but none of the other choices expresses the annoyance that Diana's brother apparently feels.

4. **(C)** If you do not understand this, you might be guilty of making the same mistake Diana made.

5. **(B)** To "discharge a shaft" is to shoot an arrow.

6. **(E)** Each choice is either a synonym for *train* or something of which a train might be a part, but only *entourage* names something of which the sisters could logically be constituent.

7. **(A)** The first three paragraphs deal with the life of Orion and his death and resurrection in constellation form. The last tells about the formation of the Pleiads.

8. **(C)** Most myths explain natural phenomena, and this one is no exception. It does not teach a lesson (A), and it mentions only a few Greek gods (B).

TEST 3

1. **(A)** He does not say exactly this, but he does say it is *peculiar* (line 2), an exact synonym.

2. **(D)** The patients do not seem to exhibit the outright rudeness implied by (C) or (E); they are simply ornery. (D) comes closest to this shade of meaning.

3. **(C)** Only (C) works in context.

4. **(D)** Be sure to read all the choices. The patients certainly behave in a way contrary to a doctor's expectations (A), but they also get worse just when they seem to be getting better (B). The answer, therefore, is (D).

5. **(A)** The illness is getting worse; it is intensifying.

6. **(D)** Rereading the entire sentence reveals the antecedent for *its approach:* "recovery."

7. **(B)** If (A) were true, the syndrome would not be "peculiar." Freud may believe (C), but he never says so. Answer (B) is supported by lines 33–36.

8. **(E)** The patient's sense of guilt tells him nothing; it is silent, or dumb.

9. **(D)** Beware of choices that are not entirely correct. Freud may believe that patients are in love with their illness (A), but that does not mean they should skip analysis. Only (D) is supported by the text.

10. **(C)** Look for the best and most specific title. (A) is too broad, as are (B) and (D). (E) is too narrow.

TEST 4

1. **(A)** The words appear in a list of children's tasks and clearly describe the harm those tasks do.

2. **(C)** Rereading the quote itself proves that the topic is the length of time growing minds should spend on a task.

3. **(E)** This is an unusual word used unusually. If (A) or (B) were true, the children would not be "hardened." (C) and (D) make little sense. Children might be "hardened" by "unwholesome conditions."

4. **(B)** Do not read more into this than is there. Markham merely speaks of a simple shift in "shackles" or servitude, not an improvement in status.

5. **(D)** *Maw* means "jaws," particularly of a meat-eating animal. Even if you did not know this, the underlying monster theme in the passage might give you a clue.

6. **(B)** The Bastille is a French prison. Using the context of the sentence, you can determine that children "hobbling in lock-step" are likely to be headed for prison.

7. **(D)** Both of these metaphors exist throughout the passage.

8. **(B)** Having compared them to human prisoners, Markham now compares them to animals "penned in narrow little lanes."

9. **(C)** Nothing you have read would lead you to believe (B) or (D), and there is no evidence to support (E). (A) may be true in a way, but (C) is the better answer.

10. **(B)** Drudgery is Markham's focus. Realizing that helps you understand the use of this repetition to parallel the repetition of the children's dreary days.

TEST 5

1. **(D)** Emerson is marveling at the writer's and reader's sympathetic natures—they might be the same person (but they clearly are not).

2. **(D)** Of the many synonyms for *abstraction,* only the meaning that relates to removal works here.

3. **(A)** Rereading the passage makes the connection clear: Just as insects store food for young they may never see, so do writers store knowledge for readers they may never know.

4. **(B)** Most of the paragraph deals with the work involved in being a creative reader.

5. **(A)** Emerson believes that reading requires a certain amount of application if it is to be fruitful. In other words, one must bring something to a passage in order to extract something from it.

6. **(E)** The meaning that parallels "supports" is the best choice here.

7. **(A)** This is a tricky passage and may require the rereading of the entire paragraph. Emerson says that creative reading allows a reader to bring to a passage all the references of his or her own background knowledge.

8. **(B)** If you had any doubt, the use of the word *seer* in line 38 should clarify your thinking.

9. **(D)** Even if you do not know this connotation for *office,* you should be able to tell that no other choice makes sense.

10. **(C)** He may well believe (A) and (B), but only (C) is supported by the text (in lines 49–53).

LEVEL B

TEST 1

1. **(A)** Only one choice really fits the context of the sentence.

2. **(D)** Wearing long pants is not a big deal today, but at the time Toomer describes, a young man's graduation to long pants was a rite of passage. Clearly, then, the events took place long ago (A), and the boys were young (B). There is no evidence to support (C).

3. **(A)** To *whittle* is to cut or carve. Rereading the paragraph clarifies what the boys are doing.

4. **(E)** He feels that "something deep in me responded to the trees, the young trees that whinnied like colts impatient to be let free… " (lines 15–16).

5. **(D)** *Flat* has many meanings, but only its relation to lodging makes sense in this context.

6. **(C)** You can choose the correct answer by plugging the choices into the sentence in question. The narrator is desperate for Avey to notice him.

7. **(B)** The boys might have felt wounded or pained, but more that this, they felt angry. Only the narrator did not, and he feels this proves his love.

8. **(C)** *Unrequited* means "unanswered." The narrator's love for Avey appears to be entirely one-sided.

TEST 2

1. **(B)** To understand this archaic construction, it may be necessary to go back and reread the paragraph in which it is found. Clearly, the doctor does *not* want the narrator to go out, although he never threatens them as in (A).

2. **(D)** *Fast* is another multiple-meaning word. All of the choices are potential synonyms, but only one could apply to windows.

3. **(A)** Again, it is easiest to decipher an archaic construction when you use the context surrounding it. The narrator is telling about his inability to keep indoors entirely due to his family's need for provisions.

4. **(E)** Remembering that the family was urged to remain indoors, try these synonyms in place of the specified word, and it becomes clear that the narrator refers to the refuge that is his house.

5. **(A)** Rereading the context reveals that *distemper* is just one of the narrator's euphemisms for the plague.

6. **(E)** Although other people repeat "with great assurance" that the provisions are not infected, the narrator has "great reason to believe" that they are (lines 34–36).

7. **(E)** The word *sound* is here contrasted with *unsound;* the healthy people meet the unhealthy, plague-ridden people at the markets and come home sick.

8. **(D)** The first line of the last paragraph gives the paragraph's main idea; you need not read further. If you do, however, you will see that the narrator discusses several means of protecting oneself against disease. He mentions the poor only in the final sentence, so (A) cannot be considered the main point of discussion.

9. **(C)** This is really the main point of the passage—that despite people's desire to protect themselves, their need to buy food led them into danger.

10. **(E)** He talks about people who live in the city (A), but the narrator never states that those people are worse off than those in the country. He does, however, in paragraphs 3 and 4, mention the fact that poor people could not protect themselves from disease.

TEST 3

1. **(B)** It is not a "great expedition"; it is only a small family going to market, but it is a big event for them. Jewett uses the words ironically; she means to point out the contradiction between the actual event and the excitement surrounding it.

2. **(E)** Substitute the choices into the sentence if you have any question. (D) is close, but (E) is better.

3. **(A)** John's "Sunday best" is unseasonal and plain, demonstrating that he is not a man of means.

4. **(E)** Find the point in the story where this comparison takes place (line 23). At that point, the mother is clucking over her children.

5. **(C)** She never mentions (A) or (B) in her litany of advice, but the mother does tell her children not to point or stare at folks, "or they'll know you come from the country" (lines 27–28). She does not want the children taken for what they are—country hicks.

6. **(D)** The word refers to something John might buy, but there is no evidence to support (B), (C), or (E).

7. **(B)** She understands them well, so (E) is incorrect. She seems sympathetic, so neither (A) nor (C) can be true. The mood is fairly humorous and upbeat, so (D) is out. Generally, the author's attitude is affectionate; she laughs at the characters, but kindly.

8. **(E)** *Far out, very long time, lost to sight,* and *lonelier* are all clues to the emphasis on isolation.

TEST 4

1. **(E)** Lumumba mentions (D), but that is certainly not his main point. The example of Guinea is a positive example of a liberated African country running its own affairs.

2. **(A)** Lumumba would never imply that his people were (B) or (C). Their desire is strong, it is *impassioned.*

3. **(E)** This is the main idea of paragraph 2. If Belgium understands the Congolese, "she will be entitled to our friendship" (lines 21–22). If not, "the Congolese people are liable to say...'we're going our own separate way'" (lines 38–42). Since both (B) and (C) are correct, the answer must be (E).

4. **(C)** The threat is barely under the surface of paragraph 2. The Congo is "going to gain our independence, come what may" (lines 37–38). It will do this with or without Belgian support, but Lumumba makes clear the ways in which Belgian support would be the best solution.

5. **(D)** The "gentleman's agreement" to which Lumumba refers is the unspoken understanding that a citizen will be protected under the laws of whatever country he finds himself in.

6. **(E)** Paragraph 3 is brief and to the point. It is a synopsis of Lumumba's purpose in addressing the crowd.

7. **(C)** This multiple-meaning word has only one connotation that fits the sentence.

8. **(C)** There is no support for (A) or (B) in the text of this speech. Lumumba addresses the concerns of financiers and colonialists who fear losing their property in the takeover.

TEST 5

1. **(E)** The discovery of species, Agassiz says, is "now almost the lowest kind of scientific work" (lines 3–4). Other things are more important.

2. **(B)** He reveals his focus in the first line of paragraph 2—number of species is not as important as the way in which species relate to one another.

3. **(A)** Reread the entire sentence to understand this unfamiliar word. (C) and (E) cannot be correct; Agassiz is talking about animals.

4. **(E)** He calls the origin of life "the great question of the day" (line 19). If that is not clue enough, Agassiz's list of questions that follow (lines 20–34) support this choice.

5. **(B)** Even if you do not know the word *dispersion,* the process of elimination should invalidate the remaining choices.

6. **(D)** Read all the choices before deciding. Only (D) corresponds to the whole meaning of the excerpted sentence.

7. **(B)** *Common* has many meanings. In this case, Agassiz means a home that species have *in common*.

8. **(A)** Agassiz is contrasting the haphazard accuracy of previous scientists with his desired accuracy. He notes that when some scientists *were* accurate, this was considered "marvellous" or remarkable.

9. **(C)** The only urging Agassiz gives his aides is to be accurate in recording their specimens. He wants precision, careful labeling, and meticulous record-keeping.

10. **(D)** Reread the sentence if you have a question here. Agassiz wants the fishes of different rivers kept "perfectly distinct"—absolutely separate.

LEVEL C

TEST 1

1. **(E)** Whoever the "soul-destroyers" are, we know that they tore Bradley from his mother's arms and carried him to a ship. The best answer is (E).

2. **(C)** He was "considered" wonderfully kind (A), and Bradley was treated "better than most" (B), but Bradley was also kicked and knocked about by his master.

3. **(E)** The last sentence makes this cause-and-effect evident.

4. **(B)** Stanton means that a mother's love for her child is the strongest and truest love there is.

5. **(A)** Do not confuse the root of this word with that of *sanctity* (B). Plugging the choices into the sentence proves that only (A) fits.

6. **(D)** The word *infest* is deliberately chosen to remind us of disease and corruption. Although Stanton discusses drink, (C) is not supported by the text, so (D) must be the answer.

7. **(A)** Of (A), (B), and (C), only a man striking a child echoes Bradley's experience. Since he deplored his treatment at the hands of his master, he would probably agree with Stanton.

8. **(C)** She certainly does not believe (D) and would seem to contradict (B). Neither (A) nor (E) is supported by the text, although Stanton might agree with them. Her main thesis is that a mother's desire and right to protect her child (especially from that child's father) are countermanded by the nation's laws.

9. **(D)** Be sure to read all the choices. Abuse of power (A) is clearly a theme in both passages. Bradley saw that his own mother was unable to protect him (B). Since (A) and (B) are correct, the answer is (D).

10. **(E)** Look for the phrase that produces a parallelism, and you will have the correct answer. (A) and (C) are true, according to Stanton, but they are not parallel. (B) and (D) are unsupported by the text. Only (E) provides a supported parallelism.

TEST 2

1. **(C)** In fact, the villagers go forth to greet the man, old and unknown as he is, until they see his sores.

2. **(B)** *Minister* has many meanings. Here it is used as a verb that means "tend."

3. **(D)** A name cannot be any of these choices *except* exalted, or glorified.

4. **(A)** If you do not know this word, trying out the choices in context will lead you to the correct answer. (C), (D), and (E) are synonyms for *cured,* not *procured.*

5. **(D)** Again, context gives you the clue you need to determine the meaning of this possibly unfamiliar phrase.

6. **(E)** In the last paragraph, Quarara makes a prediction that is more of a benediction, or blessing. He tells the woman that her kindness has led to her family's being favored.

7. **(D)** The sons will be chiefs (line 39), but the family as a whole will be "healers," or medicine men and women (lines 56–58).

8. **(C)** Only (C) makes sense in the context of many generations living under one roof.

9. **(D)** The question asks you to find a difference between the passages—something that is true for one but not for the other. On the contrary, (A), (B), and (C) are true for both, and (E) is true for neither—both take place in the past, feature people ignoring an old man, and teach a moral. Only the issue of illness is in Passage A but not in Passage B.

10. **(B)** Both the introduction to the passages and the passages themselves confirm this moral. In Passage A, the woman and her family are rewarded for her kindness. In Passage B, the man sees that his kindness now will be rewarded when he himself is old.

LEVEL D

TEST 1

1. **(D)** Muir is referring to the plates on a pine cone. Only (D) comes close to this meaning.

2. **(E)** The reference is to average length of pine cones on certain trees—most likely those having enough sun and water to grow properly.

3. **(A)** Your clues include the height "without a limb" and the list of other elements—bark, limbs, and crown. The parallel element is the trunk.

4. **(B)** It's an unusual use of the word *port,* but (B) is the only choice that works in context.

5. **(E)** This comparison occurs in lines 20–21. "No palm … displays such majesty" (B). The pine is "silent and thoughtful" or "wide-awake"—certainly human characteristics (C). Since (B) and (C) are correct, the answer must be (E).

6. **(D)** No mention is given of (C), but (A) is covered in lines 30 and 32, and (B) is mentioned in line 16.

7. **(B)** Neither (A) nor (D) is supported by the text. (C) is far too broad, and (E) is too narrow.

8. **(A)** He waxes rhapsodic about the tree's character and appearance. He seems *deferential,* or respectful.

9. **(B)** The phrase is literal: "She cooked for from twenty-five to thirty-five [people]."

10. **(B)** The scene troubled Curry. None of the other choices makes sense.

11. **(C)** It was some unimportant thing about the dinner that caused the girl to strike Curry's mother.

12. **(B)** This archaic phrase may be deciphered by plugging the choices into the context.

13. **(E)** He was certainly not *apathetic,* or indifferent, even if he did not dare to respond. Curry felt both helpless (B) and horrified (C).

14. **(E)** Raicharan does not have the same *job* (A) as his master, but he does belong to the same *class,* even if he is acting as a servant.

15. **(A)** It is too humorous to be called "dark" (B), and it does not appear to foreshadow anything (C). However, the description of baby activities as "an epoch in human history" is surely ironic.

16. **(E)** Choices A to C are synonyms for *depot.* The child is a young slave-driver.

17. **(A)** By referring to the child as "my lord," "his lordship," and "little despot," the author makes his feelings clear.

18. **(C)** Simply substituting the choices in the sentence will give you the correct response.

19. **(E)** The introduction gives you a big hint. Only Passage A fits (A) and (C). (B) relates only to Passage B. Colonialism (D) is only potentially an issue in Passage B, and "inhuman conditions" is somewhat exaggerated, anyway. (E) is the only choice that fits both passages.

20. **(A)** We never have a sense how the characters in Passage A feel about their job, but it is unlikely to be positive. Raicharan, on the other hand, dotes on his young charge. He does not take care of girls (B), and the characters in Passage A do not earn a salary (C).

TEST 2

1. **(C)** Each choice is a possible synonym for *familiar,* but only *informal* has the correct shade of meaning.

2. **(E)** Rereading the sentence in which this phrase appears should make your choice evident.

3. **(D)** Familiar style, says Hazlitt, rejects pomp, but it also rejects low, *cant* phrases—jargon.

4. **(E)** "To write a genuine familiar style … is to write as any one would speak in common conversation" (lines 13–15).

5. **(A)** The fact that Hazlitt is listing *good* qualities of writing should allow you to eliminate all but (A) here.

6. **(E)** The parallel is with "ordinary life," so "everyday" seems a reasonable choice.

7. **(D)** This is a main theme of the passage, and its focus is clear if you reread the sentence that precedes the reference. Hazlitt does not think writing should be pompous *or* vulgar, but somewhere in between.

8. **(D)** He is saying something he believes, but Hazlitt tempers his lecture with lines such as "any one may … get on stilts to tell his thoughts" and "it is easy … to use a word twice as big as the thing you wish to express."

9. **(E)** It may be a hard sentence to wade through, but understanding it is key to understanding the passage.

10. **(A)** He does *not* believe (B), and there is no evidence to support (C). He never says (D) or (E), although he may well believe them.

11. **(E)** She reminds him that she is his mother and loves him as such, that she bore him and nourished him—Agrippina is appealing to Nero's feelings as a son.

12. **(B)** Reading the line that precedes this line will help you understand that Agrippina is referring to court and the dangers that lie there.

13. **(C)** Agrippina lists the things she "knows": that "lust for empire corrupts" and that "ambition disregards wrong," but she does not admit her own wrongdoing.

14. **(E)** While saying she won't do so, Agrippina reminds Nero of all she has done to put him where he is today.

15. **(A)** Although she is "not skilled in the way of addressing kings," Browning has, through her study, "grown used to great men," especially those who are dead!

16. **(C)** This paragraph announces Browning's purpose: to petition the king.

17. **(D)** She never says (A), and she denies (B). She never says (C), and she contradicts (E). The only reason Napoleon III should forgive Hugo is because Napoleon should not be remembered as the king who exiled France's great poet.

18. **(C)** The writing for which Hugo was condemned should not affect so great a personage; what should affect him is his reputation and his son's opinion.

19. **(B)** Both plead for mercy (A), but only Agrippina is pleading her own cause.

20. **(A)** Neither one apologizes (B), and only Agrippina denies the crime (C). Browning, unlike Agrippina, speaks from what she calls a position of weakness.

PART

TWO

EVERYTHING YOU NEED!

Practice Verbal Reasoning Tests

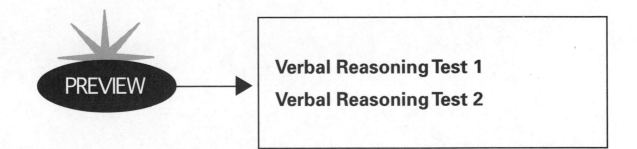

PREVIEW ➝ **Verbal Reasoning Test 1**

Verbal Reasoning Test 2

Verbal Reasoning Tests

Answer Sheet

Test 1

1. Ⓐ Ⓑ Ⓒ Ⓓ Ⓔ
2. Ⓐ Ⓑ Ⓒ Ⓓ Ⓔ
3. Ⓐ Ⓑ Ⓒ Ⓓ Ⓔ
4. Ⓐ Ⓑ Ⓒ Ⓓ Ⓔ
5. Ⓐ Ⓑ Ⓒ Ⓓ Ⓔ
6. Ⓐ Ⓑ Ⓒ Ⓓ Ⓔ
7. Ⓐ Ⓑ Ⓒ Ⓓ Ⓔ
8. Ⓐ Ⓑ Ⓒ Ⓓ Ⓔ
9. Ⓐ Ⓑ Ⓒ Ⓓ Ⓔ
10. Ⓐ Ⓑ Ⓒ Ⓓ Ⓔ
11. Ⓐ Ⓑ Ⓒ Ⓓ Ⓔ
12. Ⓐ Ⓑ Ⓒ Ⓓ Ⓔ
13. Ⓐ Ⓑ Ⓒ Ⓓ Ⓔ
14. Ⓐ Ⓑ Ⓒ Ⓓ Ⓔ
15. Ⓐ Ⓑ Ⓒ Ⓓ Ⓔ
16. Ⓐ Ⓑ Ⓒ Ⓓ Ⓔ
17. Ⓐ Ⓑ Ⓒ Ⓓ Ⓔ
18. Ⓐ Ⓑ Ⓒ Ⓓ Ⓔ
19. Ⓐ Ⓑ Ⓒ Ⓓ Ⓔ
20. Ⓐ Ⓑ Ⓒ Ⓓ Ⓔ
21. Ⓐ Ⓑ Ⓒ Ⓓ Ⓔ
22. Ⓐ Ⓑ Ⓒ Ⓓ Ⓔ
23. Ⓐ Ⓑ Ⓒ Ⓓ Ⓔ
24. Ⓐ Ⓑ Ⓒ Ⓓ Ⓔ
25. Ⓐ Ⓑ Ⓒ Ⓓ Ⓔ
26. Ⓐ Ⓑ Ⓒ Ⓓ Ⓔ
27. Ⓐ Ⓑ Ⓒ Ⓓ Ⓔ
28. Ⓐ Ⓑ Ⓒ Ⓓ Ⓔ
29. Ⓐ Ⓑ Ⓒ Ⓓ Ⓔ
30. Ⓐ Ⓑ Ⓒ Ⓓ Ⓔ

Test 2

1. Ⓐ Ⓑ Ⓒ Ⓓ Ⓔ
2. Ⓐ Ⓑ Ⓒ Ⓓ Ⓔ
3. Ⓐ Ⓑ Ⓒ Ⓓ Ⓔ
4. Ⓐ Ⓑ Ⓒ Ⓓ Ⓔ
5. Ⓐ Ⓑ Ⓒ Ⓓ Ⓔ
6. Ⓐ Ⓑ Ⓒ Ⓓ Ⓔ
7. Ⓐ Ⓑ Ⓒ Ⓓ Ⓔ
8. Ⓐ Ⓑ Ⓒ Ⓓ Ⓔ
9. Ⓐ Ⓑ Ⓒ Ⓓ Ⓔ
10. Ⓐ Ⓑ Ⓒ Ⓓ Ⓔ
11. Ⓐ Ⓑ Ⓒ Ⓓ Ⓔ
12. Ⓐ Ⓑ Ⓒ Ⓓ Ⓔ
13. Ⓐ Ⓑ Ⓒ Ⓓ Ⓔ
14. Ⓐ Ⓑ Ⓒ Ⓓ Ⓔ
15. Ⓐ Ⓑ Ⓒ Ⓓ Ⓔ
16. Ⓐ Ⓑ Ⓒ Ⓓ Ⓔ
17. Ⓐ Ⓑ Ⓒ Ⓓ Ⓔ
18. Ⓐ Ⓑ Ⓒ Ⓓ Ⓔ
19. Ⓐ Ⓑ Ⓒ Ⓓ Ⓔ
20. Ⓐ Ⓑ Ⓒ Ⓓ Ⓔ
21. Ⓐ Ⓑ Ⓒ Ⓓ Ⓔ
22. Ⓐ Ⓑ Ⓒ Ⓓ Ⓔ
23. Ⓐ Ⓑ Ⓒ Ⓓ Ⓔ
24. Ⓐ Ⓑ Ⓒ Ⓓ Ⓔ
25. Ⓐ Ⓑ Ⓒ Ⓓ Ⓔ
26. Ⓐ Ⓑ Ⓒ Ⓓ Ⓔ
27. Ⓐ Ⓑ Ⓒ Ⓓ Ⓔ
28. Ⓐ Ⓑ Ⓒ Ⓓ Ⓔ
29. Ⓐ Ⓑ Ⓒ Ⓓ Ⓔ
30. Ⓐ Ⓑ Ⓒ Ⓓ Ⓔ

Verbal Reasoning Test 1

30 QUESTIONS · TIME—30 MINUTES

(Answers on page 213)

> **Directions:** Each of the following questions consists of an incomplete sentence followed by five words or pairs of words. Choose that word or pair of words which, when substituted for the blank space or spaces, best completes the meaning of the sentence, and mark the letter of your choice on your answer sheet.

Example

> In view of the extenuating circumstances and the defendant's youth, the judge recommended ----.
>
> (A) conviction
>
> (B) a defense
>
> (C) a mistrial
>
> (D) leniency
>
> (E) life imprisonment
>
> (A) (B) (C) ● (E)

1. Her character was completely ----; she was totally devoid of ----.

    (A) prosaic .. dullness

    (B) prudent .. affection

    (C) passive .. inertia

    (D) impassive .. emotion

    (E) saintly .. virtue

2. To succeed in the training program requires great ----; you have to endure many months of rigorous exercise.

    (A) reluctance

    (B) creativity

    (C) diffidence

    (D) insensitivity

    (E) tenacity

3. Since eating that ---- amount of food I have become ----.

    (A) substantial .. unchanged

    (B) miniscule .. corpulent

    (C) gargantuan .. emaciated

    (D) prodigious .. bilious

    (E) impeccable .. fastidious

4. The performer was exceedingly ----; she could juggle three apples at once.

    (A) inept

    (B) contentious

    (C) complacent

    (D) adroit

    (E) astute

5. I am ---- about the job; although the atmosphere is pleasant, the work is boring.

    (A) ambivalent

    (B) exultant

    (C) timorous

    (D) laconic

    (E) reticent

6. Herbert had none of the social graces; he was appallingly ----.

    (A) unlimbered

    (B) underrated

    (C) unfettered

    (D) uncluttered

    (E) uncouth

GO ON TO THE NEXT PAGE

7. The ---- shantytown was infested with vermin and ---- with disease.

   (A) attractive .. riddled

   (B) spurious .. infected

   (C) squalid .. rife

   (D) tidy .. inoculated

   (E) lugubrious .. fraught

8. The gathering was anything but ----; the partygoers were in a(n) ---- mood.

   (A) aggressive .. pushy

   (B) modest .. humble

   (C) gregarious .. loquacious

   (D) mournful .. ebullient

   (E) hostile .. frenetic

9. The entering class was fairly ----; nearly all the students came from a ---- background.

   (A) hostile .. receptive

   (B) homogeneous .. similar

   (C) formidable .. fastidious

   (D) exemplary .. related

   (E) parochial .. redundant

Directions: Each of the following questions consists of a capitalized pair of words followed by five pairs of words lettered A to E. The capitalized words bear some meaningful relationship to each other. Choose the lettered pair of words whose relationship is most similar to that expressed by the capitalized pair and mark its letter on your answer sheet.

Example:

DAY : SUN ::

   (A) sunlight : daylight

   (B) ray : sun

   (C) night : moon

   (D) heat : cold

   (E) moon : star

   Ⓐ Ⓑ ● Ⓓ Ⓔ

10. PALLOR : COLOR ::

   (A) exhaustion : energy

   (B) din : tumult

   (C) palette : brush

   (D) light : dark

   (E) tint : hue

11. GAZELLE : SWIFT ::

   (A) horse : slow

   (B) wolf : sly

   (C) swan : graceful

   (D) elephant : gray

   (E) cat : clumsy

12. LIBRARY : SILENCE ::

   (A) table : grace

   (B) arena : roof

   (C) home : strife

   (D) school : bar

   (E) government : anarchy

13. PLATITUDE : STALENESS ::

   (A) bakery : mold

   (B) library : mildew

   (C) anarchy : disorder

   (D) speech : acrimony

   (E) man : wickedness

14. EYE : HURRICANE ::

(A) spoke : wheel

(B) axis : coordinate

(C) hub : wheel

(D) hub : spoke

(E) centripetal : center

15. PARTIALITY : NEUTRAL ::

(A) heresy : heretic

(B) silence : teacher

(C) corruption : degenerate

(D) enthusiasm : thinker

(E) excitability : phlegmatic

Directions: Each reading passage below is followed by a set of questions. Read the passage and answer the accompanying questions, basing your answers on what is stated or implied in the passage. Mark the letter of your choice on your answer sheet.

QUESTIONS 16–23 ARE BASED ON THE FOLLOWING PASSAGE.

Oliver Goldsmith (1730–1774) wrote criticism, plays, novels, biographies, travelogues, and nearly every other conceivable kind of composition. This good-humored essay is from a series published in the Public Ledger and then in book form as The Citizen of the World (1762).

Were we to estimate the learning of the English by the number of books that are every day published among them, perhaps no country, not even China itself, could equal them in this particular. I have
(5) reckoned not less than twenty-three new books published in one day, which, upon computation, makes eight thousand three hundred and ninety-five in one year. Most of these are not confined to one single science, but embrace the whole circle. History,
(10) politics, poetry, mathematics, metaphysics, and the philosophy of nature, are all comprised in a manual not larger than that in which our children are taught the letters. If then, we suppose the learned of England to read but an eighth part of the works which
(15) daily come from the press (and surely none can pretend to learning upon less easy terms), at this rate every scholar will read a thousand books in one year. From such a calculation, you may conjecture what an amazing fund of literature a man must be
(20) possessed of, who thus reads three new books every day, not one of which but contains all the good things that ever were said or written.

And yet I know not how it happens, but the English are not, in reality so learned as would seem
(25) from this calculation. We meet but few who know all arts and sciences to perfection; whether it is that the generality are incapable of such extensive

knowledge, or that the authors of those books are not adequate instructors. In China, the Emperor himself
(30) takes cognizance of all the doctors in the kingdom who profess authorship. In England, every man may be an author, that can write; for they have by law a liberty, not only of saying what they please, but of being also as dull as they please.

(35) Yesterday, as I testified to my surprise, to the man in black, where writers could be found in sufficient number to throw off the books I saw daily crowding from the press. I at first imagined that their learned seminaries might take this method of in-
(40) structing the world. But, to obviate this objection, my companion assured me that the doctors of colleges never wrote, and that some of them had actually forgot their reading. "But if you desire," continued he, "to see a collection of authors, I fancy I can
(45) introduce you to a club, which assembles every Saturday at seven...." I accepted his invitation; we walked together, and entered the house some time before the usual hour for the company assembling. My friend took this opportunity of letting me into
(50) the characters of the principal members of the club....

The first person," said he, "of our society is Doctor Nonentity, a metaphysician. Most people think him a profound scholar, but, as he seldom speaks, I cannot be positive in that particular; he
(55) generally spreads himself before the fire, sucks his pipe, talks little, drinks much, and is reckoned very good company. I'm told he writes indexes to perfection: he makes essays on the origin of evil, philosophical inquiries upon any subject, and draws up
(60) an answer to any book upon 24 hours' warning...."

GO ON TO THE NEXT PAGE

16. Goldsmith's disdainful attitude toward English authors is best explicated in
    (A) lines 9–13
    (B) lines 28–29
    (C) lines 31–34
    (D) lines 40–42
    (E) lines 58–61

17. Goldsmith believes that
    (A) we can tell how knowledgeable English authors are by counting the number of books they publish
    (B) the number of books published in England is not up to standards set in China
    (C) the number of books published in England says nothing about English scholarship
    (D) most English writers are better-educated than their Chinese counterparts
    (E) every scholar reads a thousand books a year

18. Why does Goldsmith calculate the number of books published in England?
    (A) To impress his readers with English erudition
    (B) To make the point that anyone can be an author
    (C) As defense for his argument that England is better than China
    (D) To show that most English publications are foreign
    (E) As a comparison with publication quotas in other lands

19. The tone of paragraph 2 may best be described as
    (A) self-satisfied
    (B) awestruck
    (C) affectionate
    (D) sardonic
    (E) solemn

20. Goldsmith first assumes that English writers come from
    (A) foreign lands
    (B) seminaries
    (C) China
    (D) clubs
    (E) the press

21. The word *obviate* (line 40) means
    (A) clarify
    (B) obscure
    (C) turn
    (D) negate
    (E) facilitate

22. Goldsmith's opinion of the first member of the club is illuminated by
    (A) his conversation with the character
    (B) his name for the character
    (C) his friend's description of the character
    (D) both A and B
    (E) both B and C

23. One of Goldsmith's major objections to English authors is to their
    (A) deficiency in language skills
    (B) inclination to drink
    (C) tendency to write about everything at once
    (D) refusal to attend the seminary
    (E) inability to retain information

QUESTIONS 24–30 ARE BASED ON THE FOLLOWING PASSAGE.

Pauline Johnson (1861–1913) was the daughter of Mohawk leader George Henry Martin; her mother was English. Johnson was known in her time as a poet and performer. For years she toured throughout Canada giving dramatic readings. Late in her life she turned to writing short stories. This excerpt is from "A Red Girl's Reasoning," first published in 1893.

How interesting—do tell us some more of your old home, Mrs. McDonald; you so seldom speak of your life at the post, and we fellows so often wish to hear of it all," said Logan eagerly.

(5)   "Why do you not ask me of it, then?"

"Well—er, I'm sure I don't know; I'm fully interested in the Ind—in your people—your mother's people, I mean, but it always seems so personal, I suppose; and—a—a—"

(10)   "Perhaps you are, like all other white people, afraid to mention my nationality to me."

The captain winced, and Mrs. Stuart laughed uncasily. Joe McDonald was not far off, and he was listening, and chuckling, and saying to himself,

(15) "That's you, Christie, lay 'em out; it won't hurt 'em to know how they appear once in a while."

"Well, Captain Logan," she was saying, "what is it you would like to hear—of my people, or my parents, or myself?"

(20)   "All, all, my dear," cried Mrs. Stuart clamorously. "I'll speak for him—tell us of yourself and your mother—your father is delightful, I am sure—but then he is only an ordinary Englishman, not half so interesting as a foreigner, or—or, perhaps I

(25) should say, a native."

Christie laughed. "Yes," she said, "my father often teases my mother now about how *very* native she was when he married her; then, how could she have been otherwise? She did not know a word of

(30) English, and there was not another English-speaking person besides my father and his two companions within sixty miles."

"Two companions, eh? One a Catholic priest and the other a wine merchant, I suppose, and with your

(35) father in the Hudson Bay, they were good representatives of the pioneers in the New World," remarked Logan, waggishly.

"Oh, no, they were all Hudson Bay men. There were no rumsellers and no missionaries in that part

(40) of the country then."

Mrs. Stuart looked puzzled. *"No missionaries?"* she repeated with an odd intonation.

Christie's insight was quick. There was a peculiar expression of interrogation in the eyes of her

(45) listeners, and the girl's blood leapt angrily up into her temples as she said hurriedly, "I know what you mean; I know what you are thinking. You are wondering how my parents were married—"

"Well—er, my dear, it seems peculiar—if there

(50) was no priest, and no magistrate, why—a—" Mrs. Stuart paused awkwardly.

"The marriage was performed by Indian rites," said Christie.

"Oh, do tell about it; is the ceremony very inter-

(55) esting and quaint—are your chieftains anything like Buddhist priests?" It was Logan who spoke.

"Why, no," said the girl in amazement at that gentleman's ignorance. "There is no ceremony at all, save a feast. The two people just agree to live

(60) only with and for each other, and the man takes his wife to his home, just as you do. There is no ritual to bind them; they need none; an Indian's word was his law in those days, you know."

Mrs. Stuart stepped backwards. "Ah!" was all

(65) she said. Logan removed his eye-glass and stared blankly at Christie. "And did McDonald marry you in this singular fashion?" he questioned.

"Oh, no, we were married by Father O'Leary. Why do you ask?"

(70)   "Because if he had, I'd have blown his brains out tomorrow."

Mrs. Stuart's partner, who had heretofore been silent, coughed and began to twirl his cuff stud nervously, but nobody took any notice of him.

(75) Christie had risen, slowly, ominously—risen, with the dignity and pride of an empress.

"Captain Logan," she said, "what do you dare to say to me? What do you dare to mean? Do you presume to think it would not have been lawful for

(80) Joe to marry me according to my people's rites? Do you for one instant dare to question that my parents were not as legally—"

"Don't, dear, don't," interrupted Mrs. Stuart hurriedly, "it is bad enough now, goodness knows;

(85) don't make—" Then she broke off blindly.

GO ON TO THE NEXT PAGE

24. The word *post* (line 3) probably means

    (A) register

    (B) trading headquarters

    (C) mailroom

    (D) assignment

    (E) stake

25. What is Joe McDonald's initial reaction to his wife's attitude toward the captain and Mrs. Stuart?

    (A) He supports her frankness.

    (B) He is horrified at her rudeness.

    (C) He is amused by her formality.

    (D) He wishes he were more like her.

    (E) He challenges her disrespectful behavior.

26. Why is Mrs. Stuart not particularly interested in hearing about Christie's father?

    (A) He is not an interesting man.

    (B) She cares little about tradespeople.

    (C) She, too, is from England.

    (D) He is not exotic enough for her taste.

    (E) He leads a life that is different from hers.

27. Mrs. Stuart's "odd intonation" (line 42) apparently results from

    (A) an inability to pronounce the words she is saying

    (B) her alarm at Christie's words

    (C) her anger at Logan's implications

    (D) ignorance and lack of vocabulary

    (E) a sudden loss of the powers of speech

28. As Mrs. Stuart steps backward (line 64), we sense that she

    (A) has fallen ill

    (B) is drunk

    (C) is having difficulty standing

    (D) wants to distance herself from Christie

    (E) was pushed or pulled away by her partner

29. Logan might have killed Christie's husband if

    (A) McDonald had shamed her by marrying Indian-style

    (B) Christie had maintained her ties to the tribe

    (C) McDonald had married a native in a church ceremony

    (D) Christie had been a full-blooded Indian

    (E) an Indian's word had not been "his law"

30. As the story continues, Joe McDonald is appalled and angry at Christie for "shocking" Logan and Mrs. Stuart. Based on the story so far, how would you expect Christie to react to Joe's disapproval?

    (A) She would probably acquiesce and apologize to Joe.

    (B) She would ask Joe to intercede for her with Logan and Mrs. Stuart.

    (C) She would tell Logan and Mrs. Stuart that she made up the whole story.

    (D) She would humbly beg Mrs. Stuart's pardon.

    (E) She would deny that she had done anything wrong.

STOP

IF YOU FINISH BEFORE THE TIME IS UP,
GO BACK AND CHECK YOUR WORK.

Verbal Reasoning Test 2

30 QUESTIONS · TIME—30 MINUTES

(Answers on page 213)

> **Directions:** Each of the following questions consists of an incomplete sentence followed by five words or pairs of words. Choose that word or pair of words which, when substituted for the blank space or spaces, best completes the meaning of the sentence, and mark the letter of your choice on your answer sheet.

Example:

In view of the extenuating circumstances and the defendant's youth, the judge recommended ----.

(A) conviction

(B) a defense

(C) a mistrial

(D) leniency

(E) life imprisonment

Ⓐ Ⓑ Ⓒ ● Ⓔ

1. When you are restive, you don't have much ----.
   (A) restlessness
   (B) animosity
   (C) equanimity
   (D) motion
   (E) equilibrium

2. With speculative investments like oil wells and horse races, money is more easily made or lost; the gain is ---- with the risk.
   (A) less
   (B) greater
   (C) equal
   (D) better
   (E) commensurate

3. To tremble in the face of a storm is to ----.
   (A) glower
   (B) cower
   (C) shower
   (D) tower
   (E) flower

4. Eleanor steadfastly refused to change her stubborn ways; she remained ---- to the end.
   (A) embattled
   (B) regurgitating
   (C) recalcitrant
   (D) decalcified
   (E) concomitant

5. Benjamin Franklin said that ---- is not always a virtue; there are times when you must speak up for yourself.
   (A) pride
   (B) forthrightness
   (C) sham
   (D) prudery
   (E) modesty

6. They ---- their offer of aid when they became disillusioned with the project.
   (A) expanded
   (B) redoubled
   (C) bolstered
   (D) constrained
   (E) rescinded

7. The firm's books were out of balance; there was a(n) ---- between the amount of physical inventory and the amount of calculated inventory.
   (A) anachronism
   (B) enigma
   (C) discredit
   (D) discrepancy
   (E) dissension

GO ON TO THE NEXT PAGE ➤

8. As a ---- he was a disaster, for his students rarely understood his lectures; yet he was a ---- scholar.

   (A) dean .. banal

   (B) philosopher .. failed

   (C) teacher .. formidable

   (D) professor .. second-rate

   (E) speaker .. contemptuous

9. Far from the ---- crowds of the city, I find refuge at my ---- cabin on Big Lake.

   (A) pervasive .. dominant

   (B) aggressive .. listless

   (C) petrified .. motivating

   (D) overwhelming .. secluded

   (E) extensive .. scanty

Directions: Each of the following questions consists of a capitalized pair of words followed by five pairs of words lettered A to E. The capitalized words bear some meaningful relationship to each other. Choose the lettered pairs of words whose relationship is most similar to that expressed by the capitalized pair and mark its letter on your answer sheet.

Example:

DAY : SUN ::

   (A) sunlight : daylight

   (B) ray : sun

   (C) night : moon

   (D) heat : cold

   (E) moon : star

10. PARAGON : EMULATE ::

   (A) reprobate : admire

   (B) ingrate : imitate

   (C) pariah : despise

   (D) conspirator : praise

   (E) thief : abet

11. HOCKEY : BLADES ::

   (A) baseball : diamond

   (B) football : cleats

   (C) skating : ice

   (D) basketball : hoop

   (E) wrestling : mat

12. ERUDITE : IGNORANT ::

   (A) amiable : friendly

   (B) remorseful : greedy

   (C) clever : guileless

   (D) merciful : tolerant

   (E) spontaneous : creative

13. TYRO : INEXPERIENCE ::

   (A) demagogue : restraint

   (B) professional : skill

   (C) neophyte : experience

   (D) dictator : benevolence

   (E) martinet : sense

14. SQUELCH : RUMOR ::

   (A) ruin : reputation

   (B) whisper : retort

   (C) sue : surrogate

   (D) testify : defendant

   (E) suppress : revolt

15. GENEROUS : MAGNANIMOUS ::

   (A) faithful : teeming

   (B) genteel : magnificent

   (C) lively : relevant

   (D) rich : opulent

   (E) abundant : ostentatious

Directions: Each reading passage below is followed by a set of questions. Read the passage and answer the accompanying questions, basing your answers on what is stated or implied in the passage. Mark the letter of your choice on your answer sheet.

QUESTIONS 16–24 ARE BASED ON THE FOLLOWING PASSAGE.

George Washington served as president of the Constitutional Convention in 1787, and was then elected (40) President of the United States in 1789. This is from his first address to Congress.

Such being the impressions under which I have, in obedience to the public summons, repaired to the present station, it would be peculiarly improper to omit, in this first official act, my fervent suppli-
(5) cations to the Almighty Being, who rules over the universe, who presides in the councils of nations, and whose providential aids can supply every human defect, that his benediction may consecrate to the liberties and happiness of the people of the
(10) United States a government instituted by themselves for these essential purposes, and may enable every instrument employed in its administration to execute with success the functions allotted to his charge. In tendering this homage to the great Author
(15) of every public and private good, I assure myself that it expresses your sentiments not less than my own; nor those of my fellow-citizens at large, less than either. No people can be bound to acknowledge and adore the invisible hand, which conducts the
(20) affairs of men, more than the people of the United States. Every step, by which they have advanced to the character of an independent nation, seems to have been distinguished by some token of providential agency. And, in the important revolution just
(25) accomplished in the system of their united government, the tranquil deliberations and voluntary consent of so many distinct communities, from which the event has resulted, cannot be compared with the means by which most governments have been es-
(30) tablished, without some return of pious gratitude along with an humble anticipation of the future blessings which the past seems to presage. These reflections, arising out of the present crisis, have forced themselves too strongly on my mind to be
(35) suppressed. You will join with me, I trust, in thinking that there are none, under the influence of which the proceedings of a new and free government can more auspiciously commence.

By the article establishing the executive depart-
(40) ment, it is made the duty of the President "to recommend to your consideration such measures as he shall judge necessary and expedient." The circumstances, under which I now meet you, will acquit me from entering into that subject farther than to refer
(45) you to the great constitutional charter under which we are assembled; and which, in defining your powers, designates the objects to which your attention is to be given. It will be more consistent with those circumstances, and far more congenial with
(50) the feelings which actuate me, to substitute, in place of a recommendation of particular measures, the tribute that is due to the talents, the rectitude, and the patriotism, which adorn the characters selected to devise and adopt them. In these honorable qualifica-
(55) tions I behold the surest pledges, that as, on one side, no local prejudices or attachments, no separate views or party animosities, will misdirect the comprehensive and equal eye, which ought to watch over this great assemblage of communities and
(60) interests; so, on another, that the foundations of our national policy will be laid in the pure and immutable principles of private morality, and the preeminence of a free government be exemplified by all the attributes, which can win the affections of its citi-
(65) zens, and command the respect of the world.

16. Washington's first official act is to

(A) refer Congress to the constitutional charter

(B) pay tribute to the uprightness of the Founding Fathers

(C) pray for divine guidance

(D) lay the foundations of national policy in the province of private morality

(E) obtain the voluntary consent of several communities

GO ON TO THE NEXT PAGE

17. According to Washington, "the invisible hand which conducts the affairs of men"

    (A) is that of the President

    (B) should be, but isn't, that of Congress

    (C) is the constitution

    (D) should be revered, especially by Americans

    (E) should be respected and adored by all peoples

18. Acting as chief executive, Washington feels that it is appropriate to

    (A) follow faithfully the article establishing the executive department

    (B) recommend to Congress consideration of certain measures

    (C) pay tribute to those who "devise and adopt" particular measures

    (D) announce that there shall be no interparty strife

    (E) impose the morality of the United States on the world at large

19. Washington foresees a national policy that will

    (A) preclude partisan interests

    (B) impose American morality on the world

    (C) "misdirect the comprehensive and equal eye"

    (D) be restricted to American interests

    (E) put the United States in charge of the world

20. When Washington says that "in obedience to the public summons" he has "repaired to the present station," he means that he

    (A) volunteered for his current duties

    (B) has been elected to this office

    (C) was haled before this court to testify

    (D) intends to correct the mistakes of his predecessors

    (E) will step down as required by law

21. The word *acquit* (line 43) is used to mean

    (A) act

    (B) sentence

    (C) excuse

    (D) discontinue

    (E) reject

22. The "comprehensive and equal eye" that is to watch over Congress is

    (A) the eye of God

    (B) the will of the people

    (C) a "Big Brother" figure in government

    (D) Congress's unbiased objectivity

    (E) the power of the press

23. Washington chooses not to lay out expedient measures to Congress because he

    (A) has no new ideas to impart

    (B) believes the Constitution outlines Congress's duties

    (C) relies on Congress to act in the public interest

    (D) prefers to act as a figurehead

    (E) wishes to spend his time delineating national policy

24. Washington's attitude toward Congress is one of

    (A) respectful admiration

    (B) fatherly concern

    (C) intermittent disappointment

    (D) solemn uneasiness

    (E) polite defiance

QUESTIONS 25–30 ARE BASED ON THE FOLLOWING PASSAGE.

He was born a slave, but T. Thomas Fortune (1856–1928) went on to become a journalist, editor, and civil rights activist, founding several early black newspapers and a civil rights organization that predated W. E. B. DuBois' Niagara Movement (later the NAACP). Like many black leaders of his time, Fortune was torn between the radical leanings of DuBois and the more conservative ideology of Booker T. Washington. This 1884 essay, "The Negro and the Nation," dates from his more militant period.

The war of the Rebellion settled only one question: It forever settled the question of chattel slavery in this country. It forever choked the life out of the infamy of the Constitutional right of one man to rob
(5) another, by purchase of his person, or of his honest share of the produce of his own labor. But this was the only question permanently and irrevocably settled. Nor was this *the* all-absorbing question involved. The right of a state to secede from the so-
(10) called *Union* remains where it was when the treasonable shot upon Fort Sumter aroused the people to all the horrors of internecine war. And the measure of protection which the national government owes the individual members of states, a right imposed
(15) upon it by the adoption of the Fourteenth Amendment to the Constitution, remains still to be affirmed.

It was not sufficient that the federal government should expend its blood and treasure to unfetter the
(20) limbs of four millions of people. There can be a slavery more odious, more galling, than mere chattel slavery. It has been declared to be an act of charity to enforce ignorance upon the slave, since to inform his intelligence would simply be to make his
(25) unnatural lot all the more unbearable. Instance the miserable existence of Æsop, the great black moralist. But this is just what the manumission of the black people of this country has accomplished. They are more absolutely under the control of the
(30) Southern whites; they are more systematically robbed of their labor; they are more poorly housed, clothed and fed, than under the slave régime; and they enjoy, practically, less of the protection of the laws of the state or of the federal government. When

(35) they appeal to the federal government they are told by the Supreme Court to go to the state authorities— as if they would have appealed to the one had the other given them that protection to which their sovereign citizenship entitles them!
(40) Practically, there is no law in the United States which extends its protecting arm over the black man and his rights. He is, like the Irishman in Ireland, an alien in his native land. There is no central or auxiliary authority to which he can appeal for pro-
(45) tection. Wherever he turns he finds the strong arm of constituted authority powerless to protect him. The farmer and the merchant rob him with absolute immunity, and irresponsible ruffians murder him without fear of punishment, undeterred by the law,
(50) or by public opinion—which connives at, if it does not inspire, the deeds of lawless violence. Legislatures of states have framed a code of laws which is more cruel and unjust than any enforced by a former slave state.
(55) The right of franchise has been practically annulled in every one of the former slave states, in not one of which, today, can a man vote, think, or act as he pleases. He must conform his views to the views of the men who have usurped every function of
(60) government—who, at the point of the dagger, and with shotgun, have made themselves masters in defiance of every law or precedent in our history as a government. They have usurped government with the weapons of the cowards and assassins, and they
(65) maintain themselves in power by the most approved practices of the most odious of tyrants. These men have shed as much innocent blood as the bloody triumvirate of Rome. Today, red-handed murderers and assassins sit in the high places of power, and
(70) bask in the smiles of innocence and beauty.

25. The only solution the Civil War provided, according to Fortune, was to the problem of

    (A) mutually destructive war

    (B) protection

    (C) slavery

    (D) secession

    (E) constitutional rights

GO ON TO THE NEXT PAGE

26. The word *manumission* (line 27) means
    (A) emancipation
    (B) duty
    (C) possessions
    (D) forgiveness
    (E) transportation

27. Now that slavery has been abolished, Fortune believes, black people
    (A) are chattel
    (B) have fewer rights than before
    (C) are protected by laws
    (D) can succeed in the white man's world
    (E) inspire lawless violence

28. Fortune uses the example of the Irishman to show that
    (A) famine is not alien to people in the United States
    (B) one can be treated as a foreigner in the land of one's birth
    (C) some people have a native land; others have none
    (D) one can be born to slavery but rise above it
    (E) people may be treated more fairly in a monarchy than in a democracy

29. According to Fortune, public opinion
    (A) is responsible for punishing criminal acts
    (B) can protect a freed slave
    (C) is the voice of authority
    (D) supports violence against black people
    (E) has no power to guard against evil

30. The triumvirate of Rome is introduced as a parallel to
    (A) the tyranny of the postwar power structure
    (B) the civility of the antebellum South
    (C) the fall of the Old South in war
    (D) the outdated, ineffectual government
    (E) the helplessness of the freed slaves

STOP

IF YOU FINISH BEFORE THE TIME IS UP,
GO BACK AND CHECK YOUR WORK.

Answer Key

For explanations see page 214.

TEST 1

1. D	7. C	13. C	19. D	25. A
2. E	8. D	14. C	20. B	26. D
3. D	9. B	15. E	21. D	27. B
4. D	10. A	16. C	22. E	28. D
5. A	11. C	17. C	23. C	29. A
6. E	12. A	18. B	24. B	30. E

For explanations see page 215.

TEST 2

1. C	7. D	13. B	19. A	25. C
2. E	8. C	14. E	20. B	26. A
3. B	9. D	15. D	21. C	27. B
4. C	10. C	16. D	22. D	28. B
5. E	11. B	17. D	23. B	29. D
6. E	12. C	18. C	24. A	30. A

Explanatory Answers

TEST 1

1. **(D)** To be *impassive* (without feelings) is to be totally devoid of (lacking in) *emotion*.

2. **(E)** To endure many months of training you need great *tenacity,* or persistence.

3. **(D)** If you eat a *substantial* amount of food, you will *not* be *unchanged* (unaffected). If you eat a *miniscule* amount, you will not become *corpulent* (excessively fat). If you eat a *gargantuan* (suitable to a giant) amount, you will certainly not become *emaciated* (thin to the point of starvation). But if you eat a *prodigious* (unusually enormous) amount, you are very likely to become *bilious* (sick to the stomach).

4. **(D)** If the performer could juggle three apples at once, she is remarkably skillful, or *adroit.*

5. **(A)** A job that is both pleasant and boring is likely to arouse feelings that are mixed, or *ambivalent.*

6. **(E)** Having no *social graces* means to be rude, or crude. The obvious answer is *uncouth* (uncultured, crude, boorish).

7. **(C)** A shantytown is a collection of ramshackle dwellings that are often miserable, dirty, or *squalid.* Such places are likely to be *rife,* or filled, with disease.

8. **(D)** The "anything but" construction calls for words that are opposites. The only answer choice that offers a pair of opposites is (D), *mournful* (sad) .. *ebullient* (joyful).

9. **(B)** Since the second clause of the sentence defines the first, the only possible answer must be a pair of synonyms. The only such pair is answer (B), *homogeneous* (alike) and *similar.*

10. **(A)** A *pallor* is a lack of *color,* especially in the face, on account of fear or ill health. *Exhaustion* is a lack of *energy.*

11. **(C)** A *gazelle* is known to be *swift;* a *swan* is known to be *graceful.*

12. **(A)** It is customary to maintain *silence* in many a *library,* as it is customary to say *grace* at many a *table.* It is not customary to have a *roof* on an *arena, strife* at *home,* a *bar* at a *school,* or *anarchy* in *government.*

13. **(C)** A *platitude* (commonplace or trite remark) is usually characterized by *staleness* (lack of freshness or originality), just as *anarchy* (without government) is usually characterized by *disorder* (chaos).

14. **(C)** The *eye* of a *hurricane* is a circular region surrounding the center of its rotation; the *hub* of a *wheel* surrounds the axle, which is at the center of the wheel's rotation.

15. **(E)** *Partiality* is not shown by *neutral* persons. *Excitability* is not shown by *phlegmatic* individuals.

16. **(C)** The statement in lines 31–34, that writers can write whatever they please and be as dull as they please, is Goldsmith's way of expressing his contempt for modern authors. Anyone can declare himself an author; few have anything intelligent to say.

17. **(C)** Goldsmith begins by saying "Were we to estimate the learning of the English by the number of books that are published …" but goes on to conclude that "… the English are not, in reality so learned as would seem from this calculation."

18. **(B)** Goldsmith's point is that England publishes an astonishing number of books, but the number has little to do with the quality.

19. **(D)** The whole tone of the piece is ironic; Goldsmith is making his point through dry, sardonic wit.

20. **(B)** He states this in line 39, but quickly dispels the notion when his companion assures him that "doctors of colleges never wrote."

21. **(D)** Goldsmith suggests that seminaries might be publishing this glut of books to educate the world, but his friend voids that argument in the next line.

22. **(E)** Doctor Nonentity is so named to show his uselessness as a scholar. The fact that he "never speaks" keeps anyone from knowing whether he is clever, and it seems, according to Goldsmith's friend, that he is able to write on nearly anything without taking time for thought.

23. **(C)** This objection is made tongue-in-cheek in lines 8–9. It may seem learned to write on "the whole circle" of sciences, but Goldsmith believes it makes for shallow, dull works.

24. **(B)** Christie lived at the "post," and references to Hudson Bay make this the only sensible answer.

25. **(A)** Lines 14–16 demonstrate Joe's approval.

26. **(D)** An "ordinary Englishman" cannot be fascinating to Mrs. Stuart.

27. **(B)** Mrs. Stuart is eager to be shocked; Christie's words imply something shocking to her.

28. **(D)** Having been shocked, Mrs. Stuart now believes Christie has an immoral background. Her backward step moves her away from this indecent person.

29. **(A)** This response follows from what precedes the line about "blowing his brains out" (line 71). Logan is appalled by the unseemly Indian marriage Christie describes; he cannot accept that Christie and Joe might have been married in this way.

30. **(E)** Christie's frankness and pride are stressed throughout the passage. There is little to allow a reader to predict that she would apologize, lie, or rely on her husband. In fact, she leaves Joe when he refuses to support her in this.

TEST 2

1. **(C)** When you are *restive* (nervous, upset), you may have at the same time *restlessness, animosity, motion,* or *equilibrium,* but you cannot have *equanimity* (evenness, peace of mind, or tranquility).

2. **(E)** In speculation, a gain is not necessarily *greater* or *less* or *better* with risk. It may *occasionally* be *equal* with the risk, but it is most usually *commensurate* (corresponding in extent of degree) with it.

3. **(B)** "To tremble in the face of a storm" is to show fear or discomfort in a special way. *Glower* (to stare or scowl with sullen anger) does not connote fear or trembling; neither do *shower, tower,* or *flower.* To cower is to crouch, as from fear or cold, or to shrink and tremble.

4. **(C)** *Embattled* (fighting), *regurgitating* (bringing partly digested food back to the mouth), *decalcified* (having calcium removed from the system), and *concomitant* (accompanying, attendant) do not in any way suggest a steadfast refusal to submit to change. The only possible choice is *recalcitrant* (refusing to obey authority, stubbornly defiant).

5. **(E)** The context of this sentence suggests that "not speaking up for yourself" is *not* always good; in other words, the missing term has something to do with self-effacement. Only *modesty* can fill this gap properly.

6. **(E)** The sentence describes people who are disillusioned with a project. They are therefore most likely to *rescind,* or withdraw, their offer of aid.

7. **(D)** If the "books were out of balance," there had to be some sort of differential between the two inventories. Only the last two choices pertain to any differential. *Dissension,* however, is a difference in feelings; *discrepancy* (inconsistency) fits the context.

8. **(C)** *Yet* indicates that the second clause will have a meaning that contrasts with that of the first clause. In the first clause, someone is a disaster. The only choice for the second blank that contrasts with that idea is *formidable,* meaning that he was a first-rate scholar.

9. **(D)** The logic of this sentence is based on contrast; the clues are *crowds, refuge,* and *cabin.* In choices (A) and (B), the first substitution works, but the second is meaningless. In choices (C) and (E), neither word makes sense in context.

10. **(C)** A *paragon* is an admirable person with qualities that people copy, or *emulate*. A *pariah* is an outcast with qualities that people *despise.*

11. **(B)** *Hockey* players have *blades* on their skates; *football* players have *cleats* on their shoes. None of the other choices refers to what players wear on their feet.

12. **(C)** A person who is *erudite* is well-educated, not *ignorant.* Similarly, a person who is *clever* is crafty, not *guileless* (lacking in cunning).

13. **(B)** A *tyro* is an amateur characterized by *inexperience.* A *professional* is a trained worker characterized by *skill.* A *demagogue* is a political rabble-rouser not characterized by *restraint.* A *neophyte* is another type of beginner. A *martinet* is a strict disciplinarian.

14. **(E)** To *squelch* a *rumor* means to put a stop to it. To *suppress* a *revolt* is to put an end to it by defeating it.

15. **(D)** To be *magnanimous* is to be extremely *generous,* just as to be *opulent* is to be extremely *rich.*

16. **(D)** The last six lines constitute the only part of the speech that could be called an "official act." (E) was part of the "revolution just accomplished." (A) and (C) are simply a referral and a prayer. (B) is a trap: He is paying tribute not to the Founding Fathers but to the legislators in his audience.

17. **(D)** Because every step they have taken "seems to have been distinguished by some token of providential agency."

18. **(C)** He gets nowhere near (E). He sees "surest pledges"—but certainly can't "announce"—that there "shall be no interparty strife" (D). He doesn't mention any need to "follow faithfully" that article; he simply refers to it (A). And rather than recommend "certain measures" (B), he prefers to "pay tribute" (C).

19. **(A)** He says nothing like (E) or (D), and the morality he hopes for is *not* "American" (B) but private, and *not* to be imposed on anybody. And because of the "honorable qualifications" of his audience, he sees *nothing* that will "misdirect the comprehensive and equal eye" (C). The one thing among these choices he truly does foresee is that there will be "no … party animosities" (A).

20. **(B)** Washington is politely intimating that he would never be where he is had "the public summons" not called him to this "station." He has been summoned by the will of the people.

21. **(C)** Washington says that present circumstances mean that he need not "enter into [the] subject" of recommending measures to Congress; he is excused from that duty.

22. **(D)** A careful reading of lines 55–60 shows that Washington is concerned that Congress must be unbiased and impartial, guided by the "principles of private morality." If "local prejudices" or "party animosities" interfere, Congress's "equal eye" will be "misdirected."

23. **(B)** Although (C) is discussed, the reason that Washington decides not to "enter into [the] subject" (line 44) is that the Constitution "designates the objects to which your attention is to be given" (lines 47–48).

24. **(A)** In line 52, Washington gives a "tribute … to the talents, the rectitude, and the patriotism" of Congress.

25. **(C)** The first sentence contains this answer; the paragraph goes on to explain what was *not* settled by the war.

26. **(A)** You can deduce this answer by reading the whole paragraph carefully. Fortune talks about "a slavery more odious … than chattel slavery." Even after being liberated, or *emancipated,* black people remain in chains.

27. **(B)** Paragraphs 2 and 3 are entirely in support of this.

28. **(B)** No law protects the black man; he is, "like the Irishman in Ireland, an alien in his native land" (lines 42–43).

29. **(D)** Black people are robbed and murdered, and neither law nor public opinion deters the criminals. See lines 47–51.

30. **(A)** The usurpers of government are as tyrannical and bloodthirsty as this historical trio of dictators.

The SAT Word List

VOCABULARY: DOES IT MATTER?

In a word: Yes.

Vocabulary *as such* is not tested on the SAT. Until a few years ago, the exam included antonym questions, which required you to pick a word whose meaning was the opposite of some other word. Those questions have been eliminated. So the most direct and obvious form of a vocabulary question on the SAT is no more.

That leaves *indirect* and *hidden* vocabulary questions—of which there are plenty.

1. Reading comprehension passages now include vocabulary-in-context questions. These focus on particular words in the passage and ask you to determine their meaning *in the passage*. Sometimes the words chosen are obviously "hard" words (*latent, replete,* and *eminent,* to name three real examples). More often, they are seemingly "easy" words that are tricky because they have so *many* possible meanings (*camp, idea,* and *hard*, for example). In both cases, the broader, more varied, and more accurate your vocabulary knowledge, the better your chances are of answering these questions quickly and correctly.

2. Analogy questions obviously depend to a large extent on vocabulary. It's difficult—though not impossible, as we discuss in Chapter Five—to decipher the analogy relationships unless you understand the words that are involved. One typical group of thirteen analogy items includes the words *proficiency, embellish, carping, reclusive, tactile, criterion, intransigent,* and *strenuous,* among others. (How many of these can you define?) You don't have to throw up your hands in despair if an analogy item contains a word or two you don't know; there's more than one way to skin that cat. But the process will be a lot easier and faster if you know most of the words used, or at least have a nodding acquaintance with them.

3. The better your vocabulary knowledge, the easier you'll find it to understand both the critical reading passages and the sentence completion items (which are, in effect, mini-reading passages, each one sentence long). Even an occasional math item is made a little more complicated by the use of a challenging vocabulary word.

Therefore, vocabulary knowledge makes a clear and significant difference in your performance on the SAT. Fortunately, the kinds of words that regularly appear on the SAT, as with so much else on the exam, fall into definite patterns.

The SAT is basically a test of "book learning." It's written and edited by bookish people for the benefit of the other bookish people who run colleges and universities. It's designed to test your ability to handle the kinds of academic tasks college students usually have to master: reading textbooks, finding information in reference books, deciphering scholarly journals, studying research abstracts, writing impressive-sounding term papers, etc.

The hard words on the SAT are hard words of a particular sort: scholastic words that deal, broadly speaking, with the manipulation and communication of *ideas*— words like *ambiguous, amplify, arbitrary,* and *arcane.* The better you master this sort of vocabulary, the better you'll do on the exam.

Fortunately, you don't need to find these words on your own. We've done the spadework for you. By examining actual SAT exams from the last several years, we've been able to list the words most commonly used in reading passages, analogies, and sentence completions, including both the question stems and the answer choices. This list became the basis of the SAT Word List. It includes about 500 primary words that are most likely to appear in one form or another on your SAT exam. It also includes hundreds of related words—words that are either variants of the primary words (*ambiguity* as a variant of *ambiguous,* for example) or that share a common word root (like *ample, amplify,* and *amplitude*).

If you make yourself acquainted with all the words in the SAT Word List, you will absolutely learn a number of new words that will appear on your SAT. You'll earn extra points as a result.

THE SIX BEST VOCABULARY-BUILDING TIPS FOR THE SAT

Study Vocabulary Daily

There are some topics you can easily cram. Vocabulary isn't one of them. In general, words don't stay in mind until the fourth or fifth time you learn them. Try to begin your vocabulary study several weeks before the exam. Take 15 or 20 minutes a day to learn new words. Periodically review all the words you've previously studied; quiz yourself, or have a friend quiz you. This simple regimen can enable you to learn several hundred new words before you take the SAT.

Learn a Few Words at a Time

Don't try to gobble dozens of words in one sitting. They're likely to blur into an indistinguishable mass. Instead, pick a reasonable quantity—say, 10 to 15 words—and study them in some depth. Learn the definition of each word; examine the sample sentence provided in the word list; learn the related words; and try writing a couple of sentences of your own that include the word. Refer to your own dictionary for further information if you like.

Learn Words in Families

Language is a living thing. Words are used by humans, innately creative beings who constantly twist, reshape, invent, and recombine words. (Think of the jargon of your favorite sport or hobby, or the new language currently blossoming in cyberspace, for some examples.) As a result, most words belong to families, in which related ideas are expressed through related words. This makes it possible to learn several words each time you learn one.

In the SAT Word List, we've provided some of the family linkages to help you. For example, you'll find the adjective *anachronistic* in the word list. It means "out of the proper time," as illustrated by the sample sentence: The reference, in Shakespeare's *Julius Caesar,* to "the clock striking twelve" is anachronistic, since there were no striking timepieces in ancient Rome.

When you meet this word, you should also get to know its close kinfolk. The noun *anachronism* means something that is out of its proper time. The clock in *Julius Caesar,* for example, is an anachronism; in another way, so are the knickers worn by modern baseball players, which reflect a style in men's fashions that went out of date generations ago. When you learn the adjective, learn the noun (and/or verb) that goes with it at the same time.

Become a Word Root Tracer

The two words we just discussed—*anachronistic* and *anachronism*—are like brother and sister. Slightly more distant relatives can be located and learned through the Word Origin feature you'll find near many of the words in the list. The origin for *anachronistic* connects this word to its source from another language: The Greek word *chronos* = time. Ultimately, this is the root from which the English word *anachronistic* grows.

As you explore the Word Origins, you'll find that many words—especially bookish SAT words—come from roots in Latin and Greek. There are complicated (and interesting) historical reasons for this, but the nub is that, for several centuries, learned people in England and America knew ancient Latin and Greek and deliberately imported words from those languages into English.

They rarely imported just one word from a given root. Thus, many word roots can enable you to learn several English words at once. The Word Origin for anachronistic tells you that *chronos* is also the source of the English words *chronic, chronicle, chronograph, chronology,* and *synchronize.* All have to do with the concept of time:

> *chronic* = lasting a long time
> *chronicle* = a record of events over a period of time
> *chronograph* = a clock or watch
> *chronology* = a timeline
> *synchronize* = to make two things happen at the same time

Learning the word root *chronos* can help you in several ways. It will make it easier to learn all the words in the *chronos* family, as opposed to trying to learn them one at a time. It will help you to remember the meanings of *chronos* words if they turn up on the exam, and it may even help you to guess the meaning of an entirely new *chronos* word when you encounter it.

Use the Words You Learn

Make a deliberate effort to include the new words you're learning in your daily speech and writing. It will impress people (teachers, bosses, friends and enemies) and it will help solidify your memory of the words and their meanings. Maybe you've heard this tip about meeting new people: if you use a new acquaintance's name several times, you're unlikely to forget it. The same is true with new words: use them, and you won't lose them.

Create Your Own Word List

Get into the habit of reading a little every day with your dictionary nearby. When you encounter a new word in a newspaper, magazine, or book, look it up. Then jot down the new word, its definition, and the sentence in which you encountered it in a notebook set aside for this purpose. Review your vocabulary notebook periodically—say, once a week. This is a great way to supplement our SAT Word List, because it's personally tailored. Your notebook will reflect the kinds of things you read and the words you find most difficult. The fact that you've taken the time and made the effort to write down the words and their meanings will help to fix them in your memory. Chances are good that you'll encounter a few words from your vocabulary notebook on the exam.

The Word List

Word Origin
Latin *brevis* = short. Also found in English *brevity*.

abbreviate (verb)   to make briefer, to shorten. *Because time was running out, the speaker had to abbreviate his remarks.* **abbreviation** (noun).

abrasive (adjective)   irritating, grinding, rough. *The manager's rude, abrasive way of criticizing the workers was bad for morale.* **abrasion** (noun).

abridge (verb)   to shorten, to reduce. *The Bill of Rights is designed to prevent Congress from abridging the rights of Americans.* **abridgment** (noun).

absolve (verb)   to free from guilt, to exonerate. *The criminal jury absolved the man of the murder of his ex-wife.* **absolution** (noun).

abstain (verb)   to refrain, to hold back. *After his heart attack, he was warned by the doctor to abstain from smoking, drinking, and over-eating.* **abstinence** (noun), **abstemious** (adjective).

accentuate (verb)   to emphasize, to stress. *The overcast skies and chill winds accentuated our gloomy mood.*

acrimonious (adjective)   biting, harsh, caustic. *The election campaign became acrimonious, as the candidates traded insults and accusations.* **acrimony** (noun).

adaptable (adjective)   able to be changed to be suitable for a new purpose. *Some scientists say that the mammals outlived the dinosaurs because they were more adaptable to a changing climate.* **adapt** (verb), **adaptation** (noun).

adulation (noun)   extreme admiration. *Few young actors have received greater adulation than did Marlon Brando after his performance in* A Streetcar Named Desire. **adulate** (verb), **adulatory** (adjective).

adversary (noun)   an enemy or opponent. *When the former Soviet Union became an American ally, the United States lost its last major adversary.*

adversity (noun)   misfortune. *It's easy to be patient and generous when things are going well; a person's true character is revealed under adversity.* **adverse** (adjective).

aesthetic (adjective)   relating to art or beauty. *Mapplethorpe's photos may be attacked on moral grounds, but no one questions their aesthetic value—they are beautiful.* **aestheticism** (noun).

affected (adjective)   false, artificial. *At one time, Japanese women were taught to speak in an affected high-pitched voice, which was thought girlishly attractive.* **affect** (verb), **affectation** (noun).

aggressive (adjective)   forceful, energetic, and attacking. *A football player needs a more aggressive style of play than a soccer player.* **aggression** (noun).

alacrity (noun)   promptness, speed. *Thrilled with the job offer, he accepted with alacrity—"Before they can change their minds!" he thought.*

allege (verb)   to state without proof. *Some have alleged that the actor was murdered, but all the evidence points to suicide.* **allegation** (noun).

alleviate (verb)   to make lighter or more bearable. *Although no cure for AIDS has been found, doctors are able to alleviate the sufferings of those with the disease.* **alleviation** (noun).

ambiguous (adjective)   having two or more possible meanings. *The phrase, "Let's table that discussion" is ambiguous; some think it means, "Let's discuss it now," while others think it means, "Let's save it for later."* **ambiguity** (noun).

Word Origin
Latin *acer* = sharp. Also found in English *acerbity*, *acrid*, *exacerbate*.

Word Origin
Latin *levis* = light. Also found in English *levitate*, *levity*.

ambivalent (adjective)   having two or more contradictory feelings or attitudes; uncertain. *She was ambivalent toward her impending marriage; at times she was eager to go ahead, while at other times she wanted to call it off.* **ambivalence** (noun).

Word Origin
Latin *amare* = love. Also found in English *amicable, amity, amorous.*

amiable (adjective)   likable, agreeable, friendly. *He was an amiable lab partner, always smiling, on time, and ready to work.* **amiability** (verb).

amicable (adjective)   friendly, peaceable. *Although they agreed to divorce, their settlement was amicable and they remained friends afterward.*

amplify (verb)   to enlarge, expand, or increase. *Uncertain as to whether they understood, the students asked the teacher to amplify his explanation.* **amplification** (noun).

Word Origin
Greek *chronos* = time. Also found in English *chronic, chronicle, chronograph, chronology, synchronize.*

anachronistic (adjective)   out of the proper time. *The reference, in Shakespeare's Julius Caesar, to "the clock striking twelve" is anachronistic, since there were no striking timepieces in ancient Rome.* **anachronism** (noun).

anarchy (noun)   absence of law or order. *For several months after the Nazi government was destroyed, there was no effective government in parts of Germany, and anarchy ruled.* **anarchic** (adjective).

anomaly (noun)   something different or irregular. *The tiny planet Pluto, orbiting next to the giants Jupiter, Saturn, and Neptune, has long appeared to be an anomaly.* **anomalous** (adjective).

antagonism (noun)   hostility, conflict, opposition. *As more and more reporters investigated the Watergate scandal, antagonism between Nixon and the press increased.* **antagonistic** (adjective), **antagonize** (verb).

antiseptic (adjective)   fighting infection; extremely clean. *A wound should be washed with an antiseptic solution. The all-white offices were bare and almost antiseptic in their starkness.*

apathy (noun)   lack of interest, concern, or emotion. *American voters are showing increasing apathy over politics; fewer than half voted in the last election.* **apathetic** (adjective).

arable (adjective)   able to be cultivated for growing crops. *Rocky New England has relatively little arable farmland.*

arbiter (noun)   someone able to settle dispute; a judge or referee. *The public is the ultimate arbiter of commercial value: It decides what sells and what doesn't.*

arbitrary (adjective)   based on random or merely personal preference. *Both computers cost the same and had the same features, so in the end I made an arbitrary decision about which to buy.*

Word Origin
Latin *arbiter* = judge. Also found in English *arbitrage, arbitrary, arbitrate.*

arcane (adjective)   little-known, mysterious, obscure. *Eliot's "Waste Land" is filled with arcane lore, including quotations in Latin, Greek, French, German, and Sanskrit.* **arcana** (noun, plural).

ardor (noun)   a strong feeling of passion, energy, or zeal. *The young revolutionary proclaimed his convictions with an ardor that excited the crowd.* **ardent** (adjective).

arid (adjective)   very dry; boring and meaningless. *The arid climate of Arizona makes farming difficult. Some find the law a fascinating topic, but for me it is an arid discipline.* **aridity** (noun).

ascetic (adjective)   practicing strict self-discipline for moral or spiritual reasons. *The so-called Desert Fathers were hermits who lived an ascetic life of fasting, study, and prayer.* **asceticism** (verb).

assiduous (verb)   working with care, attention, and diligence. *Although Karen is not a naturally gifted math student, by assiduous study she managed to earn an A in trigonometry.* **assiduity** (noun).

astute (adjective)   observant, intelligent, and shrewd. *Alan's years of experience in Washington and his personal acquaintance with many political insiders make him an astute commentator on politics.*

atypical (adjective)   not typical; unusual. *In* The Razor's Edge, *Bill Murray, best known as a comic actor, gave an atypical dramatic performance.*

audacious (adjective)   bold, daring, adventurous. *Her plan to cross the Atlantic single-handed in a twelve-foot sailboat was audacious, if not reckless.* **audacity** (noun).

audible (adjective)   able to be heard. *Although she whispered, her voice was picked up by the microphone, and her words were audible throughout the theater.* **audibility** (noun).

Word Origin
Latin *audire* = to hear. Also found in English *audition, auditorium, auditory.*

auspicious (adjective)   promising good fortune; propitious. *The news that a team of British climbers had reached the summit of Everest seemed an auspicious sign for the reign of newly crowned Queen Elizabeth II.*

authoritarian (adjective)   favoring or demanding blind obedience to leaders. *Despite Americans' belief in democracy, the American government has supported authoritarian regimes in other countries.* **authoritarianism** (noun)

belated (adjective)   delayed past the proper time. *She called her mother on January 5th to offer her a belated "Happy New Year."*

belie (verb)   to present a false or contradictory appearance. *Julie's youthful appearance belies her long, distinguished career in show business.*

benevolent (adjective)   wishing or doing good. *In old age, Carnegie used his wealth for benevolent purposes, donating large sums to found libraries and schools.* **benevolence** (noun).

> **Word Origin**
> Latin *bene* = well. Also found in English *benediction, benefactor, beneficent, beneficial, benefit, benign.*

berate (verb)   to scold or criticize harshly. *The judge angrily berated the two lawyers for their unprofessional behavior.*

bereft (adjective)   lacking or deprived of something. *Bereft of parental love, orphans sometimes grow up insecure.*

bombastic (adjective)   inflated or pompous in style. *Old-fashioned bombastic political speeches don't work on television, which demands a more intimate style of communication.* **bombast** (noun).

bourgeois (adjective)   middle-class or reflecting middle-class values. *The Dadaists of the 1920s produced art deliberately designed to offend bourgeois art collectors, with their taste for respectable, refined, uncontroversial pictures.* **bourgeois** (noun).

buttress (noun)   something that supports or strengthens. *The endorsement of the American Medical Association is a powerful buttress for the claims made about this new medicine.* **buttress** (verb).

camaraderie (noun)   a spirit of friendship. *Spending long days and nights together on the road, the members of a traveling theater group develop a strong sense of camaraderie.*

candor (noun)   openness, honesty, frankness. *In his memoir, the former defense secretary describes his mistakes with remarkable candor.* **candid** (adjective).

capricious (adjective)   unpredictable, willful, whimsical. *The pop star has changed her image so many times that each new transformation now appears capricious rather than purposeful.* **caprice** (noun).

> **Word Origin**
> Latin *vorare* = to eat. Also found in English *devour, omnivorous, voracious.*

carnivorous (adjective)   meat-eating. *The long, dagger-like teeth of the Tyrannosaurus make it obvious that this was a carnivorous dinosaur.* **carnivore** (noun).

carping (adjective)   unfairly or excessively critical; querulous. *The newspaper is famous for its demanding critics, but none is harder to please than the carping McNamera, said to have single-handedly destroyed many acting careers.* **carp** (verb).

catalytic (adjective)   bringing about, causing, or producing some result. *The conditions for revolution existed in America by 1765; the disputes about taxation that arose later were the catalytic events that sparked the rebellion.* **catalyze** (verb).

caustic (adjective)   burning, corrosive. *No one was safe when the satirist H.L. Mencken unleashed his caustic wit.*

Word Origin
Greek *kaustikos* = burning. Also found in English *holocaust*.

censure (noun)   blame, condemnation. *The news that the senator had harassed several women brought censure from many feminists.* **censure** (verb).

chaos (noun)   disorder, confusion, chance. *The first few moments after the explosion were pure chaos: no one was sure what had happened, and the area was filled with people running and yelling.* **chaotic** (adjective).

circuitous (adjective)   winding or indirect. *We drove to the cottage by a circuitous route so we could see as much of the surrounding countryside as possible.*

Word Origin
Latin *circus* = circle. Also found in English *circumference, circumnavigate, circumscribe, circumspect, circumvent*.

circumlocution (noun)   speaking in a roundabout way; wordiness. *Legal documents often contain circumlocutions which make them difficult to understand.*

circumscribe (verb)   to define by a limit or boundary. *Originally, the role of the executive branch of government was clearly circumscribed, but that role has greatly expanded over time.* **circumscription** (noun).

circumvent (verb)   to get around. *When Jerry was caught speeding, he tried to circumvent the law by offering the police officer a bribe.*

clandestine (adjective)   secret, surreptitious. *As a member of the underground, Balas took part in clandestine meetings to discuss ways of sabotaging the Nazi forces.*

cloying (adjective)   overly sweet or sentimental. *The deathbed scenes in the novels of Dickens are famously cloying: as Oscar Wilde said, "One would need a heart of stone to read the death of Little Nell without laughing."*

cogent (adjective)   forceful and convincing. *The committee members were won over to the project by the cogent arguments of the chairman.* **cogency** (noun).

Word Origin
Latin *cognoscere* = to know. Also found in English *cognition, cognitive, incognito, recognize*.

cognizant (adjective)   aware, mindful. *Cognizant of the fact that it was getting late, the master of ceremonies cut short the last speech.* **cognizance** (noun).

cohesive (adjective)   sticking together, unified. *An effective military unit must be a cohesive team, all its members working together for a common goal.* **cohere** (verb), **cohesion** (noun).

collaborate (verb)   to work together. *To create a truly successful movie, the director, writers, actors, and many others must collaborate closely.* **collaboration** (noun), **collaborative** (adjective).

colloquial (adjective)   informal in language; conversational. *Some expressions from Shakespeare, such as the use of thou and thee, sound formal today but were colloquial English in Shakespeare's time.*

competent (adjective)   having the skill and knowledge needed for a particular task; capable. *Any competent lawyer can draw up a will.* **competence** (noun).

complacent (adjective)   smug, self-satisfied. *During the 1970s, American auto makers became complacent, believing that they would continue to be successful with little effort.* **complacency** (noun).

composure (noun)   calm, self-assurance. *The president managed to keep his composure during his speech even when the TelePrompTer broke down, leaving him without a script.* **composed** (adjective).

Word Origin
Latin *caedere* = to cut. Also found in English *decide, excise, incision, precise*.

conciliatory (adjective)   seeking agreement, compromise, or reconciliation. *As a conciliatory gesture, the union leaders agreed to postpone a strike and to continue negotiations with management.* **conciliate** (verb), **conciliation** (noun).

concise (adjective)   expressed briefly and simply; succinct. *Less than a page long, the Bill of Rights is a concise statement of the freedoms enjoyed by all Americans.* **concision** (noun).

condescending (adjective)   having an attitude of superiority toward another; patronizing. *"What a cute little car!" she remarked in a condescending style. "I suppose it's the nicest one someone like you could afford!"* **condescension** (noun).

Word Origin
Latin *dolere* = to feel pain. Also found in English *dolorous, indolent*.

condolence (noun)   pity for someone else's sorrow or loss; sympathy. *After the sudden death of the princess, thousands of messages of condolence were sent to her family.* **condole** (verb).

confidant (noun)   someone entrusted with another's secrets. *No one knew about Janee's engagement except Sarah, her confidant.* **confide** (verb), **confidential** (adjective).

conformity (noun)   agreement with or adherence to custom or rule. *In my high school, conformity was the rule: everyone dressed the same, talked the same, and listened to the same music.* **conform** (verb), **conformist** (adjective).

consensus (noun)   general agreement among a group. *Among Quakers, voting traditionally is not used; instead, discussion continues until the entire group forms a consensus.*

consolation (noun)   relief or comfort in sorrow or suffering. *Although we miss our dog very much, it is a consolation to know that she died quickly, without suffering.* **console** (verb).

consternation (noun)   shock, amazement, dismay. *When a voice in the back of the church shouted out, "I know why they should not be married!" the entire gathering was thrown into consternation.*

consummate (verb)   to complete, finish, or perfect. *The deal was consummated with a handshake and the payment of the agreed-upon fee.* **consummate** (adjective), **consummation** (noun).

contaminate (verb)   to make impure. *Chemicals dumped in a nearby forest had seeped into the soil and contaminated the local water supply.* **contamination** (noun).

contemporary (adjective)   modern, current; from the same time. *I prefer old-fashioned furniture rather than contemporary styles. The composer Vivaldi was roughly contemporary with Bach.* **contemporary** (noun).

> **Word Origin**
> Latin *tempus = time*. Also found in English *temporal, temporary, temporize*.

contrite (adjective)   sorry for past misdeeds. *The public is often willing to forgive celebrities who are involved in some scandal, as long as they appear contrite.* **contrition** (noun).

conundrum (noun)   a riddle, puzzle, or problem. *The question of why an all-powerful, all-loving God allows evil to exist is a conundrum many philosophers have pondered.*

convergence (noun)   the act of coming together in unity or similarity. *A remarkable example of evolutionary convergence can be seen in the shark and the dolphin, two sea creatures that developed from different origins to become very similar in form.* **converge** (verb).

> **Word Origin**
> Latin *volvere* = to roll. Also found in English *devolve, involve, revolution, revolve, voluble*.

convoluted (adjective)   twisting, complicated, intricate. *Tax law has become so convoluted that it's easy for people to accidentally violate it.* **convolute** (verb), **convolution** (noun).

corroborating (adjective)   supporting with evidence; confirming. *A passerby who had witnessed the crime gave corroborating testimony about the presence of the accused person.* **corroborate** (verb), **corroboration** (noun).

corrosive (adjective)   eating away, gnawing, or destroying. *Years of poverty and hard work had a corrosive effect on her beauty.* **corrode** (verb), **corrosion** (noun).

credulity (noun)   willingness to believe, even with little evidence. *Con artists fool people by taking advantage of their credulity.* **credulous** (adjective).

Word Origin
Greek *krinein* = to choose. Also found in English *criticize, critique.*

criterion (noun)   a standard of measurement or judgment. (The plural is criteria.) *In choosing a design for the new taxicabs, reliability will be our main criterion.*

critique (noun)   a critical evaluation. *The editor gave a detailed critique of the manuscript, explaining its strengths and its weaknesses.* **critique** (verb).

culpable (adjective)\mdeserving blame, guilty. *Although he committed the crime, because he was mentally ill he should not be considered culpable for his actions.* **culpability** (noun).

cumulative (adjective)   made up of successive additions. *Smallpox was eliminated only through the cumulative efforts of several generations of doctors and scientists.* **accumulation** (noun), **accumulate** (verb).

curtail (verb)   to shorten. *Because of the military emergence, all soldiers on leave were ordered to curtail their absences and return to duty.*

debased (adjective)   lowered in quality, character, or esteem. *The quality of TV journalism has been debased by the many new tabloid-style talk shows.* **debase** (verb).

debunk (verb)   to expose as false or worthless. *The magician loves to debunk psychics, mediums, clairvoyants, and others who claim supernatural powers.*

decorous (adjective)   having good taste; proper, appropriate. *The once reserved and decorous style of the British monarchy began to change when the chic, flamboyant young Diana Spencer joined the family.* **decorum** (noun).

Word Origin
Latin *ducere* = to lead. Also found in English *ductile, induce, produce, reduce.*

decry (verb)   to criticize or condemn. *Cigarette ads aimed at youngsters have led many to decry the marketing tactics of the tobacco industry.*

deduction (noun)   a logical conclusion, especially a specific conclusion based on general principles. *Based on what is known about the effects of greenhouse gases on atmospheric temperature, scientists have made several deductions about the likelihood of global warming.* **deduce** (verb).

delegate (verb)   to give authority or responsibility. *The president delegated the vice-president to represent the administration at the peace talks.* **delegate** (noun).

deleterious (adjective)   harmful. *About thirty years ago, scientists proved that working with asbestos could be deleterious to one's health, producing cancer and other diseases.*

delineate (verb)   to outline or describe. *Naturalists had long suspected the fact of evolution, but Darwin was the first to delineate a process—natural selection—through which evolution could occur.*

demagogue (noun)   a leader who plays dishonestly on the prejudices and emotions of his followers. *Senator Joseph McCarthy was a demagogue who used the paranoia of the anti-Communist 1950s as a way of seizing fame and power in Washington.* **demagoguery** (noun).

demure (adjective)   modest or shy. *The demure heroines of Victorian fiction have given way to today's stronger, more opinionated, and more independent female characters.*

denigrate (verb)   to criticize or belittle. *The firm's new president tried to explain his plans for improving the company without seeming to denigrate the work of his predecessor.* **denigration** (noun).

depose (verb)   to remove from office, especially from a throne. *Iran was formerly ruled by a monarch called the Shah, who was deposed in 1976.*

derelict (adjective)   neglecting one's duty. *The train crash was blamed on a switchman who was derelict, having fallen asleep while on duty.* **dereliction** (noun).

derivative (adjective)   taken from a particular source. *When a person first writes poetry, her poems are apt to be derivative of whatever poetry she most enjoys reading.* **derivation** (noun), **derive** (verb).

desolate (adjective)   empty, lifeless, and deserted; hopeless, gloomy. *Robinson Crusoe was shipwrecked and had to learn to survive alone on a desolate island. The murder of her husband left Mary Lincoln desolate.* **desolation** (noun).

destitute (adjective)   very poor. *Years of rule by a dictator who stole the wealth of the country had left the people of the Philippines destitute.* **destitution** (noun).

deter (verb)   to discourage from acting. *The best way to deter crime is to insure that criminals will receive swift and certain punishment.* **deterrence** (noun), **deterrent** (adjective).

> *Word Origin*
> Latin *delere* = to destroy. Also found in English *delete*.

detractor (noun)   someone who belittles or disparages. *The singer has many detractors who consider his music boring, inane, and sentimental.* **detract** (verb).

deviate (verb)   to depart from a standard or norm. *Having agreed upon a spending budget for the company, we mustn't deviate from it; if we do, we may run out of money soon.* **deviation** (noun).

devious (adjective)   tricky, deceptive. *The stockbroker's devious financial tactics were designed to enrich his firm while confusing or misleading government regulators.*

didactic (adjective)   intended to teach, instructive. *The children's TV show "Sesame Street" is designed to be both entertaining and didactic.*

diffident (adjective)   hesitant, reserved, shy. *Someone with a diffident personality should pursue a career that involves little public contact.* **diffidence** (noun).

diffuse (verb)   to spread out, to scatter. *The red dye quickly became diffused through the water, turning it a very pale pink.* **diffusion** (noun).

digress (verb)   to wander from the main path or the main topic. *My high school biology teacher loved to digress from science into personal anecdotes about his college adventures.* **digression** (noun), **digressive** (adjective).

dilatory (adjective)   delaying, procrastinating. *The lawyer used various dilatory tactics, hoping that his opponent would get tired of waiting for a trial and drop the case.*

diligent (adjective)   working hard and steadily. *Through diligent efforts, the townspeople were able to clear away the debris from the flood in a matter of days.* **diligence** (noun).

diminutive (adjective)   unusually small, tiny. *Children are fond of Shetland ponies because their diminutive size makes them easy to ride.* **diminution** (noun).

discern (verb)   to detect, notice, or observe. *I could discern the shape of a whale off the starboard bow, but it was too far away to determine its size or species.* **discernment** (noun).

disclose (verb)   to make known; to reveal. *Election laws require candidates to disclose the names of those who contribute money to their campaigns.* **disclosure** (noun).

discomfit (verb)   to frustrate, thwart, or embarrass. *Discomfited by the interviewer's unexpected question, Peter could only stammer in reply.* **discomfiture** (noun).

disconcert (verb)   to confuse or embarrass. *When the hallway bells began to ring halfway through her lecture, the speaker was disconcerted and didn't know what to do.*

discredit (verb)   to cause disbelief in the accuracy of some statement or the reliability of a person. *Although many people still believe in UFOs, among scientists the reports of "alien encounters" have been thoroughly discredited.*

discreet (adjective)   showing good judgment in speech and behavior. *Be discreet when discussing confidential business matters—don't talk among strangers on the elevator, for example.* **discretion** (noun).

discrepancy (noun)   a difference or variance between two or more things. *The discrepancies between the two witnesses' stories show that one of them must be lying.* **discrepant** (adjective).

disdain (noun)   contempt, scorn. *The millionaire was disliked by many people because she treated "little people" with such disdain.* **disdain** (verb), **disdainful** (adjective).

disingenuous (adjective)   pretending to be candid, simple, and frank. *When the Texas billionaire ran for president, many considered his "jest plain folks" style disingenuous.*

disparage (verb)   to speak disrespectfully about, to belittle. *Many political ads today both praise their own candidate and disparage his or her opponent.* **disparagement** (noun), **disparaging** (adjective).

disparity (noun)   difference in quality or kind. *There is often a disparity between the kind of high-quality television people say they want and the low-brow programs they actually watch.* **disparate** (adjective).

disregard (verb)   to ignore, to neglect. *If you don't write a will, when you die, your survivors may disregard your wishes about how your property should be handled.* **disregard** (noun).

disruptive (adjective)   causing disorder, interrupting. *When the senator spoke at our college, angry demonstrators picketed, heckled, and engaged in other disruptive activities.* **disrupt** (verb), **disruption** (noun).

dissemble (verb)   to pretend, to simulate. *When the police questioned her about the crime, she dissembled innocence.*

dissipate (verb)   to spread out or scatter. *The windows and doors were opened, allowing the smoke that had filled the room to dissipate.* **dissipation** (noun).

Word Origin
Latin *credere* = to believe. Also found in English *credential*, *credible*, *credit*, *credo*, *credulous*, *incredible*.

Word Origin
Latin *sonare* = to sound. Also found in English *consonance*, *sonar*, *sonic*, *sonorous*.

dissonance (noun)   lack of music harmony; lack of agreement between ideas. *Most modern music is characterized by dissonance, which many listeners find hard to enjoy. There is a noticeable dissonance between two common beliefs of most conservatives: their faith in unfettered free markets and their preference for traditional social values.* **dissonant** (adjective).

diverge (verb)   to move in different directions. *Frost's poem "The Road Less Traveled" tells of the choice he made when "Two roads diverged in a yellow wood."* **divergence** (noun), **divergent** (adjective).

diversion (noun)   a distraction or pastime. *During the two hours he spent in the doctor's waiting room, his hand-held computer game was a welcome diversion.* divert (verb).

divination (noun)   the art of predicting the future. *In ancient Greece, people wanting to know their fate would visit the priests at Delphi, supposedly skilled at divination.* **divine** (verb).

divisive (adjective)   causing disagreement or disunity. *Throughout history, race has been the most divisive issue in American society.*

divulge (verb)   to reveal. *The people who count the votes for the Oscar awards are under strict orders not to divulge the names of the winners.*

dogmatic (adjective)   holding firmly to a particular set of beliefs with little or no basis. *Believers in Marxist doctrine tend to be dogmatic, ignoring evidence that contradicts their beliefs.* **dogmatism** (noun).

> **Word Origin**
> Latin *durare* = to last. Also found in English *durance, duration, endure.*

dominant (adjective)   greatest in importance or power. *The historian suggests that the existence of the frontier had a dominant influence on American culture.* **dominate** (verb), **domination** (noun).

dubious (adjective)   doubtful, uncertain. *Despite the chairman's attempts to convince the committee members that his plan would succeed, most of them remained dubious.* **dubiety** (noun).

durable (adjective)   long-lasting. *Denim is a popular material for work clothes because it is strong and durable.*

duress (noun)   compulsion or restraint. *Fearing that the police might beat him, he confessed to the crime, not willingly but under duress.*

eclectic (adjective)   drawn from many sources; varied, heterogeneous. *The Mellon family art collection is an eclectic one, including works ranging from ancient Greek sculptures to modern paintings.* **eclecticism** (noun).

efficacious (adjective)   able to produce a desired effect. *Though thousands of people today are taking herbal supplements to treat depression, researchers have not yet proved them efficacious.* **efficacy** (noun).

effrontery (noun)   shameless boldness. *The sports world was shocked when a pro basketball player had the effrontery to choke his head coach during a practice session.*

effusive (adjective)   pouring forth one's emotions very freely. *Having won the Oscar for Best Actress, Sally Field gave an effusive acceptance speech in which she marveled, "You like me! You really like me!"* **effusion** (noun).

egoism (noun)   excessive concern with oneself; conceit. *Robert's egoism was so great that all he could talk about was the importance—and the brilliance—of his own opinions.* **egoistic** (adjective).

egregious (adjective)   obvious, conspicuous, flagrant. *It's hard to imagine how the editor could allow such an egregious error to appear.*

elated (adjective)   excited and happy; exultant. *When the Green Bay Packers' last, desperate pass was dropped, the elated fans of the Denver Broncos began to celebrate.* **elate** (verb), **elation** (noun).

elliptical (adjective)   very terse or concise in writing or speech; difficult to understand. *Rather than speak plainly, she hinted at her meaning through a series of nods, gestures, and elliptical half-sentences.*

elusive (adjective)   hard to capture, grasp, or understand. *Though everyone thinks they know what "justice" is, when you try to define the concept precisely, it proves to be quite elusive.*

embezzle (verb)   to steal money property that has been entrusted to your care. *The church treasurer was found to have embezzled thousands of dollars by writing phony checks on the church bank account.* **embezzlement** (noun).

emend (verb)   to correct. *Before the letter is mailed, please emend the two spelling errors.* **emendation** (noun).

emigrate (verb)   to leave one place or country to settle elsewhere. *Millions of Irish emigrated to the New World in the wake of the great Irish famines of the 1840s.* **emigrant** (noun), **emigration** (noun).

eminent (adjective)   noteworthy, famous. *Vaclav Havel was an eminent author before being elected president of the Czech Republic.* **eminence** (noun).

Word Origin
Latin *grex* = herd. Also found in English *aggregate, congregate, gregarious.*

Word Origin
Latin *ludere* = to play. Also found in English *delude, illusion, interlude, ludicrous.*

emissary (noun)   someone who represents another. *In an effort to avoid a military showdown, Carter was sent as an emissary to Korea to negotiate a settlement.*

emollient (noun)   something that softens or soothes. *She used a hand cream as an emollient on her dry, work-roughened hands.* **emollient** (adjective).

empathy (noun)   imaginative sharing of the feelings, thoughts, or experiences of another. *It's easy for a parent to have empathy for the sorrow of another parent whose child has died.* **empathetic** (adjective).

empirical (adjective)   based on experience or personal observation. *Although many people believe in ESP, scientists have found no empirical evidence of its existence.* **empiricism** (noun).

emulate (verb)   to imitate or copy. *The British band Oasis admitted their desire to emulate their idols, the Beatles.* **emulation** (noun).

encroach (verb)   to go beyond acceptable limits; to trespass. *By quietly seizing more and more authority, Robert Moses continually encroached on the powers of other government leaders.* **encroachment** (noun).

enervate (verb)   to reduce the energy or strength of someone or something. *The stress of the operation left her feeling enervated for about two weeks.*

engender (verb)   to produce, to cause. *Countless disagreements over the proper use of national forests have engendered feelings of hostility between ranchers and environmentalists.*

enhance (verb)   to improve in value or quality. *New kitchen appliances will enhance your house and increase the amount of money you'll make when you sell it.* **enhancement** (noun).

enmity (noun)   hatred, hostility, ill will. *Long-standing enmity, like that between the Protestants and Catholics in Northern Ireland, is difficult to overcome.*

enthrall (verb)   to enchant or charm. *When the Swedish singer Jenny Lind toured America in the nineteenth century, audiences were enthralled by her beauty and talent.*

ephemeral (adjective)   quickly disappearing; transient. *Stardom in pop music is ephemeral; most of the top acts of ten years ago are forgotten today.*

equanimity (noun)   calmness of mind, especially under stress. *Roosevelt had the gift of facing the great crises of his presidency—the Depression, the Second World War—with equanimity and even humor.*

Word Origin
Latin *anima* = mind, spirit. Also found in English *animate, magnanimous, pusillanimous, unanimous.*

eradicate (verb)   to destroy completely. *American society has failed to eradicate racism, although some of its worst effects have been reduced.*

espouse (verb)   to take up as a cause; to adopt. *No politician in American today will openly espouse racism, although some behave and speak in racially prejudiced ways.*

euphoric (adjective)   a feeling of extreme happiness and well-being; elation. *One often feels euphoric during the earliest days of a new love affair.* **euphorial** (noun).

evanescent (adjective)   vanishing like a vapor; fragile and transient. *As she walked by, the evanescent fragrance of her perfume reached me for just an instant.*

exacerbate (verb)   to make worse or more severe. *The roads in our town already have too much traffic; building a new shopping mall will exacerbate the problem.*

> **Word Origin**
> Latin *asper* = rough. Also found in English *asperity*.

exasperate (verb)   to irritate or annoy. *Because she was trying to study, Sharon was exasperated by the yelling of her neighbors' children.*

exculpate (verb)   to free from blame or guilt. *When someone else confessed to the crime, the previous suspect was exculpated.* **exculpation** (noun), **exculpatory** (adjective).

exemplary (adjective)   worthy to serve as a model. *The Baldrige Award is given to a company with exemplary standards of excellence in products and service.* **exemplar** (noun), **exemplify** (verb).

exonerate (verb)   to free from blame. *Although he was suspected at first of being involved in the bombing, later evidence exonerated him.* **exoneration** (noun), **exonerative** (adjective).

expansive (adjective)   broad and large; speaking openly and freely. *The LBJ Ranch is located on an expansive tract of land in Texas. Over dinner, she became expansive in describing her dreams for the future.*

expedite (verb)   to carry out promptly. *As the flood waters rose, the governor ordered state agencies to expedite their rescue efforts.*

expertise (noun)   skill, mastery. *The software company was eager to hire new graduates with programming expertise.*

> **Word Origin**
> Latin *proprius* = own. Also found in English *appropriate, property, proprietary, proprietor.*

expiate (verb)   to atone for. *The president's apology to the survivors of the notorious Tuskegee experiments was his attempt to expiate the nation's guilt over their mistreatment.* **expiation** (noun).

expropriate (verb)   to seize ownership of. *When the Communists came to power in China, they expropriated most businesses and turned them over to government-appointed managers.* **expropriation** (noun).

extant (adjective)   currently in existence. *Of the seven ancient "Wonders of the World," only the pyramids of Egypt are still extant.*

extenuate (verb)   to make less serious. *Karen's guilt is extenuated by the fact that she was only twelve when she committed the theft.* **extenuating** (adjective), **extenuation** (noun).

extol (verb)   to greatly praise. *At the party convention, speaker after speaker rose to extol their candidate for the presidency.*

extricate (verb)   to free from a difficult or complicated situation. *Much of the humor in the TV show I Love Lucy comes in watching Lucy try to extricate herself from the problems she creates by fibbing or trickery.* **extricable** (adjective).

extrinsic (adjective)   not an innate part or aspect of something; external. *The high price of old baseball cards is due to extrinsic factors, such as the nostalgia felt by baseball fans for the stars of their youth, rather than the inherent beauty or value of the cards themselves.*

Word Origin
Latin *facere* = to do. Also found in English *facility, factor, facsimile, faculty.*

exuberant (adjective)   wildly joyous and enthusiastic. *As the final seconds of the game ticked away, the fans of the winning team began an exuberant celebration.* **exuberance** (noun).

facile (adjective)   easy; shallow or superficial. *The one-minute political commercial favors a candidate with facile opinions rather than serious, thoughtful solutions.* **facilitate** (verb), **facility** (noun).

fallacy (noun)   an error in fact or logic. *It's a fallacy to think that "natural" means "healthful"; after all, the deadly poison arsenic is completely natural.* **fallacious** (adjective).

felicitous (adjective)   pleasing, fortunate, apt. *The sudden blossoming of the dogwood trees on the morning of Matt's wedding seemed a felicitous sign of good luck.* **felicity** (noun).

feral (adjective)   wild. *The garbage dump was inhabited by a pack of feral dogs, which had escaped from their owners and become completely wild.*

fervent (adjective)   full of intense feeling; ardent, zealous. *In the days just after his religious conversion, his piety was at its most fervent.* **fervid** (adjective), **fervor** (noun).

flagrant (adjective)   obviously wrong; offensive. *Nixon was forced to resign the presidency after a series of flagrant crimes against the U.S. Constitution.* **flagrancy** (noun).

flamboyant (adjective)   very colorful, showy, or elaborate. *At Mardi Gras, partygoers compete to show off the most wild and flamboyant outfits.*

florid (adjective)   flowery, fancy; reddish. *The grand ballroom was decorated in a florid style. Years of heavy drinking had given him a florid complexion.*

foppish (adjective)   describing a man who is foolishly vain about his dress or appearance. *The foppish character of the 1890s wore bright-colored spats and a top hat; in the 1980s, he wore fancy suspenders and a shirt with a contrasting collar.* **fop** (noun).

formidable (adjective)   awesome, impressive, or frightening. *According to his plaque in the Baseball Hall of Fame, pitcher Tom Seaver turned the New York Mets "from lovable losers into formidable foes."*

fortuitous (adjective)   lucky, fortunate. *Although the mayor claimed credit for the falling crime rate, it was really caused by several fortuitous trends.*

fractious (adjective)   troublesome, unruly. *Members of the British Parliament are often fractious, shouting insults and sarcastic questions during debates.*

> **Word Origin**
> Latin *frater* = brother. Also found in English *fraternal, fraternity, fratricide.*

fragility (noun)   the quality of being easy to break; delicacy, weakness. *Because of their fragility, few stained glass windows from the early Middle Ages have survived.* **fragile** (adjective).

fraternize (verb)   to associate with on friendly terms. *Although baseball players aren't supposed to fraternize with their opponents, players from opposing teams often chat before games.* **fraternization** (noun).

frenetic (adjective)   chaotic, frantic. *The floor of the stock exchange, filled with traders shouting and gesturing, is a scene of frenetic activity.*

frivolity (noun)   lack of seriousness; levity. *The frivolity of the Mardi Gras carnival is in contrast to the seriousness of the religious season of Lent which follows.* **frivolous** (adjective).

frugal (adjective)   spending little. *With our last few dollars, we bought a frugal dinner: a loaf of bread and a piece of cheese.* **frugality** (noun).

fugitive (noun)   someone trying to escape. *When two prisoners broke out of the local jail, police were warned to keep an eye out for the fugitives.* **fugitive** (adjective).

gargantuan (adjective)   huge, colossal. *The building of the Great Wall of China was one of the most gargantuan projects ever undertaken.*

genial (adjective)   friendly, gracious. *A good host welcomes all visitors in a warm and genial fashion.*

grandiose (adjective)   overly large, pretentious, or showy. *Among Hitler's grandiose plans for Berlin was a gigantic building with a dome several times larger than any ever built.* **grandiosity** (noun).

gratuitous (adjective)   given freely or without cause. *Since her opinion was not requested, her harsh criticism of his singing seemed a gratuitous insult.*

gregarious (adjective)   enjoying the company of others; sociable. *Marty is naturally gregarious, a popular member of several clubs and a sought-after lunch companion.*

guileless (adjective)   without cunning; innocent. *Deborah's guileless personality and complete honesty make it hard for her to survive in the harsh world of politics.*

gullible (adjective)   easily fooled. *When the sweepstakes entry form arrived bearing the message, "You may be a winner!" my gullible neighbor tried to claim a prize.* **gullibility** (noun).

hackneyed (adjective)   without originality, trite. *When someone invented the phrase, "No pain, no gain," it was clever, but now it is so commonly heard that it seems hackneyed.*

haughty (adjective)   overly proud. *The fashion model strode down the runway, her hips thrust forward and a haughty expression, like a sneer, on her face.* **haughtiness** (noun).

hedonist (noun)   someone who lives mainly to pursue pleasure. *Having inherited great wealth, he chose to live the life of a hedonist, traveling the world in luxury.* **hedonism** (noun), **hedonistic** (adjective).

heinous (adjective)   very evil, hateful. *The massacre by Pol Pot of over a million Cambodians is one of the twentieth century's most heinous crimes.*

hierarchy (noun)   a ranking of people, things, or ideas from highest to lowest. *A cabinet secretary ranks just below the president and vice president in the hierarchy of the executive branch.* **hierarchical** (adjective).

hypocrisy (noun)   a false pretense of virtue. *When the sexual misconduct of the television preacher was exposed, his followers were shocked at his hypocrisy.* **hypocritical** (adjective).

iconoclast (noun)   someone who attacks traditional beliefs or institutions. *The comedian enjoys his reputation as an iconoclast, though people in power often resent his satirical jabs.* **iconoclasm** (noun), **iconoclastic** (adjective).

idiosyncratic (adjective)   peculiar to an individual; eccentric. *She sings pop music in an idiosyncratic style, mingling high-pitched whoops and squeals with throaty gurgles.* **idiosyncrasy** (noun).

idolatry (noun)   the worship of a person, thing, or institution as a god. *In Communist China, Chairman Mao was the subject of idolatry; his picture was displayed everywhere, and millions of Chinese memorized his sayings.* **idolatrous** (adjective).

impartial (adjective)   fair, equal, unbiased. *If a judge is not impartial, then all of her rulings are questionable.* **impartiality** (noun).

impeccable (adjective)   flawless. *The crooks printed impeccable copies of the Super Bowl tickets, making it impossible to distinguish them from the real things.*

impetuous (adjective)   acting hastily or impulsively. *Ben's resignation was an impetuous act; he did it without thinking, and he soon regretted it.* **impetuosity** (noun).

impinge (verb)   to encroach upon, touch, or affect. *You have a right to do whatever you want, so long as your actions don't impinge on the rights of others.*

implicit (adjective)   understood without being openly expressed; implied. *Although most clubs had no rules excluding blacks and Jews, many had an implicit understanding that no blacks or Jews would be allowed to join.*

impute (verb)   to credit or give responsibility to; to attribute. *Although Sarah's comments embarrassed me, I don't impute any ill will to her; I think she didn't realize what she was saying.* **imputation** (noun).

inarticulate (adjective)   unable to speak or express oneself clearly and understandably. *A skilled athlete may be an inarticulate public speaker, as demonstrated by many post-game interviews.*

incisive (adjective)   expressed clearly and directly. *Franklin settled the debate with a few incisive remarks that summed up the issue perfectly.*

> *Word Origin*
> Latin *articulus* = joint, division. Also found in English *arthritis, articulate.*

incompatible (adjective)   unable to exist together; conflicting. *Many people hold seemingly incompatible beliefs: for example, supporting the death penalty while believing in the sacredness of human life.* **incompatibility** (noun).

inconsequential (adjective)   of little importance. *When the stereo was delivered, it was a different shade of gray than I expected, but the difference was inconsequential.*

incontrovertible (adjective)   impossible to question. *The fact that Sheila's fingerprints were the only ones on the murder weapon made her guilt seem incontrovertible.*

incorrigible (adjective)   impossible to manage or reform. *Lou is an incorrigible trickster, constantly playing practical jokes no matter how much his friends complain.*

incremental (adjective)   increasing gradually by small amounts. *Although the initial cost of the Medicare program was small, the incremental expenses have grown to be very large.* **increment** (noun).

incriminate (adjective)   to give evidence of guilt. *The fifth amendment to the Constitution says that no one is required to reveal information that would incriminate him in a crime.* **incriminating** (adjective).

incumbent (noun)   someone who occupies an office or position. *It is often difficult for a challenger to win a seat in Congress from the incumbent.* **incumbency** (noun), **incumbent** (adjective).

indeterminate (adjective)   not definitely known. *The college plans to enroll an indeterminate number of students; the size of the class will depend on the number of applicants and how many accept offers of admission.* **determine** (verb).

indifferent (adjective)   unconcerned, apathetic.*The mayor's small proposed budget for education suggests that he is indifferent to the needs of our schools.* **indifference** (noun).

indistinct (adjective)   unclear, uncertain. *We could see boats on the water, but in the thick morning fog their shapes were indistinct.*

indomitable (adjective)   unable to be conquered or controlled. *The world admired the indomitable spirit of Nelson Mandela; he remained courageous despite years of imprisonment.*

induce (verb)   to cause. *The doctor prescribed a medicine which is supposed to induce a lowering of the blood pressure.* **induction** (noun).

ineffable (adjective)   difficult to describe or express. *He gazed in silence at the sunrise over the Taj Mahal, his eyes reflecting an ineffable sense of wonder.*

inevitable (adjective)   unable to be avoided. *Once the Japanese attacked Pearl Harbor, American involvement in World War Two was inevitable.* **inevitability** (noun).

inexorable (adjective)   unable to be deterred; relentless. *It's difficult to imagine how the mythic character of Oedipus could have avoided his evil destiny; his fate appears inexorable.*

ingenious (adjective)   showing cleverness and originality. *The Post-It note is an ingenious solution to a common problem—how to mark papers without spoiling them.* **ingenuity** (noun).

inherent (adjective)   naturally part of something. *Compromise is inherent in democracy, since everyone cannot get his way.* **inhere** (verb), **inherence** (noun).

innate (adjective)   inborn, native. *Not everyone who takes piano lessons becomes a fine musician, which shows that music requires innate talent as well as training.*

innocuous (adjective)   harmless, inoffensive. *I was surprised that Andrea took offense at such an innocuous joke.*

inoculate (verb)   to prevent a disease by infusing with a disease-causing organism. *Pasteur found he could prevent rabies by inoculating patients with the virus that causes the disease.* **inoculation** (noun).

insipid (adjective)   flavorless, uninteresting. *Most TV shows are so insipid that you can watch them while reading without missing a thing.* **insipidity** (noun).

insolence (noun)   an attitude or behavior that is bold and disrespectful. *Some feel that news reporters who shout questions at the president are behaving with insolence.* **insolent** (adjective).

insular (adjective)   narrow or isolated in attitude or viewpoint. *New Yorkers are famous for their insular attitudes; they seem to think that nothing important has ever happened outside of their city.* **insularity** (noun).

insurgency (noun)   uprising, rebellion. *The angry townspeople had begun an insurgency bordering on downright revolution; they were collecting arms, holding secret meetings, and refusing to pay certain taxes.* **insurgent** (adjective).

Word Origin
Latin *loqui* = to speak. Also found in English *colloquial, colloquy, eloquent, grandiloquent, locution, loquacious.*

integrity (noun)   honesty, uprightness; soundness, completeness. *"Honest Abe" Lincoln is considered a model of political integrity. Inspectors examined the building's support beams and foundation and found no reason to doubt its structural integrity.*

interlocutor (noun)   someone taking part in a dialogue or conversation. *Annoyed by the constant questions from someone in the crowd, the speaker challenged his interlocutor to offer a better plan.* **interlocutory** (adjective).

interlude (noun)   an interrupting period or performance. *The two most dramatic scenes in King Lear are separated, strangely, by a comic interlude starring the king's jester.*

interminable (adjective)   endless or seemingly endless. *Addressing the United Nations, Castro announced, "We will be brief"—then delivered an interminable 4-hour speech.*

Word Origin
Latin *trepidus = alarmed.* Also found in English *trepidation.*

intransigent (adjective)   unwilling to compromise. *Despite the mediator's attempts to suggest a fair solution, the two parties were intransigent, forcing a showdown.* **intransigence** (noun).

intrepid (adjective)   fearless and resolute. *Only an intrepid adventurer is willing to undertake the long and dangerous trip by sled to the South Pole.* **intrepidity** (noun).

intrusive (adjective)   forcing a way in without being welcome. *The legal requirement of a search warrant is supposed to protect Americans from intrusive searches by the police.* **intrude** (verb), **intrusion** (noun).

Word Origin
Latin *varius* = various. Also found in English *prevaricate, variable, variance, variegated, vary.*

intuitive (adjective)   known directly, without apparent thought or effort. *An experienced chess player sometimes has an intuitive sense of the best move to make, even if she can't explain it.* **intuit** (verb), **intuition** (noun).

inundate (verb)   to flood; to overwhelm. *As soon as playoff tickets went on sale, eager fans inundated the box office with orders.*

invariable (adjective)   unchanging, constant. *When writing a book, it was her invariable habit to rise at 6 and work at her desk from 7 to 12.* **invariability** (noun).

inversion (noun)   a turning backwards, inside-out, or upside-down; a reversal. *Latin poetry often features inversion of word order; for example, the first line of Vergil's* Aeneid: *"Arms and the man I sing."* **invert** (verb), **inverted** (adjective).

inveterate (adjective)   persistent, habitual. *It's very difficult for an inveterate gambler to give up the pastime.* **inveteracy** (noun).

invigorate (verb)   to give energy to, to stimulate. *As her car climbed the mountain road, Lucinda felt invigorated by the clear air and the cool breezes.*

invincible (adjective)   impossible to conquer or overcome. *For three years at the height of his career, boxer Mike Tyson seemed invincible.*

inviolable (adjective)   impossible to attack or trespass upon. *In the president's remote hideaway at Camp David, guarded by the Secret Service, his privacy is, for once, inviolable.*

irrational (adjective)   unreasonable. *Charles knew that his fear of insects was irrational, but he was unable to overcome it.* **irrationality** (noun).

irresolute (adjective)   uncertain how to act, indecisive. *When McGovern first said he supported his vice president candidate "one thousand percent," then dropped him from the ticket, it made McGovern appear irresolute.* **irresolution** (noun).

jeopardize (verb)   to put in danger. *Terrorist attacks jeopardize the fragile peace in the Middle East.* **jeopardy** (noun).

juxtapose (verb)   to put side by side. *It was strange to see the old-time actor Charlton Heston and rock icon Bob Dylan juxtaposed at the awards ceremony.* **juxtaposition** (noun).

languid (adjective)   without energy; slow, sluggish, listless. *The hot, humid weather of late August can make anyone feel languid.* **languish** (verb), **languor** (noun).

latent (adjective)   not currently obvious or active; hidden. *Although he had committed only a single act of violence, the psychiatrist who examined him said he had probably always had a latent tendency toward violence.* **latency** (noun).

laudatory (adjective)   giving praise. *The ads for the movie are filled with laudatory comments from critics.*

> **Word Origin**
> Latin *laus* = praise. Also found in English *applaud, laud, laudable, plaudit.*

lenient (adjective)   mild, soothing, or forgiving. *The judge was known for his lenient disposition; he rarely imposed long jail sentences on criminals.* **leniency** (noun).

lethargic (adjective)   lacking energy; sluggish. *Visitors to the zoo are surprised that the lions appear so lethargic, but in the wild lions sleep up to 18 hours a day.* **lethargy** (noun).

liability (noun)   an obligation or debt; a weakness or drawback. *The insurance company had a liability of millions of dollars after the town was destroyed by a tornado. Slowness afoot is a serious liability in an aspiring basketball player.* **liable** (adjective).

lithe (adjective)   flexible and graceful. *The ballet dancer was almost as lithe as a cat.*

longevity (noun)   length of life; durability. *The reduction in early deaths from infectious diseases is responsible for most of the increase in human longevity over the past two centuries.*

lucid (adjective)   clear and understandable. *Hawking's A Short History of the Universe is a lucid explanation of modern scientific theories about the origin of the universe.* **lucidity** (noun).

> **Word Origin**
> Latin *malus* = bad. Also found in English *malefactor, malevolence, malice, malicious.*

lurid (adjective)   shocking, gruesome. *While the serial killer was on the loose, the newspapers were filled with lurid stories about his crimes.*

malediction (noun)   curse. *In the fairy tale "Sleeping Beauty," the princess is trapped in a death-like sleep because of the malediction uttered by an angry witch.*

malevolence (noun)   hatred, ill will. *Critics say that Iago, the villain in Shakespeare's Othello, seems to exhibit malevolence with no real cause.* **malevolent** (noun).

malinger (verb)   to pretend illness to avoid work. *During the labor dispute, hundreds of employees malingered, forcing the company to slow production and costing it millions in profits.*

> **Word Origin**
> Latin *mandare* = entrust, order. Also found in English *command, demand, remand.*

malleable (adjective)   able to be changed, shaped, or formed by outside pressures. *Gold is a very useful metal because it is so malleable. A child's personality is malleable and deeply influenced by the things her parents say and do.* **malleability** (noun).

mandate (noun)   order, command. *The new policy on gays in the military went into effect as soon as the president issued his mandate about it.* **mandate** (verb), **mandatory** (adjective).

> **Word Origin**
> Latin *medius* = middle. Also found in English *intermediate, media, medium.*

maturation (noun)   the process of becoming fully grown or developed. *Free markets in the former Communist nations are likely to operate smoothly only after a long period of maturation.* **mature** (adjective and verb), **maturity** (noun).

mediate (verb)   to reconcile differences between two parties. *During the baseball strike, both the players and the club owners were willing to have the president mediate the dispute.* **mediation** (noun).

mediocrity (noun)   the state of being middling or poor in quality. *The New York Mets, who'd finished in ninth place in 1968, won the world's championship in 1969, going from horrible to great in a single year and skipping mediocrity.* **mediocre** (adjective).

mercurial (adjective)   changing quickly and unpredictably. *The mercurial personality of Robin Williams, with his many voices and styles, made him perfect for the role of the ever-changing genie in* Aladdin.

meticulous (adjective)   very careful with details. *Repairing watches calls for a craftsperson who is patient and meticulous.*

mimicry (noun)   imitation, aping. *The continued popularity of Elvis Presley has given rise to a class of entertainers who make a living through mimicry of "The King."* **mimic** (noun and verb).

misconception (noun)   a mistaken idea. *Columbus sailed west under the misconception that he would reach the shores of Asia that way.* **misconceive** (verb).

mitigate (verb)   to make less severe; to relieve. *Wallace certainly committed the assault, but the verbal abuse he'd received helps to explain his behavior and somewhat mitigates his guilt.* **mitigation** (noun).

modicum (noun)   a small amount. *The plan for your new business is well designed; with a modicum of luck, you should be successful.*

mollify (verb)   to soothe or calm; to appease. *Carla tried to mollify the angry customer by promising him a full refund.*

morose (adjective)   gloomy, sullen. *After Chuck's girlfriend dumped him, he lay around the house for a couple of days, feeling morose.*

mundane (adjective)   everyday, ordinary, commonplace. *Moviegoers in the 1930s liked the glamorous films of Fred Astaire because they provided an escape from the mundane problems of life during the Great Depression.*

munificent (adjective)   very generous; lavish. *The billion-dollar donation to the United Nations is probably the most munificent act of charity in history.* **munificence** (noun).

mutable (adjective)   likely to change. *A politician's reputation can be highly mutable, as seen in the case of Harry Truman—mocked during his lifetime, revered afterward.*

narcissistic (adjective)   showing excessive love for oneself; egoistic. *Andre's room, decorated with photos of himself and the sports trophies he has won, suggests a narcissistic personality.* **narcissism** (noun).

Word Origin
Latin *modus* = measure. Also found in English *immoderate, moderate, modest, modify, modulate.*

Word Origin
Latin *mutare* = to change. Also found in English *immutable, mutant, mutation.*

nocturnal (adjective)   of the night; active at night. *Travelers on the Underground Railroad escaped from slavery to the North by a series of nocturnal flights. The eyes of nocturnal animals must be sensitive in dim light.*

nonchalant (adjective)   appearing to be unconcerned. *Unlike the other players on the football team, who pumped their fists when their names were announced, John ran on the field with a nonchalant wave.* **nonchalance** (noun).

nondescript (adjective)   without distinctive qualities; drab. *The bank robber's clothes were nondescript; none of the witnesses could remember their color or style.*

Word Origin
Latin *novus* = new. Also found in English *innovate, novelty, renovate.*

notorious (adjective)   famous, especially for evil actions or qualities. *Warner Brothers produced a series of movies about notorious gangsters such as John Dillinger and Al Capone.* **notoriety** (noun).

novice (noun)   beginner, tyro. *Lifting your head before you finish your swing is a typical mistake committed by the novice at golf.*

nuance (noun)   a subtle difference or quality. *At first glance, Monet's paintings of water lilies all look much alike, but the more you study them, the more you appreciate the nuances of color and shading that distinguish them.*

Word Origin
Latin *durus* = hard. Also found in English *durable, endure.*

nurture (verb)   to nourish or help to grow. *The money given by the National Endowment for the Arts helps nurture local arts organizations throughout the country.* **nurture** (noun).

obdurate (adjective)   unwilling to change; stubborn, inflexible. *Despite the many pleas he received, the governor was obdurate in his refusal to grant clemency to the convicted murderer.*

objective (adjective)   dealing with observable facts rather than opinions or interpretations. *When a legal case involves a shocking crime, it may be hard for a judge to remain objective in her rulings.*

oblivious (adjective)   unaware, unconscious. *Karen practiced her oboe with complete concentration, oblivious to the noise and activity around her.* **oblivion** (noun), **obliviousness** (noun).

obscure (adjective)   little known; hard to understand. *Mendel was an obscure monk until decades after his death, when his scientific work was finally discovered. Most people find the writings of James Joyce obscure; hence the popularity of books that explain his books.* **obscure** (verb), **obscurity** (noun).

obsessive (adjective) haunted or preoccupied by an idea or feeling. *His concern with cleanliness became so obsessive that he washed his hands twenty times every day.* **obsess** (verb), **obsession** (noun).

obsolete (adjective) no longer current; old-fashioned. *W. H. Auden said that his ideal landscape would include water wheels, wooden grain mills, and other forms of obsolete machinery.* **obsolescence** (noun).

obstinate (adjective) stubborn, unyielding. *Despite years of effort, the problem of drug abuse remains obstinate.* **obstinacy** (noun).

obtrusive (adjective) overly prominent. *Philip should sing more softly; his bass is so obtrusive that the other singers can barely be heard.* **obtrude** *(verb)*, **obtrusion** (noun).

ominous (adjective) foretelling evil. *Ominous black clouds gathered on the horizon, for a violent storm was fast approaching.* **omen** (noun).

onerous (adjective) heavy, burdensome. *The hero Hercules was ordered to clean the Augean Stables, one of several onerous tasks known as "the labors of Hercules."* **onus** (noun).

opportunistic (adjective) eagerly seizing chances as they arise. *When Princess Diana died suddenly, opportunistic publishers quickly released books about her life and death.* **opportunism** (noun).

opulent (adjective) rich, lavish. *The mansion of newspaper tycoon Hearst is famous for its opulent decor.* **opulence** (noun).

ornate (adjective) highly decorated, elaborate. *Baroque architecture is often highly ornate, featuring surfaces covered with carving, sinuous curves, and painted scenes.*

ostentatious (adjective) overly showy, pretentious. *To show off his wealth, the millionaire threw an ostentatious party featuring a full orchestra, a famous singer, and tens of thousands of dollars worth of food.*

ostracize (verb) to exclude from a group. *In Biblical times, those who suffered from the disease of leprosy were ostracized and forced to live alone.* **ostracism** (noun).

pallid (adjective) pale; dull. *Working all day in the coal mine had given him a pallid complexion. The new musical offers only pallid entertainment: the music is lifeless, the acting dull, the story absurd.*

parched (adjective)   very dry; thirsty. *After two months without rain, the crops were shriveled and parched by the sun.* **parch** (verb).

pariah (noun)   outcast. *Accused of robbery, he became a pariah; his neighbors stopped talking to him, and people he'd considered friends no longer called.*

partisan (adjective)   reflecting strong allegiance to a particular party or cause. *The vote on the president's budget was strictly partisan: every member of the president's party voted yes, and all others voted no.* **partisan** (noun).

pathology (noun)   disease or the study of disease; extreme abnormality. *Some people believe that high rates of crime, are symptoms of an underlying social pathology.* **pathological** (adjective).

pellucid (adjective)   very clear; transparent; easy to understand. *The water in the mountain stream was cold and pellucid. Thanks to the professor's pellucid explanation, I finally understand relativity theory.*

penitent (adjective)   feeling sorry for past crimes or sins. *Having grown penitent, he wrote a long letter of apology, asking forgiveness.*

penurious (adjective)   extremely frugal; stingy. *Haunted by memories of poverty, he lived in penurious fashion, driving a twelve-year-old car and wearing only the cheapest clothes.* **penury** (noun).

perfunctory (adjective)   unenthusiastic, routine, or mechanical. *When the play opened, the actors sparkled, but by the thousandth night their performance had become perfunctory.*

permeate (verb)   to spread through or penetrate. *Little by little, the smell of gas from the broken pipe permeated the house.*

perceptive (adjective)   quick to notice, observant. *With his perceptive intelligence, Holmes was the first to notice the importance of this clue.* **perceptible** (adjective), **perception** (noun).

perfidious (adjective)   disloyal, treacherous. *Although he was one of the most talented generals of the American Revolution, Benedict Arnold is remembered today as a perfidious betrayer of his country.* **perfidy** (noun).

persevere (adjective)   to continue despite difficulties. *Although several of her teammates dropped out of the marathon, Laura persevered.* **perseverance** (noun).

Word Origin
Greek *pathos* = suffering. Also found in English *apathy, empathy, pathetic, pathos, sympathy.*

Word Origin
Latin *fides* = faith. Also found in English *confide, confidence, fidelity, infidel.*

perspicacity (noun)   keenness of observation or understanding. *Journalist Murray Kempton was famous for the perspicacity of his comments on social and political issues.* **perspicacious** (adjective).

peruse (verb)   to examine or study. *Mary-Jo perused the contract carefully before she signed it.* **perusal** (noun).

pervasive (adjective)   spreading throughout. *As news of the disaster reached the town, a pervasive sense of gloom could be felt everywhere.* **pervade** (verb).

phlegmatic (adjective)   sluggish and unemotional in temperament. *It was surprising to see Tom, who is normally so phlegmatic, acting excited.*

placate (verb)   to soothe or appease. *The waiter tried to placate the angry customer with the offer of a free dessert.* **placatory** (adjective).

plastic (adjective)   able to be molded or reshaped. *Because it is highly plastic, clay is an easy material for beginning sculptors to use.*

plausible (adjective)   apparently believable. *The idea that a widespread conspiracy to kill President Kennedy has been kept secret for over thirty years hardly seems plausible.* **plausibility** (noun).

polarize (adjective)   to separate into opposing groups or forces. *For years, the abortion debate polarized the American people, with many people voicing extreme views and few trying to find a middle ground.* **polarization** (noun).

portend (verb)   to indicate a future event; to forebode. *According to folklore, a red sky at dawn portends a day of stormy weather.*

potentate (noun)   a powerful ruler. *Before the Russian Revolution, the Tsar was one of the last hereditary potentates of Europe.*

pragmatism (noun)   a belief in approaching problems through practical rather than theoretical means. *Roosevelt's approach toward the Great Depression was based on pragmatism: "Try something," he said; "If it doesn't work, try something else."* **pragmatic** (adjective).

preamble (noun)   an introductory statement. *The preamble to the Constitution begins with the famous words, "We the people of the United States of America ..."*

precocious (adjective)   mature at an unusually early age. *Picasso was so precocious as an artist that, at nine, he is said to have painted far better pictures than his teacher.* **precocity** (noun).

> **Word Origin**
> Latin *ambulare* = to walk. Also found in English *ambulatory, circumambulate, perambulate.*

predatory (adjective)   living by killing and eating other animals; exploiting others for personal gain. *The tiger is the largest predatory animal native to Asia. The corporation has been accused of predatory business practices that prevent other companies from competing with them.* **predation** (noun), **predator** (noun).

Word Origin
 Latin *dominare* = to rule. Also found in English *dominate, domineer, dominion, indomitable.*

predilection (noun)   a liking or preference. *To relax from his presidential duties, Kennedy had a predilection for spy novels featuring James Bond.*

predominant (adjective)   greatest in numbers or influence. *Although hundreds of religions are practiced in India, the predominant faith is Hinduism.* **predominance** (noun), **predominate** (verb).

prepossessing (adjective)   attractive. *Smart, lovely, and talented, she has all the prepossessing qualities that mark a potential movie star.*

presumptuous (adjective)   going beyond the limits of courtesy or appropriateness. *The senator winced when the presumptuous young staffer addressed him as "Chuck."* **presume** (verb), **presumption** (noun).

pretentious (adjective)   claiming excessive value or importance. *For an ordinary shoe salesman to call himself a "Personal Foot Apparel Consultant" seems awfully pretentious.* **pretension** (noun).

procrastinate (verb)   to put off, to delay. *If you habitually procrastinate, try this technique: never touch a piece of paper without either filing it, responding to it, or throwing it out.* **procrastination** (noun).

profane (adjective)   impure, unholy. *It seems inappropriate to have such profane activities as roller blading and disco dancing in a church.* **profane** (verb), **profanity** (noun).

proficient (adjective)   skillful, adept. *A proficient artist, Louise quickly and accurately sketched the scene.* **proficiency** (noun).

proliferate (verb)   to increase or multiply. *Over the past fifteen years, high-tech companies have proliferated in northern California, Massachusetts, and other regions.* **proliferation** (noun).

prolific (adjective)   producing many offspring or creations. *With over three hundred books to his credit, Isaac Asimov was one of the most prolific writers of all time.*

prominence (noun)   the quality of standing out; fame. *Kennedy's victory in the West Virginia primary gave him a position of prominence among the Democratic candidates for president.* **prominent** (adjective).

promulgate (verb)   to make public, to declare. *Lincoln signed the proclamation that freed the slaves in 1862, but he waited several months to promulgate it.*

propagate (verb)   to cause to grow; to foster. *John Smithson's will left his fortune for the founding of an institution to propagate knowledge, without saying whether that meant a university, a library, or a museum.* **propagation** (noun).

propriety (noun)   appropriateness. *Some people had doubts about the propriety of Clinton's discussing his underwear on MTV.*

prosaic (adjective)   everyday, ordinary, dull. *"Paul's Case" tells the story of a boy who longs to escape from the prosaic life of a clerk into a world of wealth, glamour, and beauty.*

protagonist (noun)   the main character in a story or play; the main supporter of an idea. *Leopold Bloom is the protagonist of James Joyce's great novel Ulysses.*

provocative (adjective)   likely to stimulate emotions, ideas, or controversy. *The demonstrators began chanting obscenities, a provocative act that they hoped would cause the police to lose control.* **provoke** (verb), **provocation** (noun).

> **Word Origin**
> Latin *vocare* = to call. Also found in English *evoke, invoke, revoke, vocal, vocation.*

proximity (noun)   closeness, nearness. *Neighborhood residents were angry over the proximity of the sewage plant to the local school.* **proximate** (adjective).

prudent (adjective)   wise, cautious, and practical. *A prudent investor will avoid putting all of her money into any single investment.* **prudence** (noun), **prudential** (adjective).

> **Word Origin**
> Latin *proximus* = near, next. Also found in English *approximate.*

pugnacious (adjective)   combative, bellicose, truculent; ready to fight. *Ty Cobb, the pugnacious outfielder for the Detroit Tigers, got into more than his fair share of brawls, both on and off the field.* **pugnacity** (noun).

punctilious (adjective)   very concerned about proper forms of behavior and manners. *A punctilious dresser like James would rather skip the party altogether than wear the wrong color tie.* **punctilio** (noun).

pundit (noun)   someone who offers opinions in an authoritative style. *The Sunday afternoon talk shows are filled with pundits, each with his or her own theory about this week's political news.*

> **Word Origin**
> Latin *pungere* = to jab, to prick. Also found in English *pugilist, punctuate, puncture, pungent.*

punitive (adjective)   inflicting punishment. *The jury awarded the plaintiff one million dollars in punitive damages, hoping to teach the defendant a lesson.*

purify (verb)   to make pure, clean, or perfect. *The new plant is supposed to purify the drinking water provided to everyone in the nearby towns.* **purification** (noun).

quell (verb)   to quiet, to suppress. *It took a huge number of police to quell the rioting.*

querulous (adjective)   complaining, whining. *The nursing home attendant needed a lot of patience to care for the three querulous, unpleasant residents on his floor.*

rancorous (adjective)   expressing bitter hostility. *Many Americans are disgusted by recent political campaigns, which seem more rancorous than ever before.* **rancor** (noun).

rationale (noun)   an underlying reason or explanation. *At first, it seemed strange that several camera companies would freely share their newest technology; but their rationale was that offering one new style of film would benefit them all.*

raze (verb)   to completely destroy; demolish. *The old Coliseum building will soon be razed to make room for a new hotel.*

reciprocate (verb)   to make a return for something. *If you'll baby-sit for my kids tonight, I'll reciprocate by taking care of yours tomorrow.* **reciprocity** (noun).

reclusive (adjective)   withdrawn from society. *During the last years of her life, actress Greta Garbo led a reclusive existence, rarely appearing in public.* **recluse** (noun).

reconcile (verb)   to make consistent or harmonious. *Roosevelt's greatness as a leader can be seen in his ability to reconcile the demands and values of the varied groups that supported him.* **reconciliation** (noun).

recriminate (verb)   to accuse, often in response to an accusation. *Divorce proceedings sometimes become bitter, as the two parties recriminate each other over the causes of the breakup.* **recrimination** (noun), **recriminatory** (adjective).

recuperate (verb)   to regain health after an illness. *Although she left the hospital two days after her operation, it took her a few weeks to fully recuperate.* **recuperation** (noun), **recuperative** (adjective).

redoubtable (adjective)   inspiring respect, awe, or fear. *Johnson's knowledge, experience, and personal clout made him a redoubtable political opponent.*

refurbish (verb)   to fix up; renovate. *It took three days' work by a team of carpenters, painters, and decorators to completely refurbish the apartment.*

refute (adjective)   to prove false. *The company invited reporters to visit their plant in an effort to refute the charges of unsafe working conditions.* **refutation** (noun).

relevance (noun)   connection to the matter at hand; pertinence. *Testimony in a criminal trial may be admitted only if it has clear relevance to the question of guilt or innocence.* **relevant** (adjective).

remedial (adjective)   serving to remedy, cure, or correct some condition. *Affirmative action can be justified as a remedial step to help minority members overcome the effects of past discrimination.* **remediation** (noun), **remedy** (verb).

remorse (noun)   a painful sense of guilt over wrongdoing. *In Poe's story "The Tell-Tale Heart," a murderer is driven insane by remorse over his crime.* **remorseful** (adjective).

remuneration (noun)   pay. *In a civil lawsuit, the attorney often receives part of the financial settlement as his or her remuneration.* **remunerate** (verb), **remunerative** (adjective).

renovate (verb)   to renew by repairing or rebuilding. *The television program "This Old House" shows how skilled craftspeople renovate houses.* **renovation** (noun).

renunciation (noun)   the act of rejecting or refusing something. *King Edward VII's renunciation of the British throne was caused by his desire to marry an American divorcee, something he couldn't do as king.* **renounce** (verb).

replete (adjective)   filled abundantly. *Graham's book is replete with wonderful stories about the famous people she has known.*

reprehensible (adjective)   deserving criticism or censure. *Although the athlete's misdeeds were reprehensible, not all fans agree that he deserves to be excluded from the Baseball Hall of Fame.* **reprehend** (verb), **reprehension** (noun).

repudiate (verb)   to reject, to renounce. *After it became known that the congressman had been a leader of the Ku Klux Klan, most politicians repudiated him.* **repudiation** (noun).

reputable (adjective)   having a good reputation; respected. *Find a reputable auto mechanic by asking your friends for recommendations based on their own experiences.* **reputation** (noun), **repute** (noun).

resilient (adjective)   able to recover from difficulty. *A pro athlete must be resilient, able to lose a game one day and come back the next with confidence and enthusiasm.* **resilience** (adjective).

resplendent (adjective)   glowing, shining. *In late December, midtown New York is resplendent with holiday lights and decorations.* **resplendence** (noun).

Word Origin
Latin *putare* = to reckon. Also found in English *compute, dispute, impute, putative.*

responsive (adjective)　reacting quickly and appropriately. *The new director of the Internal Revenue Service has promised to make the agency more responsive to public complaints.* **respond** (verb), **response** (noun).

restitution (noun)　return of something to its original owner; repayment. *Some Native American leaders are demanding that the U.S. government make restitution for the lands taken from them by white settlers.*

revere (verb)　to admire deeply, to honor. *Millions of people around the world revered Mother Teresa for her saintly generosity.* **reverence** (noun), **reverent** (adjective).

rhapsodize (verb)　to praise in a wildly emotional way. *That critic is such a huge fan of Toni Morrison that she will surely rhapsodize over the writer's next novel.* **rhapsodic** (adjective).

Word List
Latin *sanctus* = holy. Also found in English *sanctify, sanction, sanctity, sanctuary.*

sagacious (adjective)　discerning, wise. *Only a leader as sagacious as Nelson Mandela could have united South Africa so successfully and peacefully.* **sagacity** (noun).

salvage (verb)　to save from wreck or ruin. *After the earthquake destroyed her home, she was able to salvage only a few of her belongings.* **salvage** (noun), **salvageable** (adjective).

sanctimonious (adjective)　showing false or excessive piety. *The sanctimonious prayers of the TV preacher were interspersed with requests that the viewers send him money.* **sanctimony** (noun).

scapegoat (noun)　someone who bears the blame for others' acts; someone hated for no apparent reason. *Although Buckner's error was only one reason the Red Sox lost, many fans made him the scapegoat, booing him mercilessly.*

scrupulous (adjective)　acting with extreme care; painstaking. *Disney theme parks are famous for their scrupulous attention to small details.* **scruple** (noun).

Word List
Latin *sedere* = to sit. Also found in English *sedate, sedative, sediment.*

scrutinize (verb)　to study closely. *The lawyer scrutinized the contract, searching for any sentence that could pose a risk for her client.* **scrutiny** (noun).

secrete (verb)　to emit; to hide. *Glands in the mouth secrete saliva, a liquid that helps in digestion. The jewel thieves secreted the necklace in a tin box buried underground.*

sedentary (adjective)　requiring much sitting. *When Officer Samson was given a desk job, she had trouble getting used to sedentary work after years on the street.*

sequential (adjective)   arranged in an order or series. *The courses for the chemistry major are sequential; you must take them in the order, since each course builds on the previous ones.* **sequence** (noun).

serendipity (noun)   the ability to make lucky accidental discoveries. *Great inventions sometimes come about through deliberate research and hard work, sometimes through pure serendipity.* **serendipitous** (adjective).

servile (adjective)   like a slave or servant; submissive. *The tycoon demanded that his underlings behave in a servile manner, agreeing quickly with everything he said.* **servility** (noun).

simulated (adjective)   imitating something else; artificial. *High-quality simulated gems must be examined under a magnifying glass to be distinguished from real ones.* **simulate** (verb), **simulation** (noun).

solace (verb)   to comfort or console. *There was little the rabbi could say to solace the husband after his wife's death.* **solace** (noun).

> *Word List*
> Latin *simulare* = to resemble. Also found in English *semblance, similarity, simulacrum, simultaneous, verisimiltude.*

spontaneous (adjective)   happening without plan or outside cause. *When the news of Kennedy's assassination broke, people everywhere gathered in a spontaneous effort to share their shock and grief.* **spontaneity** (noun).

spurious (adjective)   false, fake. *The so-called Piltdown Man, supposed to be the fossil of a primitive human, turned out to be spurious, although who created the hoax is still uncertain.*

squander (verb)   to use up carelessly, to waste. *Those who had made donations to the charity were outraged to learn that its director had squandered millions on fancy dinners and first-class travel.*

staid (adjective)   sedate, serious, and grave. *This college is no "party school"; the students all work hard, and the campus has a reputation for being staid.*

stagnate (verb)   to become stale through lack of movement or change. *Having had no contact with the outside world for generations, Japan's culture gradually stagnated.* **stagnant** (adjective), **stagnation** (noun).

stimulus (noun)   something that excites a response or provokes an action. *The arrival of merchants and missionaries from the West provided a stimulus for change in Japanese society.* **stimulate** (verb).

stoic (adjective)   showing little feeling, even in response to pain or sorrow. *A soldier must respond to the death of his comrades in stoic fashion, since the fighting will not stop for his grief.* **stoicism** (noun).

strenuous (adjective)　requiring energy and strength. *Hiking in the foothills of the Rockies is fairly easy, but climbing the higher peaks can be strenuous.*

submissive (adjective)　accepting the will of others; humble, compliant. *At the end of Ibsen's play A Doll's House, Nora leaves her husband and abandons the role of submissive housewife.*

substantiated (adjective)　verified or supported by evidence. *The charge that Nixon had helped to cover up crimes was substantiated by his comments about it on a series of audio tapes.* **substantiate** (verb), **substantiation** (noun).

sully (verb)　to soil, stain, or defile. *Nixon's misdeeds as president did much to sully the reputation of the American government.*

superficial (adjective)　on the surface only; without depth or substance. *Her wound was superficial and required only a light bandage. His superficial attractiveness hides the fact that his personality is lifeless and his mind is dull.* **superficiality** (noun).

superfluous (adjective)　more than is needed, excessive. *Once you've won the debate, don't keep talking; superfluous arguments will only bore and annoy the audience.*

suppress (verb)　to put down or restrain. *As soon as the unrest began, thousands of helmeted police were sent into the streets to suppress the riots.* **suppression** (noun).

surfeit (noun)　an excess. *Most American families have a surfeit of food and drink on Thanksgiving Day.* **surfeit** (verb).

surreptitious (adjective)　done in secret. *Because Iraq has avoided weapons inspections, many believe it has a surreptitious weapons development program.*

surrogate (noun)　a substitute. *When the congressman died in office, his wife was named to serve the rest of his term as a surrogate.* **surrogate** (adjective).

sustain (verb)　to keep up, to continue; to support. *Because of fatigue, he was unable to sustain the effort needed to finish the marathon.*

tactile (adjective)　relating to the sense of touch. *The thick brush strokes and gobs of color give the paintings of Van Gogh a strongly tactile quality.* **tactility** (noun).

talisman (noun)　an object supposed to have magical effects or qualities. *Superstitious people sometimes carry a rabbit's foot, a lucky coin, or some other talisman.*

tangential (adjective)   touching lightly; only slightly connected or related. *Having enrolled in a class on African-American history, the students found the teacher's stories about his travels in South America only of tangential interest.* **tangent** (noun).

Word Origin
Latin *tangere* = to touch. Also found in English *contact, contiguous, tangent, tangible.*

tedium (noun)   boredom. *For most people, watching the Weather Channel for 24 hours would be sheer tedium.* **tedious** (adjective).

temerity (noun)   boldness, rashness, excessive daring. *Only someone who didn't understand the danger would have the temerity to try to climb Everest without a guide.* **temerarious** (adjective).

temperance (noun)   moderation or restraint in feelings and behavior. *Most professional athletes practice temperance in their personal habits; too much eating or drinking, they know, can harm their performance.* **temperate** (adjective).

tenacious (adjective)   clinging, sticky, or persistent. *Tenacious in pursuit of her goal, she applied for the grant unsuccessfully four times before it was finally approved.* **tenacity** (noun).

Word Origin
Latin *tenere* = to hold. Also found in English *retain, tenable, tenant, tenet, tenure.*

tentative (adjective)   subject to change; uncertain. *A firm schedule has not been established, but the Super Bowl in 2002 has been given the tentative date of January 20.*

terminate (verb)   to end, to close. *The Olympic Games terminate with a grand ceremony attended by athletes from every participating country.* **terminal** (noun), **termination** (noun).

terrestrial (adjective)   of the Earth. *The movie* Close Encounters *tells the story of the first contact between beings from outer space and terrestrial humans.*

therapeutic (adjective)   curing or helping to cure. *Hot-water spas were popular in the nineteenth century among the sickly, who believed that soaking in the water had therapeutic effects.* **therapy** (noun).

timorous (adjective)   fearful, timid. *The cowardly lion approached the throne of the wizard with a timorous look on his face.*

toady (noun)   someone who flatters a superior in hopes of gaining favor; a sycophant. *"I can't stand a toady!" declared the movie mogul. "Give me someone who'll tell me the truth—even if it costs him his job!"* **toady** (verb).

tolerant (adjective)   accepting, enduring. *San Franciscans have a tolerant attitude about lifestyles: "Live and let live" seems to be their motto.* **tolerate** (verb), **toleration** (noun).

toxin (noun)   poison. *DDT is a powerful toxin once used to kill insects but now banned in the U.S. because of the risk it poses to human life.* **toxic** (adjective).

tranquillity (noun)   freedom from disturbance or turmoil; calm. *She moved from New York City to rural Vermont seeking the tranquillity of country life.* **tranquil** (adjective).

transient (adjective)   passing quickly. *Long-term visitors to this hotel pay at a different rate than transient guests who stay for just a day or two.* **transience** (noun).

transgress (verb)   to go past limits; to violate. *If Iraq has developed biological weapons, then it has transgressed the United Nation's rules against weapons of mass destruction.* **transgression** (noun).

transitory (adjective)   quickly passing. *Public moods tend to be transitory; people may be anxious and angry one month, but relatively content and optimistic the next.* **transition** (noun).

translucent (adjective)   letting some light pass through. *Blocks of translucent glass let daylight into the room while maintaining privacy.*

transmute (verb)   to change in form or substance. *In the middle ages, the alchemists tried to discover ways to transmute metals such as iron into gold.* **transmutation** (noun).

treacherous (adjective)   untrustworthy or disloyal; dangerous or unreliable. *Nazi Germany proved to be a treacherous ally, first signing a peace pact with the Soviet Union, then invading. Be careful crossing the rope bridge; parts are badly frayed and treacherous.* **treachery** (noun).

tremulous (adjective)   trembling or shaking; timid or fearful. *Never having spoken in public before, he began his speech in a tremulous, hesitant voice.*

trite (adjective)   boring because of over-familiarity; hackneyed. *Her letters were filled with trite expressions, like "All's well that ends well," and "So far so good."*

truculent (adjective)   aggressive, hostile, belligerent. *Hitler's truculent behavior in demanding more territory for Germany made it clear that war was inevitable.* **truculence** (noun).

truncate (verb)   to cut off. *The manuscript of the play appeared truncated; the last page ended in the middle of a scene, halfway through the first act.*

turbulent (adjective)   agitated or disturbed. *The night before the championship match, Martina was unable to sleep, her mind turbulent with fears and hopes.* **turbulence** (noun).

Word Origin
Latin *turba* = confusion. Also found in English *disturb, perturb, turbid.*

unheralded (adjective)   little known, unexpected. *In a year of big-budget, much-hyped mega-movies, this unheralded foreign film has surprised everyone with its popularity.*

unpalatable (adjective)   distasteful, unpleasant. *Although I agree with the candidate on many issues, I can't vote for her, because I find her position on capital punishment unpalatable.*

unparalleled (adjective)   with no equal; unique. *His victory in the Masters golf tournament by a full twelve strokes was an unparalleled accomplishment.*

unstinting (adjective)   giving freely and generously. *Eleanor Roosevelt was much admired for her unstinting efforts on behalf of the poor.*

untenable (adjective)   impossible to defend. *The theory that this painting is a genuine Van Gogh became untenable when the artist who actually painted it came forth.*

untimely (adjective)   out of the natural or proper time. *The untimely death of a youthful Princess Diana seemed far more tragic than Mother Teresa's death of old age.*

unyielding (adjective)   firm, resolute, obdurate. *Despite criticism, he was unyielding in his opposition to capital punishment; he vetoed several death penalty bills as governor.*

usurper (noun)   someone who takes a place or possession without the right to do so. *Kennedy's most devoted followers tended to regard later presidents as usurpers, holding the office they felt he or his brothers should have held.* **usurp** (verb), **usurpation** (noun).

utilitarian (adjective)   purely of practical benefit. *The design of the Model T car was simple and utilitarian, lacking the luxuries found in later models.*

utopia (noun)   an imaginary, perfect society. *Those who founded the Oneida community dreamed that it could be a kind of utopia—a prosperous state with complete freedom and harmony.* **utopian** (adjective).

validate (verb)   to officially approve or confirm. *The election of the president is validated when the members of the Electoral College meet to confirm the choice of the voters.* **valid** (adjective), **validity** (noun).

variegated (adjective)   spotted with different colors. *The brilliant, variegated appearance of butterflies makes them popular among collectors.* **variegation** (noun).

venerate (verb)   to admire or honor. *In Communist China, Chairman Mao Zedong was venerated as an almost god-like figure.* **venerable** (adjective), **veneration** (noun).

verdant (adjective)   green with plant life. *Southern England is famous for its verdant countryside filled with gardens and small farms.* **verdancy** (noun).

vestige (noun)   a trace or remainder. *Today's tiny Sherwood Forest is the last vestige of a woodland that once covered most of England.* **vestigial** (adjective).

vex (verb)   to irritate, annoy, or trouble. *Unproven for generations, Fermat's last theorem was one of the most famous, and most vexing, of all mathematical puzzles.* **vexation** (noun).

vicarious (adjective)   experienced through someone else's actions by way of the imagination. *Great literature broadens our minds by giving us vicarious participation in the lives of other people.*

vindicate (verb)   to confirm, justify, or defend. *Lincoln's Gettysburg Address was intended to vindicate the objectives of the Union in the Civil War.*

virtuoso (noun)   someone very skilled, especially in an art. *Vladimir Horowitz was one of the great piano virtuosos of the twentieth century.* **virtuosity** (noun).

Word Origin
virtus = strength. Also found in English *virtue*.

vivacious (adjective)   lively, sprightly. *The role of Maria in "The Sound of Music" is usually played by a charming, vivacious young actress.* **vivacity** (noun).

volatile (adjective)   quickly changing; fleeting, transitory; prone to violence. *Public opinion is notoriously volatile; a politician who is very popular one month may be voted out of office the next.* **volatility** (noun).

whimsical (adjective)   based on a capricious, carefree, or sudden impulse or idea; fanciful, playful. *The book is filled with the kind of goofy jokes that are typical of the author's whimsical sense of humor.* **whim** (noun).

zealous (adjective)   filled with eagerness, fervor, or passion. *A crowd of the candidate's most zealous supporters greeted her at the airport with banners, signs, and a marching band.* **zeal** (noun), **zealot** (noun), **zealotry** (noun).

Notes

Notes

Notes

Notes

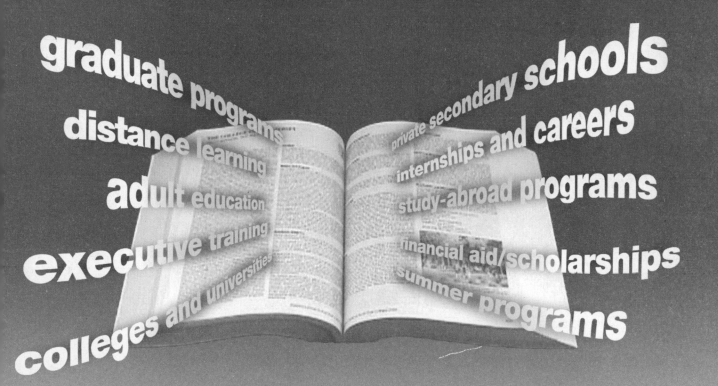